## PRAISE FOR I

'Mary Peters is exceptional. One of the kindest women I have ever met. With an unparalleled influence in sport in Northern Ireland, Mary is a massive role model and has been an inspiration to so many people for years – including myself!'

**HON. COL. DAME KELLY HOLMES MBE (MIL)**

'Mary takes her place amongst those few special sporting stars who have achieved legendary status both as an athlete and in her achievements since leaving the track. A joyful trailblazer, Mary lit up the track herself, and ever since has been working hard to change the lives of so many other athletes for the better. Her story is nothing short of inspirational.'

**DAME KATHERINE GRAINGER DBE**

'I owe so much to Mary Peters. Back when I was a young amateur with no funding, I was a beneficiary of one of her foundation's grants. For that, and for her continued support as I fought my way to professional titles, I will always be grateful. When I told my wife that I had been asked to say a few words for this book, she said, "Mary is probably the most well-liked and respected woman from this country." I absolutely agree.'

**CARL FRAMPTON MBE**

'Mary is an inspiration. She shows 100 per cent commitment in whatever she does, a trait carried though to her life after sport. She has used her success to encourage and support so many people in reaching their potential, personally demonstrating how to overcome the disappointment and to celebrate the achievements. Yet it is her kindness and non-judgemental approach that are her greatest attributes. Her honesty, sense of fairness, and warm approach are welcomed by so many people … but most of all by me. She is simply the best.'

**JOSLYN HOYTE-SMITH OLY, OLYMPIC AND COMMONWEALTH MEDALLIST**

'Mary has been a huge inspiration to me and to many other women across all sports. To win an Olympic gold medal is something special – it inspires me every day.'

**MICHAELA WALSH, COMMONWEALTH GOLD MEDALLIST, BOXER**

'Mary has paved the way for future generations of young women in sport. She showed me what a little girl from our part of the world can do. Mary has inspired athletes from all sports and from all parts of Northern Ireland. Her legacy spreads much further than her sporting prowess: she is always there with a kind word and a smile. She has been an inspiration to me to be a better athlete on the track but also a better person throughout my life. A true legend both in sport and out.'

**CIARA MAGEEAN, COMMONWEALTH SILVER MEDALLIST, RUNNER**

'Mary has had such a positive impact on sport in Northern Ireland and we are extremely grateful.'

JASON SMYTH, PARALYMPIC GOLD MEDALLIST, RUNNER

'I just want to thank Mary Peters for her endless pursuit of supporting young athletes to reach their full potential in their sport, and for supporting me throughout my whole career. She doesn't just do it for me, she does it for hundreds of athletes across the country.'

RHYS MCCLENAGHAN, COMMONWEALTH GOLD MEDALLIST, GYMNAST

'Fifty years ago Mary Peters returned to NI as an Olympic Champion and from then on she has gone on to build a legacy: a legacy of inspiring and supporting young people to achieve their hopes and dreams.
My own little piece of history at the London 2012 Olympic Games is due in no small part to that support.'

ALAN CAMPBELL, OLYMPIC BRONZE MEDALLIST, ROWER

'Mary Peters began funding me quite a few years ago to go on training camps and to get new sports equipment – there is a lot of that when you are a multi eventer. She is such an inspiration and I hope to try and follow in her footsteps.'

KATE O'CONNOR, COMMONWEALTH SILVER MEDALLIST, HEPTATHLETE

'Mary Peters is an absolute inspiration to us all. I and many other athletes all across the country are inspired by her success.'

AIDAN WALSH, OLYMPIC BRONZE MEDALLIST, BOXER

'I wouldn't be half the athlete, or gone to half the competitions to represent this incredible nation, without her support or the inspiration that she has given me. If I can be half the woman and half the athlete that she is, I know I'll be doing something right.'

DANIELLE HILL, IRISH INTERNATIONAL SWIMMER

'Lady Mary has done so much for me over the years, not only from the support I received from the Mary Peters Trust, but from the legacy that Lady Mary has left behind in sport. It is amazing that someone from a country so small can do something so big.'

EWAN MCATEER, NORTHERN IRISH INTERNATIONAL GYMNAST

'Thank you so much for supporting me on my athletic career so far and taking my dream to professional level.'

HANNAH SCOTT, GB WOMEN'S ROWING SQUAD

MY STORY

# MARY PETERS

WITH
IAN WOOLDRIDGE
AND
JIM GRACEY

First published in 2023 by Blackstaff Press
an imprint of Colourpoint Creative Ltd
Colourpoint House
Jubilee Business Park
21 Jubilee Road
Newtownards BT23 4YH

© Text, Mary Peters, 1974, 2023
© Foreword, Lord Sebastian Coe, 2023
© Photographs, Mary Peters, 2023, unless otherwise indicated

All rights reserved

Mary Peters has asserted her right under the Copyright, Designs and Patents Act 1988 to be identified as the author of this work.

Printed and bound in Northern Ireland by W&G Baird, Antrim

A CIP catalogue record for this book is available from the British Library

ISBN 978 1 78073 375 3

www.blackstaffpress.com

To my parents,
who made me who I am

# Contents

| | | |
|---|---|---|
| Foreword by Lord Sebastian Coe | | ix |
| Introduction | | xiii |
| | Prologue | 1 |
| 1 | First Steps | 5 |
| 2 | A Potential Star | 10 |
| 3 | The Big League | 19 |
| 4 | Buster McShane | 28 |
| 5 | Queen of the Workers | 41 |
| 6 | The Runner-up | 51 |
| 7 | Mexico: Myth and Reality | 60 |
| 8 | The Road to Munich | 68 |
| 9 | Survival of the Fittest | 74 |
| 10 | The Long Wait | 83 |
| 11 | The Aftermath | 92 |
| 12 | Life and Death | 109 |
| 13 | When the Running Had to Stop | 119 |
| 14 | Back to the Olympics | 131 |
| 15 | Building for the Future | 145 |
| 16 | The Mary Peters Trust | 154 |
| 17 | Life After Gold | 160 |
| 18 | Fame on the Small Screen | 169 |
| 19 | For Queen and Country | 175 |
| 20 | The Heart of the Matter | 184 |
| Acknowledgements | | 189 |
| Index | | 191 |

# Foreword

Almost a decade passed between securing the bid for and delivering the London Olympic and Paralympic Games, so it was inevitable that I would collect more than a few indelible memories along the way. Some are better than others. It has been said that if you like sausages or the Olympic Games it's best not to watch either being put together.

And there are those memories that still, by the hour, engender warmth in recollection. One of these features the subject of this remarkable autobiography, Lady Mary Peters; or Mary P. as she has been known for many more years than she probably cares to admit. And it's that easy familiarity and humanity that leaves its mark on almost everything that Mary has done in a life of such distinctive chapters.

It was really important that the Games in London were not just seen as a story about London. In our endeavours to avert that malaise, we created what we dubbed 'Nations and Regions' (Scotland, Wales, Northern Ireland and the nine English regions), and developed initiatives to bring meaningful and practical engagement with those Games to neighbourhoods, hamlets and cities. It was, on the whole, successful. The torch relay alone passed within ten miles of 95 per cent of the British populous.

And nowhere in the rich tapestry of the Union did this approach have better traction than in Northern Ireland.

On one of a number of Nations and Regions excursions, I escorted

Mary to a school in Belfast. It is hard to convey in words the outpouring of love, affection and pure admiration that Mary was met with when we were both greeted at the school's front door. There were even a few curtsies along the way. I've only ever witnessed this emotion once before and that was when HM the late Queen visited the Olympic Park in its construction phase.

Mary is royalty in Northern Ireland, and not just because at the time of our visit she was Lord-Lieutenant of Belfast – the Queen's personal representative in the city.

I had by that time come to know Mary as a close personal friend. I had always been aware of her incredible athletics career, which peaked with an Olympic pentathlon title at the Munich Games in 1972. A decade later, she was my team manager at both the Moscow and Los Angeles Olympic Games, where her warm, sensitive and fiercely protective guardianship of athletes was so refreshing in a world that tended to throw up less empathetic characters. From that role, getting on for half a century ago, she still has the most devoted following in my generation of athlete, and amongst her own competitive peers.

This book captures a time in athletics echoic of the amateur era of make and mend, when facilities were cartoonish in their archaic nature. A time when her charismatic and complex coach Buster McShane would secrete about his body lumps of steel from the shipyard where he plied his early trade, to create basic weight training equipment; and of Mary's beloved father who built a concrete shot circle in the back garden, which for many years remained the only concrete shot-putting circle in Northern Ireland. This inventiveness in the face of scarcity started when her father presented her with two tons of sand as a fifteenth birthday present to build a long jump pit. But what she also captures so graphically is a Fawlty Towers sport, chronically under-funded compared to many competitor nations, administered by decent people doing their best and coach educators who secured a pre-eminent global reputation. Reinforcing my belief that, in the matrix of need, world-class coaching sits at the top of the heap. In McShane she had the best, if alarmingly quirky and occasionally brutal, coaching. You sense through her writing that athletics didn't mean quite as much to her after his untimely death.

Her career spanned some of the most turbulent years that Northern

## Foreword

Ireland and its people have ever had to endure. She faced death threats in the aftermath of her Munich triumph, even though the book reveals her ease working on both sides of the sectarian divide. It is probably, in part, that element that allowed her to so deftly navigate and ultimately contribute so much to the lives of those in Belfast and beyond through her civic responsibilities and the trust she created in her own name.

We both enjoyed the honour of processing through Westminster Abbey on the occasion of the King's coronation in 2023. She was resplendent both in dress and stature. In the final chapter, she admonishes me for demoting her to damehood rather than a lady on a BBC interview only hours before the ceremony. That is not a mistake I will make again.

This is a wonderful book – chronicling a toweringly inspirational life so well lived. Thank you, Mary, for a life of achievement, service and an unflinching belief in our better angels.

Lord Sebastian Coe CH, KBE

# Introduction

Two questions were invariably asked of me when, in 2022, I celebrated the fiftieth anniversary of my pentathlon gold medal at the 1972 Munich Olympic Games.

The first, from a generation who hadn't been born then, was, 'Why haven't you written your autobiography?'

The answer to that would then lead on to the second question. Because in 1974, along with master wordsmith, the late Ian Wooldridge of the *Daily Mail*, I had released *Mary P. – Autobiography*. In it, I told the story of my early life, leading up to my gold medal and retirement from competitive athletics two years later.

'So why write another?' the curious would ask.

The answer to that is simple. When I looked back at the places I have been, the people I have met and the things I have done in the years since that book, I felt compelled to heed the requests from so many people to put the rest of it into writing. The original book may have dealt with the first thirty-five years of my life and the events that shaped me – chief among them the loss of my mother when I was just sixteen years old – but in the time that has passed since my gold medal win, I have lived a very different sort of life.

And perhaps serendipity played a part in that.

As I prepared these pages for publication, I met a lady at a fundraising event who had been waiting for many years to explain the cosmic significance of my racing number, 111, coincidentally given to me by a stalwart of British athletics, Sir Arthur Gold. In the cosmos, 111 signifies new opportunities, new beginnings, positive signs from a higher power and a sign of good luck. It is a symbol of visions coming true and of living one's true purpose … it can even be a sign from a deceased loved one that hard work and effort are about to pay off. When you see 111, you are being told that all things are possible, that you are connected to a bigger power and the miracles you create in your own life are evidence to those around you of what is also possible for them.

So, this book reproduces the original text by Ian Wooldridge – I couldn't think of a better way to tell that story, as it so accurately reflected how I felt in the immediate aftermath of Munich – and updates it with the story of my life and my achievements since 1974. The new material was written with the help of the incredibly talented Jim Gracey, a former group sports editor and reporter with the *Belfast Telegraph*. It covers the work I have done with my Trust, which has aided over 4,000 young athletes in the pursuit of their dreams, and with my Track, which is still fully operational and attracting more people each passing year. It conveys my great pride in having been made a Dame of the British Empire and then a Lady of the Order of the Garter, honours conferred by Her Late Majesty Queen Elizabeth II. I was also proud to play a processional role in the coronation of King Charles III and Queen Camilla in 2023.

It is a record of my life for my family in Australia as they have not known the cross sections of things I've been involved in.

But most of all, it is record for history of how a little girl, born in Liverpool and brought up in Northern Ireland without wealth or privilege, made the most of her opportunities. For the last fifty years, I have worked to inspire young people from similar backgrounds that they, too, can follow their own paths; that they can become champions if they have the desire to do so.

I hope, in reading my story, you will agree that I have fulfilled all my dreams.

# Prologue

The dawn didn't break that Sunday morning in Munich. 'Break' suggests that you have been suddenly snatched out of a long, dreamless sleep and you get up rested and relaxed and can start planning a pleasant day. For me, alone in my one-roomed flat high up in those towering white blocks of the Olympic Village, the dawn didn't break at all. It started seeping in slowly down the sides of the curtains and, God knows, it had taken long enough coming.

In fact I'd been lying there waiting for it all night. I must have dozed, for ten minutes here and there I suppose, but I don't remember it. Every time I switched the light on to look at my watch it seemed that the hands had moved backwards. Every time I couldn't help seeing the cards and good-luck telegrams stacked around the room and my mind went racing away again. There wasn't a sound outside. There were nearly 12,000 people in that Village and a couple of million out there in the great city beyond it and all but me were sleeping. You can work yourself up with sheer nerves and envy about an injustice like that, but the night wasn't without its ironic humour. Rosemary Stirling had promised to wake me at half past seven in case I overslept. I could have read the entire works of Tolstoy by then. Instead I just lay there reliving every second of the previous day. The 100m hurdles, the shot and the high jump were done and I was leading the field. Two events – the hated long jump and the 200m – were still to come.

The trouble with the pentathlon isn't so much the running and jumping and throwing as the night in between. When it's the Olympic Games and you're ahead, and you've lived and dreamed of this day for twenty years, that night is as long as a generation.

I tossed and turned, and turned and tossed, and when I gave in and got up, the bed looked like a bundle of laundry. I went across to the window and drew back the curtains. It was grey and misty and damp outside with no hint of the blazing day to come. My kit was already laid out on the second bed. I am very meticulous about things like that.

I wondered how the opposition had slept. I knew exactly who the opposition were. There was Burglinde Pollak, very blonde and very Iron-Curtain-trained, from East Germany. She was the world record holder for the pentathlon and she was lying second, right on my heels. Curiously, to those not au fait with the mathematical intricacies of time and motion on the athletics track, I was far more concerned about the opponent lying fifth. Heide Rosendahl, with her studious look and her steel-rimmed spectacles, might not have struck the uninitiated as epitomising power in sport, but I was well acquainted with her character and knew her to be a stupendous long jumper and fabulous sprinter. There was another factor too: Heide was representing West Germany. She was the local girl performing before an idolising crowd and, when they shouted, I knew that a great rising roar would pick her up and lift her as never before. Crowd power should never be underestimated. It's why so many football teams win at home.

The condemned lady did not eat a hearty breakfast. I brewed up some coffee on one of the electric rings and ate the yoghurt I had brought up from the restaurant the previous evening when I had gone to bed at about 10.30 p.m. It was a thoughtful breakfast but no more than that.

I was terribly tense but I wasn't nervous because the issue was very clear. The bronze medal, to me, was worthless. So was the silver. It had to be gold or nothing. I wanted it for me. I wanted it for my coach, Buster McShane. Above all, I wanted it for the people back home who would be watching me that day on television. I didn't mean the people of England. Back home was Belfast and Northern Ireland where it was long overdue for something good to happen. 'Mary P.', I said, which is what all my close friends call me, 'you can't let those people down.' It may sound a little trite and sentimental now, but through that long night, I'd had time to get my priorities clear.

We went down in the lift and out into the morning. The mist and the greyness had gone. The sun was rising in a clear sky and glinting already off that dragon's back roof of the Olympic Stadium. In there I would prevail or fail and by sunset, for better or for worse, it would be all over.

The longest day was about to follow the longest night of my life.

# 1

# First Steps

My accent doesn't tell the truth at all because there isn't a single drop of Irish blood in my veins. I was born in Halewood, on the outskirts of Liverpool, and both my father and mother were born near there too. We weren't even Liverpool-Irish. All four of my grandparents were English, so by birth I'm pure Lancashire. A Scouse, in fact, though I had never even heard that word before I left. It was the nomadic life of the insurance world that made us reverse the trend and move from Liverpool to Northern Ireland. My father, Arthur, was an agent selling insurance for the Liverpool Victoria Friendly Society, and three years after the war he was promoted to inspector in the Belfast area. For nearly two years he lived and worked there on his own, just coming back to Liverpool once every fortnight to see how we were getting on. He did that, as he did everything, out of a sense of responsibility to us. He was desperately ambitious for his children. My brother, John, had just won his way through to a new school and my father had the kind of selflessness needed to put up with a lonely, chaotic life so that his only son's education wouldn't be interrupted at a critical period.

I loved my father dearly. The only problem, until we moved to join him in Ireland, was that I didn't know him at all. We lived in classic, comfortable suburbia in a neat semi-detached with a neat garden and a bed of lupins at the side of the house which were so magnificent that people used to stop to admire them. It's little enough to remember about one's early life but we didn't do those spectacular things which stick in the memory. I only know that my father was never there. At first, in the war years, he worked by day and fire-watched by night. Even afterwards, the only time I really spent with him was on Saturday mornings when he sat down to make up his books for the week. I would sit there in the same room, pretending to write in my own book, but actually looking at him. He worked and I watched and, somehow, that summed up the relationship between us. There was projection on his side and admiration on mine but there was absolutely no communication between us.

I was extremely close to my mother, Hilda, who was the kind of practical lady who never threw away a torn sheet but sewed it into tea towels and aprons. She was almost the only feminine influence on my life out of school. There were no girls in our street, only boys. I had no sisters, only one brother. I became a tomboy.

Pianists always seem to be able to recall exactly when and where they struck their first note, and actors the incident which fired them to take to the stage. Quite often the talent is hereditary. This wasn't so in my case. We had no sporting traditions at all in my entire family and I don't remember either of my parents being interested. There was, a little later, to be a moment to which I can now look back and say 'That was when I became an athlete.' But a psychiatrist might see it differently. Even during those first eleven years in Liverpool, certain characteristics were emerging which are essential to the personality of the competitor. No one can teach them and few would want to, perhaps, because they are not necessarily the traits one would want to instill in a child.

There was, for example, a streak of exhibitionism. I detest show-offs and braggarts now, but I can recall showing off like mad in front of the neighbours who used to stop to gaze at our lupins. I had become pretty adept with a skipping rope and Mary P. was never abashed at putting on a free show in the front garden for the passers-by. There was also an increased determination when prizes were involved, such as at the school swimming gala where the reward for winning the width of the bath race was a sixpenny savings stamp. Unlike the Olympic Games, the prizes weren't distributed on the spot and I can remember going to knock on the headmistress's door every day for a week after that to see whether my prize had come through.

There was, too, an altogether darker side which emerged the day we were leaping into a sand pit, which is about the most accurate way I can describe the first long jump competition in which I ever took part. I was probably eight at the time and my big rival was a girl called Pauline whose face remains as clear to me today as Rosendahl's or Pollak's. Pauline was ahead of me but then got sand in her eyes and had to withdraw. My reactions were hardly those expounded by the Baron de Coubertin when he revived the modern Olympics and summoned the youth of the world to gather in an atmosphere of noble purpose and good sportsmanship. Far from it.

'Goodie,' I said to myself. 'Now maybe I shall win.'

But the tomboy environment was probably what counted most. There were no girls at birthday parties to insist we played with dolls. It was always races, organised by my mother, in the field at the back of the house. Then there was the nightly contest against the bus that brought us home from school. The bus stop was seventy yards away from our house and we used to jump off and sprint away, with our satchels thumping up and down on our backs, to reach our front gate before the driver could accelerate past us. Later, when my brother proved himself the brains of the family and got through to grammar school with its organised sport there were cross-country runs in the evenings. He must have many memories of the small figure stumbling breathlessly after him crying, 'Wait for me!'

We usually spent our annual holidays in the Isle of Man or Scarborough, but during the two years that my father was commuting between Liverpool and Northern Ireland, I paid my first visit to Belfast. We went there for a few days one Easter, and it was there that I tasted my first milkshake. Yet my affinity with Northern Ireland and its people does not go back to that trip. Instead my main impression was one of strangeness: Belfast, though barely a few miles west of Liverpool, was a new world.

I had an instinct that something big was about to happen to all of us. It proved to be right, as I discovered the evening I sat on the stairs of our Liverpool home and eavesdropped on a conversation between my parents. It was a sneaky thing to do, I suppose, but it was then that I learned that my father had been promoted again, this time as area manager to Ballymena. My brother was launched on a grammar school education and I had failed my eleven-plus so there was nothing to stop us from moving and being united again as a family. I looked forward to that, but even as my father said that we would now be moving I had this feeling that it was going to be a traumatic experience. The prospect of living in Northern Ireland was not, at least to eleven-year-old me, particularly appealing.

We arrived in Ballymena just before Christmas, with four days of the school term left. It was decided that I might as well start classes right away and, to my horror, I found that I literally couldn't understand what anyone was saying. The accent was as bewildering to me as a child from the deep south of England would have found it had they been transported overnight to the Orkney Islands. In those early days I had to have someone sit beside me in class and interpret the lessons.

But if they were strange to me, I, clearly, was even stranger to them in my St Trinian's hat and double-breasted Crombie overcoat. I was 'the English girl', an object of curiosity. I suppose most of us crave some kind of identification that will separate us from the masses, and it was at that Model School in Ballymena that I found it though, at first, it required no effort on my part. But I thrived on it. My earliest excursion into competitive sport there didn't quite make the headlines because, though I won the sack race, I was subsequently disqualified for jumping the gun. But within a few months, the tomboy years back in Liverpool had paid off and I won the junior championships in the school sports.

Academically, too, my confidence had grown. Moving to Ireland gave me a second chance at a scholarship, and this time I won my way through to join my brother at Ballymena Academy, where I was searchingly examined for my intellectual capacity, placed in the lower stream and was blissfully happy for two years. Liverpool and England were forgotten.

Looking back, I realise it to have been an important period, for when our next move came I was prepared for it. I was no longer a nonentity from the sprawling suburbs of Liverpool. I was good at sport and I had been totally accepted in Northern Ireland. So when my father was transferred to Portadown, and my brother and I were moved to Portadown College, I hurled myself into every activity there was: the hockey club, the film society, the debating society, the dancing club and the athletic club. I was never home before six in the evenings, and I still faced a pile of homework because examinations didn't come easily. But it was never a strain. We were taught that everything in life was an adventure, that everything had to be tried, that every hour had to be lived to the utmost, that discussion was better than dogma. For this I was indebted to a remarkable educationist and headmaster, Donald Woodman. I loved him as I loved my father. In fact, if I had a problem, I would take it to him before I took it to my father.

Mr Woodman had six hundred pupils in his school at any given time, and whether we were first-formers or prefects he knew every one of us by name. His methods were encouragement and persuasion. He even encouraged me to continue with Latin. He also made the decision, quite abruptly, to let me begin training as an athlete.

Sport was a haphazard business at Portadown, especially for girls. One afternoon, in the fourth year, I was standing by the boundary of a field where a number of girls were being instructed in the art of cricket, which appealed to me about as much as Latin and struck me as being even less useful for whatever life lay out ahead. I was looking wistfully through a hole in the hedge to the next field, where an exclusively male group of about a dozen were taking athletics. This was not the athletics club: it was the school squad being coached and drilled and disciplined like some crack squad of guardsmen.

It was typical of Mr Woodsman that he saw my envious glance, interpreted it correctly and acted. He simply led me through the gap in the hedge, broke down the barriers of male chauvinism fully twenty years before anyone had even heard of the phrase and said to the coach, 'Let Mary join you.' Kenny McClelland showed no surprise or irritation. He had been a pupil at the school and was back as a student teacher. I owe him much, for that afternoon I took the first short step along the road to Munich.

# 2

# A Potential Star

Our immediate neighbour in Portadown was Mr Gordon, a kind and encouraging man who owned the field behind our house and let us use it for our training. From early on he took a close interest in my progress as an athlete, even to the point where he promised to buy a goat to keep the grass short in our personal stadium. The deal was that I had to promise to drink the goat's milk to replace the calories I was burning up every evening. I couldn't face it, so he never bought the goat. But he never stopped us training or acting out our sporting fantasies on his land. It wasn't quite a Tartan track but my debt to him can never be repaid.

Usually there were three of us at these training sessions: my brother, who was desperately keen on athletics but never seemed to win much, myself and Kenny McClelland. Kenny was now something rather more than the student teacher to whom I had originally been introduced through a hole in the hedge. We were madly in love. At least, we thought we were madly in love. He was two or three years older than me but that was rather cancelled out by the fact that, in stature, I towered above him. He only came up to my shoulder and it was only subsequently that I learned that our very tender, very innocent relationship, caused a certain amount of amusement around the town. We must have been an odd-looking couple but we were almost inseparable. We never went to the cinema together because we had no need to. Athletics was our cause and it brought us together with everyone's approval. Here again I was lucky; as a coach, Kenny was years ahead of his time.

We ran everywhere we could find a flat stretch of land, including, for a short while, the Portadown Golf Club. We were given special permission for that but unfortunately it was soon revoked. Apparently my brother's startling white tracksuit had put the more dedicated golfers off their stroke. We were asked to leave. I hope those golfers won't think badly about their decision now.

Northern Ireland at that time didn't place quite the same importance on athletics as, say, the University of Southern California. There were no tracks, gymnasisa or equipment readily available in 1954. If you wanted to train, you had to find your own facilities, and if you wanted equipment you had to cadge it or make it. My technique was to tell Kenny what we needed and then Kenny would go to my father and tell him it was vitally important for the advancement of my athletics career. That's how, on the day I turned fifteen, I received from my father the somewhat unusual birthday present of two tons of sand. A lorry came and dumped it in our neighbour's drive and we had to hijack a wheelbarrow to shift it into Mr Gordon's field before he came home in his car. John, Kenny, my father and I then dug a pit, shovelled the sand into it and thus built our own long jump area.

Our high jump facilities weren't exactly Olympic standard either. We got a couple of broom handles, hammered nails into them and found a long piece of bamboo to use as the bar. This was later replaced by some really smart high jump stands, which my father bought for me. He was terribly ambitious for us and gave us many things, but his misfortune was that there was no end to the equipment I would need because, unknowingly, I was heading to become a pentathlete.

I didn't even know what the pentathlon was when I was first invited to compete in one. Kenny had to explain to me that it was a combination of five events, two of which – the hurdles and the shot – were absolutely unknown to me. Neither was in the school athletics curriculum, so my long-suffering father had to use his ingenuity all over again to shape some now rather important equipment out of the kind of everyday objects you would find lying around small Irish towns.

The hurdles proved to be no real problem. They just needed a lot of broom handles and a lot of bamboo. But the shot raised real difficulties. In the end, a local foundry shaped a wooden ball exactly the size a shot had to be and then had it cast. To this day I cannot work out how they managed to construct a shot of regulation size *and* weight (8lb 13⅖oz).

Armed with a shot, I now needed something more practical than a rude answer when I asked where I was going to put it. You don't learn much just flinging a shot around an open field. So, at the back of the house, we tied a nail to a piece of string and scraped out a correctly sized throwing circle while my father made a stop board, the wooden kerb at the front of the circle which you are not allowed to touch or pass over while in the act of putting. At first I putted there, on the grass, in spikes. Then we discovered that, while that was the general practice in Ireland, international rules permitted you to throw off a concrete base. My father reacted heroically to the discovery. More sand and some cement suddenly appeared and he was back in the building business again, constructing a throwing area as firm as an airport runway. It is a small commentary on the athletics story of the country when I add that this was the first concrete shot-putting circle in the whole of Northern Ireland.

In discovering the pentathlon, I had found two new athletics events, which ultimately turned out to be my best. It is the best argument I know for encouraging youngsters to try their hands at absolutely everything in sport before they settle for a single specialist event. There is no other way of discovering their potential. I only came across the shot by asking Kenny what a pentathlon was, yet very shortly after taking it up I was equalling, then breaking, the Northern Ireland All-Comers record. It had to be this particular record because, since I had been born in Liverpool, I was not permitted to hold native records. Practically every time I competed I added an extra couple of inches to my previous best performance, and within six months of getting that heavy black ball from the foundry I had become really quite good at putting it.

Obviously, I was doing most of my running and jumping at school, but the real, hard, tough experience was being gained outside. Almost every Saturday, somewhere in Northern Ireland, they were holding open meetings where all-comers of all ages and sizes and temperaments could compete. This was a tough, colourful world which has almost disappeared, but at the time its lessons were as valuable to the rising athlete as, say, the experience of booth-boxing is to the rising professional fighter. My father took me to dozens of these small meetings all over the country. Kenny would come along with advice, and more often than not we would go home loaded with small prizes. I loved collecting these trinkets, if only to give them to my mother. She could almost have set up as a wholesaler in sets of teaspoons and salt and pepper sets, but she would never part with any of them. I can recall how terribly upset she was when she chipped an ornate oval plate that I had won for some event or other in a meeting at Newcastle, County Down. To me it was nothing more than a plate that kept breadcrumbs off the tablecloth; to her it was a trophy that her daughter had won.

These were marvellous meetings, with all the classically Irish atmosphere one associates with country-town fairs and the make-your-own-fun of Irish life in the days before TV and rising living standards killed most of them off. They varied enormously in size and importance. In Lisburn you would find yourself sprinting on very bumpy grass where the lanes had been marked off by pieces of string instead of the usual white lines. Once, in Londonderry, at a meeting my father had seen advertised in the newspapers, I found myself running against factory girls wearing things like tennis shorts and sun-tops. I had proper shorts and proper spikes and I was so embarrassed about it that I didn't want to run at all. But my father 'wasn't driving all that way for nothing', so I had to take part. I won absolutely everything. I even ran a 440 yards, which would have killed me when I became an international athlete, and I won that, too.

One of the really big ones was the Royal Ulster Constabulary Sports at Balmoral Stadium, Belfast. There were bands and gymnastic displays and the highlight always came when the police cadets used to march out and form up to make the letters RUC. It was a great day out with enormous crowds, but even here, at the athletic event of the Ulster year, the running surface was so uneven that I suppose most of today's big names would regard it as something beneath their dignity to compete on it. I ran and loved it. My parents were there and so was Kenny, to talk to me with all the earnestness of a world-renowned coach before a race and then hold my hand like a rather proud boyfriend afterwards. We really were terribly fond of one another.

It was at one of the larger meetings in Belfast that I first ran against Thelma Hopkins, who was then a star British international. I couldn't believe how quiet and unassuming, even shy, she was. Although I was certainly three, possibly four, years younger, she found it quite difficult to say anything more than 'Hello' until we had known one another for quite some time. Mostly we would compete in handicap races in which I would be given ten or twelve yards advantage. Occasionally I would beat her and it did my standing at school no harm at all when I could say, 'Oh yes, I beat Thelma Hopkins,' carefully neglecting to add that it had been a handicap race.

Thelma and I were to become very good friends but, in those early days, she was sheer inspiration. I competed against her on the day in 1956 that she broke the world high jump record in Belfast. The London Olympiads had come over for a match against Belfast University at the Queen's University athletic ground at Cherryvale but there was also an open competition as well. The high jump, with its cinder approach and soft landing, was sheer luxury after Mr Gordon's field. I had finished jumping at 4ft 8in before Thelma actually started, and then I lay there in awe as the bar went higher and higher and she finally went over at 5ft 8½in, adding half an inch to the world record set in Kiev two years earlier by Aleksandra Chudina of Russia. Thelma, in fact, was to hold that record for only two months before it went back behind the Iron Curtain again, but the thrill of having actually competed in the same event was to have a big influence on my determination to break out of the country-town circuit and see the world through sport. Anyway, my 4ft 8in was enough to see me finish fourth to a world record. Kenny and I went back to Mr Gordon's field with visions of glory and the sounds of acclaim in our ears for we were now in contact with the mighty. Thelma was just off to compete in the Olympics.

By this stage, I was becoming a bit of celebrity at school. My name was regularly appearing in the newspapers. I started a press cuttings book and used to underline my name in ink whenever it appeared in the small print used to tabulate results. One of the earliest clipped-out photographs I put in is of Thelma Tomkins winning a sprint. I am a tiny figure in the background so I added a large inked arrow to identify myself and in the margin wrote, 'Mary Peters' in large letters.

People really began to sit up and take notice when I competed in my first pentathlon in open competition at the Ballymena Athletic Club. I was fifteen. Against a field of ten, which included the two Olympians, Thelma Hopkins and Maeve Kyle, I came third to the two major stars and was, in fact, only just beaten out of second place by the vastly experienced Maeve. The final scores, under the old points-scoring system, were: Thelma Hopkins, 3723 points; Maeve Kyle, 3324; and Mary Peters, 3253. I ran the 80m hurdles in 15.5 seconds, the 200m in 28 seconds, finished equal second in the high jump with 4ft 8¼in and, putting the shot in public for the first time, achieved just over 27ft 4½in. There is no record of my distance in the long jump. I was probably too far behind for it to have been counted.

The days were full of sunlight and friendship and the earth was at my feet, but the idyll didn't last. A traumatic experience was about to occur which was to threaten the whole security of my existence and cause me to question, not for the last time, the meaning of religious faith.

Death was always something that happened to other people in other families, and I was utterly unprepared for my mother's passing, slow and distressing though it was. I was very close to her and loved her deeply and she was such a gentle woman, with her shyness and modesty and her perfect skin and the lovely hair that stretched right down to her waist when she unplaited it, that I could not visualise an existence without her there.

She fell ill in the summer of 1956, not long after I had competed in the Belfast meeting in which Thelma Hopkins had broken the world record. We were all on holiday in a caravan at Newcastle when she began to suffer from severe swelling of the feet. My father had no faith in doctors at all, always believing that they were more interested in golf than in curing people, but by the time my mother was taken into hospital in Belfast for exploratory tests, there was nothing any doctor could do anyway.

I suppose I was the only person either in the hospital or in our family who did not realise that she had cancer. Astonishing though it will seem to any teenager of today, I had never heard the word cancer. It was not then the subject of endless television documentaries and newspaper articles. It was still a dreaded word that was kept in the dark and it explains much about the sheltered existence we led that, had I been told what my mother was suffering from I would, in my innocence, have asked whether or not it was serious.

I think she tried to warn me about what was going to happen. I knitted her a royal blue twinset and she said, 'No, you have it because I might never be able to wear it.' I refused to understand the words and I refused to understand what was happening when she became steadily heavier with gathering fluid and was then taken over to Liverpool to see Grandma Peters and the family for the last time and then returned to our home where a nurse was brought in to tend her. She had been terribly burned by radium treatment for stomach cancer, but the sheer optimism and happiness of my life until then still left me quite defenceless when she died four months later, in the early hours of New Year's Eve. I stood for a long while staring at her face which, in death, was still beautiful and reflected the goodness and gentleness of her character. She was buried in Liverpool, five days later, beside her father and mother. I felt very alone.

What followed was a deeply emotionally disturbed period of several months during which I failed to come to terms with another woman replacing my mother in our home. I write it frankly because the wounds have long since healed and I recognise, now, that the shortcomings were mine. At the time, the arrival of Doris Waterhouse, who had been my mother's bridesmaid and was my godmother, was more than I could cope with. I scarcely knew her because she had lived in Canada for many years, but my father asked me to write to her informing her of my mother's death. She arrived in Liverpool on the evening after the funeral and my father asked her to come over to Ireland as our housekeeper. She did so a few weeks later and, though I baked pies and laid out the dining table beautifully to greet her, I could not forgive her simply for not being my mother.

I was quick to resent the immediate ordering of a washing machine, while my mother had always had to make do with a washboard and mangle. My father would take Doris out on drives to some of the beauty spots of Northern Ireland and although they always asked me to go with them, I would refuse. Shopping trips to Belfast were agony. I would see my father take Doris's elbow to cross a street while I came trailing along behind. I had no resentment of Doris as a person, only for the position which circumstances had seen her assume. But I resisted her warmth and kindness and in doing so, I know I caused not a little distress. My father either did not understand my feelings or else reasoned that time would work them out of my system without any interference from him. It was a difficult time for us all.

My father and Doris Waterhouse were married in a little country church outside Portadown, six months after my mother's death. The ceremony took place at eight o'clock on a June morning and my brother and I were witnesses. We then all went into Armagh city for the reception. Eight people were there, including the bride and bridegroom, the minister, and the rotund, red-faced and very jolly taxi driver.

That summer, athletically, was not a very good one for me.

All the protective barriers were tumbling at once. My brother had moved away to Stranmillis Training College and it was fast approaching the time when I had to leave school where, as a good athlete and head girl, I had enjoyed the happiness and popularity that had come from being something of a success. My father and Mr Woodman both virtually took it for granted that I would become a physical education teacher. It seemed such an obvious choice that they even got the application forms for me to fill in. But again I defied the two people I admired the most. I reasoned that very few PE teachers ever came through as sports stars and, anyway, I loved domestic science, though admittedly was less good at the scientific side of things. I applied for a place at the Domestic Science College in Belfast and, resplendent in a new suit from C&A and armed with such invaluable advice as 'Don't cross your legs', I went for an interview.

A few weeks previously I had taken part in a *Down Your Way* programme, when BBC presenter Franklin Engelmann had visited Portadown, and this appeared to be worth at least ten marks in the opinion of one of the interviewers who had heard it. Another caught me on the trickier subject of literature which, as an outdoor tomboy, had never loomed very large in my life.

'What sort of books do you read?' he asked. I groped around wildly and suddenly clutched the name of Dickens out of mid-air. 'Do you mean to say,' he said, 'that if I gave you a copy of *The Cruel Sea* and a copy of *Bleak House* you would choose the Dickens?'

'Yes I would,' I said, and I was probably speaking the truth. So close and confined had been my small world in Portadown that, at the time, I had never heard of either *The Cruel Sea* or Nicholas Monsarrat.

I apparently impressed them enough that I had at least a future over a sewing machine or a hot stove. I came through the interview successfully, and it signalled the end of family life. My father and stepmother sold their house and moved to England, later to follow my brother to Sydney, Australia. I moved into Belfast, a place with faults and blemishes like every other city, but one that made me feel welcome when I needed love very badly.

# 3

# The Big League

Coming to terms with the larger world when you've led a sheltered life can lead to some difficult moments. Athletically I was making progress – I didn't need the Irish newspapers to tell me that – but Northern Ireland is one place and England can feel like the other side of the Pacific when you are suddenly chosen for your first 'overseas' trip.

As I have said, the year following my mother's death was not exactly a sporting milestone but by the September I was going over to Birmingham University to compete in the 1956 British pentathlon championships. You would have thought we were emigrating forever. My brother came with me as a kind of chaperone and we went via Liverpool where we stayed with my grandmother overnight. The following night we spent in the Cobden Hotel in Birmingham. I could hardly sleep. I, Mary Peters, was overseas, staying in a hotel, about to compete in national championships.

This would be the point in the movie where the heroine does something terribly sophisticated, like falling in love or bringing a crowd of 100,000 to its feet by breaking about eight world records. My only concern was not to be late. In fact I was so concerned about it that we turned up at the Birmingham University track about an hour before any of the groundsmen. This was just as well. I simply couldn't find the changing rooms so I went to the groundsmen's hut and changed there, laying out my school uniform over a wheelbarrow. I was kitted out and ready for action roughly half a morning before anyone else arrived.

Eventually the stars showed up. I knew their names, of course, and I suddenly found myself contemplating the ultimately glamorous figure of Margaret Rowley, pentathlete. She emerged wearing the dramatic all-black ensemble of Birchfield Harriers and was just the most dramatic lady I had ever seen. All at once I was conscious of the fact that my shorts came down almost to my knees. I hastily rolled them up about three turns, revealing some six inches of thigh that had not been exposed previously to the more conservative audiences of Ulster. It was a tremendous relief to see that there was one girl, whose name was something like Parrish or Parsons, who was even more nervous than I was. In the high jump she just couldn't bring herself to take off. She rocked and rolled on her feet for minutes on end and then broke away without jumping every time she reached the bar. There was a terrible moment when the university clock struck midday and seemed to go on forever. Miss Parrish-or-Parsons wouldn't jump during the distraction, and for a dreadful moment I thought the event was over. In fact it was only just starting and I was to do rather well. I finished second, only 133 points behind the gorgeous Miss Rowley. I'd come fourth in the shot, fourth in the hurdles, second in the long jump and first in both the high jump and the 200 metres.

I pasted the newspaper articles of the event into my press cuttings book – a rather bilious green-covered book bearing the imprint 'School and College Jotter issued by the Education Company Ltd of 36, Fountain Street, Belfast.' – but soon my first fan letter arrived, addressed to the *Blonde Bombshell*. It didn't do any harm now that I was alone, living in digs and studying in Belfast.

Now that my father was gone I was absolutely determined to show him what I could do. The first thing I did in the summer of 1957 was smash the Northern Ireland shot record by miles, only to be put right back in my place when it was discovered that the shot was considerably under weight. But my moment was only briefly delayed: in Ballymena, just after my eighteenth birthday, they weighed the shot beforehand to make certain it was legal and I then put it 34ft 1in, exactly one foot better than the previous Northern Ireland All-Comers' record. As comparative performances went at the time, it was pretty good. By the end of that summer I was emerging quite well as a hurdler, a high jumper and a shot-putter.

But 1958 was to be the year. At the end of the summer, luring everyone to strive their utmost, were the Commonwealth Games in Cardiff. I knew that Northern Ireland would send only a small team but that I stood a good chance of selection. What I needed was experience and that, in more ways than one, was what I was about to get.

It might seem inconceivable nowadays, but I was eighteen before I first went to London. Even then it wasn't to go and see Westminster or the Crown Jewels, but to get down to the White City, on the Wormwood Scrubs side of Shepherds Bush, and run. We stayed in a hotel near Lancaster Gate, not quite overlooking Hyde Park but almost. It was around here that famous actresses, conductors and authors took their flats when they came to London, which was all very well to write home about, but it was a very different story when I discovered that our hotel was teeming with famous athletes with whom, until now, my only connection had been when I cut their photographs out for inclusion in my scrapbook. I was terrified.

On top of that, I had little money. I had only just emerged from the days when my pocket money amounted to two shillings a week. Thelma Hopkins was an angel, however. She took complete charge of me without patronising me at all. She introduced me to Chinese cooking, and for the first time in my life I ate out in a restaurant where you didn't have to go along with a tray and select your own food. From time to time we took taxis. Thelma would pay for one and I would pay for the next. My taxi rides were agonising. I always had one eye on the meter wondering if I would have enough money to pay for it. I would have been too scared to tell Thelma that I was flat broke. We managed somehow, until we came to the White City.

The event was the Women's AAA Championships (the Amateur Athletic Association), and I was realistic enough to know that I didn't have a hope. I was there to gather experience and that is just what I got, even down to the point where a judge quietly informed me that my action in the shot-put was not only wrong but actually illegal. 'You must put it,' he said, 'not throw it.' I had to get it up under my chin. It didn't matter much. No one in the crowd had ever heard of me, no one expected me to do well and I duly obliged everyone's peace by making no impression at all on the meeting. I don't even know where I finished. But

I had learned what it felt like to go into a stadium with people thronging through turnstiles; how to mix with athletes who were household names; how to give my coat to a waiter in a restaurant; and how much to tip a taxi-driver, provided I had the money, after a two-mile journey.

I returned to Belfast a wiser, if uncelebrated, young woman, but it was destined to be a good year. In the space of ten days, this time with a shot of the correct weight and also with a legal method, I broke the Northern Ireland record twice. The second time I increased it by 10 inches. As it happened, in the final trials before the team selection for the then British Empire Games (now the Commonwealth Games), I added a further two feet to my distance. But once again, subsequent check-ups revealed that the shot I'd used had been too light. This sort of thing was becoming a sick joke long before anyone had thought of the phrase.

It didn't matter much. When they came to name the four-woman Northern Ireland track and field team for Cardiff, I was on it, along with Thelma Hopkins, javelin-thrower Bridget Robinson, and Maeve Kyle. Maeve was the only sprinter among us. The rest of us, essentially, were field-event performers, but for reasons of prestige as much as economics, we were asked if we would mind forming a 4 x 100yds relay team to go in there and compete against the rest of the Commonwealth. It was rather like designating four glider pilots to fight the Battle of Britain.

There was so much to learn, primarily that you don't go to the Commonwealth Games until you are officially kitted out. We were provided with gorgeous green blazers, complete with wire badges, and elegant white suits for the opening parade. These were so beautiful that it would have been nonsense to travel in them, so we were asked to buy ourselves grey skirts for the journey. This just showed how Avery Brundage, by now president of the International Olympic Committee, was desperately out of touch with the whole situation. He was so rich that he could have bought five million grey skirts without an issue. As a first-year domestic science student, I had to sit down and try to work out how I was going to buy one.

I did, as it happened, have a little money in my Post Office Savings book and I decided that if Northern Ireland could send me to the Games, the least I could do was show that I'd been touring abroad to places like Birmingham and London and come up with something smart. I went out and spent £5 on the most beautiful, the very latest, the most elegant grey pleated skirt you ever saw. I was so thrilled about it that I came out of the store, went straight to a phone box and rang Thelma Hopkins's mother, who was to be our team manager in Cardiff, to tell her about it. I spoke to her, put the receiver down, rushed out of the kiosk and had got all of fifty yards up the road when it dawned on me that I'd left the carrier bag containing the skirt by the telephone. I went straight back, but it had gone.

To say that I could have wept is ridiculous. I did weep. I had just enough money to go and buy another, but I knew that would be the end of my savings. I would be left with nothing for a hungry, let alone a rainy, day. Still, I went back to the store and got another one and so it was that, for the first time ever, I turned up at an athletics meeting wearing something other than a school or college uniform. It was a beautiful moment, but it would be untrue to claim that we had yet quite arrived.

By 'we' I mean Bridget Robinson and myself, the novices of the team. From start to finish we never really understood what the whole expensive expedition was about. We didn't train very much and we certainly didn't train every day. It never occurred to us that that was what one was expected to do. All we knew was that we were there because we had a certain natural talent and we were there on merit, if the definition of that was that there wasn't anyone better around in our country. We were there for a super, exciting holiday among lots of famous people, and when it came to the athletics we would do our absolute utmost and not become bitter and twisted hulks of humanity when we lost. In the meantime there were far more fundamental matters to contend with, such as inadvertently packing our white berets in our main advance luggage so that we wouldn't have to wear them on the journey to Cardiff. We both detested hats and had worked really hard on the scheme to lose them. We loved our white kid leather Van Dal shoes, though.

We knew we'd really arrived in the international set when some of the boxers took us down to Barry Island one night and gave us a super time on the dodgems and the big dipper and we all finished up dining on candyfloss which I'd never eaten before.

We shared a billet in a bottle-green Nissen hut on an RAF station. It had two beds and a locker in which we could hang our clothes, in my case, little more than my official uniform, my doubly precious grey skirt and the only tracksuit I possessed. Today's international athlete may have found it somewhat monastic, but since I didn't know the difference between Sparta and the Savoy at the time I was deliriously happy. It is only since that I've learned that sophistication can be an unsettling thing. As for food, I'd never seen anything like it. Dinner in my first digs in Belfast had comprised, on a good night, two slices of Spam, one tomato and some bread and butter. Here there were sizzling chops for lunch and delicious steak for dinner followed by puddings immersed in fresh cream.

I cried at the opening ceremony because it was all so moving and beautiful and I, Mary Elizabeth Peters, who was hopeless at Latin, was there in my own right in the presence of the Queen. Then the Games got under way and I found myself caught up in the whirlwind of movement. There were no seniors or juniors, no VIPs and also-rans. I was staggered to discover that you could be in the same restaurant queue as yesterday's gold medallist, whose photograph was in every newspaper. They would take their turn with the rest of us. If I'd known what democracy meant then, I would have decided that this was it. I even met the great sprint champion Mike Agostini, possibly the most glamorous figure at the entire Games. Sixteen years later I ran into Mike again, at the Commonwealth Games in New Zealand. 'I remember meeting you in Cardiff,' he said. 'You know, in those days I used to think the great thing in life was to go around and screw everybody. Nowadays I've got a gorgeous wife and gorgeous kids, and some gorgeous girl could come along here now and I wouldn't even be interested.' I'd liked Agostini when we'd first met, but this made me like him even more.

At some point the ceremonial and the eating and the chat had to stop and we had to get down to the Games. In those days there was no pentathlon. I was in for the shot and the high jump and, as reluctantly as at least three other members of the Northern Ireland women's team, the relay.

Well, you've got to start somewhere, and as soon as I went out to the high jump area I had the first taste of what the big league was all about. The bar was resting at 4ft 10in – which was within a fraction of the best I'd ever achieved – and no one had taken their tracksuit off yet. We warmed up and stripped down. The stars left their conversation, hopped over and came back to pick up the sentence they'd broken off a moment ago. I concentrated like hell, ran like fury and got over. Jubilation! Ecstasy! Then they moved it up to 5ft and that was me, out of the high jump. So we came to the shot. By my own standards I didn't do badly at all and I would like to point out that I didn't finish up last in the Commonwealth. Nine took part and although I don't recall now the lady's name or which country she came from, one of them actually finished behind me.

There remained the dreaded relay, which some economy-minded bureaucrat had decided we must enter. Of the four of us, only Maeve Kyle was a specialist sprinter. Thelma was the high jump queen, Bridget threw the javelin and I, as we've established, enjoyed candyfloss. But we had to face it, so we went out for our heat knowing that our only reward could be a humiliating beating. So it was. We were last by miles. But that wasn't quite the end of it. We were discreetly walking away when we were informed that one of the teams had been disqualified over a baton change. As there had been only four teams in our heat in the first place, we would be overjoyed to know, said our happy informant, that Northern Ireland's women had qualified for the final.

I repeat, it was like four gliders trying to stop the Luftwaffe; four windjammers in pursuit of the Sixth Fleet. There is a photograph somewhere showing me handing over the baton at the end of the third leg to Maeve Kyle. If you ever see it, note the classical style. Note, also, on the right-hand side of the picture, that the winners, at that precise moment, were breaking the tape. They'd broken the world record, that's all.

Cardiff had staged the most marvellous Games and every moment was a joy. I came away enriched as a person, but still athletically naive. Of course, my approach had been too matter-of-fact, but it occurs to me, knowing what I now know about the demands on the modern athlete, that we might have come too far. When victory is the result of obsession rather than dedication, when training demands submission rather than sacrifice, I am inclined to think we might have lost sight of our values. In my own case I was a free agent and chose to go along with the devouring system, but over the years I have been in contact with children, literally one third of the age I was when I competed at Cardiff, who appear to have been given no choice in the matter.

On my way home from the New Zealand Commonwealth Games in

1974, I called in at Sydney and was staying there with my brother when I received an invitation to attend a meeting of the New South Wales Little Athletes, aged six to twelve. It wasn't what the kids were doing that horrified me, it was the obvious, manic ambition of their parents that made me feel quite ill. Watching their faces, I could see a ruthlessness and determination to make certain their children emerged as winners, regardless of cost. Perhaps, in some cases, it was to compensate for their own anonymity in an adult world. But I knew as I watched that the adrenalin there was flowing in the spectators, not the tiny competitors. The aggression was between parent and parent, not runner and runner, and I had a good idea that some of those kids were going to get hell when they got home if they hadn't come up to expectation. Young Australian swimmers, of course, trained under a still more severe regime, getting up in the middle of the night to start training, then going to school, then returning to the pool as soon as lessons are over.

I know, in a small way, what parental ambitions can do to a child later in life. My father was, and remained, ambitious for me and I know that over a number of years it did not improve our relationship. What I saw at that Australian trackside was the same syndrome multiplied a hundred times. It might have yielded an extra gold medal at an Olympic Games eight, twelve or sixteen years hence, but it could just have broken a few hundred lives in the process. I concluded you have to be a small nation with a large complex of some kind to indulge in that kind of production-line madness and that it would have been a marvellous system had that kind of sustained training and competition started at the age of eleven instead of six. I expressed this opinion to one or two local officials of the scheme and felt that they didn't necessarily appreciate it.

It didn't matter much. For one thing, I would have banned those parents to a point out of harm's way the moment they opened their mouths to scream for their offspring. And for another, I had been quite amused at a small incident that had occurred when I'd arrived. 'And here,' said a sort of disc-jockey voice over the public address, 'is Miss Mary Peters, who's just been to the Commonwealth Games and won a gold for Australia.'

Ah well, I thought, you can't win 'em for everybody. If the idiot couldn't even recognise his own heroes (Australia had just won the Games and twenty-nine golds without any help from Northern Ireland) maybe he was ideally suited to his position of drill-sergeant to the infants' class.

Cardiff, for me in 1958, was absurdly different. I went there without any predetermined targets and came away without any overwhelming sense of failure. I'd just been to the Commonwealth Games, that's all. Today there would probably be a national inquiry into the reasons for my failure. That would be wrong. I don't decry any youngster being sent to one of the big ones just to get the feel of the atmosphere and get used to rubbing shoulders with the big names and knowing what you have to do to get lunch or the laundry or a letter posted. It's experience, and if you're planning to stay around for a year or two that's something you can't pick up by correspondence course.

Back in Belfast, I quit the digs with Spam on the menu and nowhere to hang your washing and strict orders never to use the telephone. I went instead to live with Granny Murray and her daughter, Helen, who welcomed me as one of the family. They were God-fearing and very kind. I had another two years at the Belfast College of Domestic Science where there were sixteen girls on our course, of whom fifteen were better than me at chemistry. My chemistry was so bad that it made my relay running look good. My only hope was to try and memorise it, parrot-wise, and hope that I could understand what the examination questions were even about. I was quite good, though, on the practical side and, in the end, all sixteen of us got through. I'd never really been in two minds about what to do as a career. I could have earned more money, perhaps, in hotel management, but I wanted to be with young people, and teaching was the obvious answer.

My first (and last) teaching job was at Graymount Girls' Secondary School, now Hazelwood Integrated. I remember on one occasion I had to instruct some pupils on improving their personal hygiene. A few days later, a letter from a parent arrived. 'I sent Maggie to school to be taught, not smelt,' it complained. I spent only four years there.

It was during that time that a short, dark-haired man named Buster McShane entered my life.

# 4

# Buster McShane

I knew very little about Buster McShane when I first saw him, except that he was a weightlifting coach to the Northern Ireland team. We had assembled in Belfast to have a group photograph taken before leaving for the Commonwealth Games of 1958. Someone said, 'That's Buster McShane' and I saw this rather funny-looking little man who seemed to be wearing all the wrong clothes. He had a habit of wearing jackets with enormously broad shoulders, trousers that tended to be so short that you could see the ankle bones above his shoes, and ties that had horizontal and not diagonal stripes. These he would tie in large Windsor knots, which were hardly part of the Belfast sartorial scene at the time. He also had the rather lengthy sideburns that were to become quite fashionable all over the British Isles something like twenty-five years later.

Buster had the virtue of not remotely caring what anyone thought of him or his style. He was a happy, amusing man who always seemed to be the centre of groups of people who were laughing. He was eight years older than me and our paths hardly crossed at all during the Games in Cardiff. It was only when I returned to Belfast that, like every other international athlete in the city, I received a letter from him saying that he was starting weightlifting courses for anyone who would like to attend them. I was very pleased to get his letter.

Quite a few of us turned up the first week, half returned the following week and eventually we were whittled down to a hard core of about four.

I loved weight training from the very start. His gym, on the third floor above a pub and a small sewing factory, was a pretty tatty place with holes in the window panes and broken floorboards, but it was a vibrant place, full of Buster's enthusiasm. His motto seemed to be *dedication with fun*. I was still very much a junior international, but we had an immediate rapport. I couldn't wait to get out of college to go there in the evenings and was often the first to arrive. That meant collecting the key from Desano's ice cream shop across the road and creeping up to the third floor without the luxury of any lights on the stairs. Then Buster would arrive. He always had a pale complexion and his hair would be slicked back from his forehead. Somehow there was something quite Teddy-boyish about his appearance but that never lessened my respect for him. As I got to know him I was able to piece together the background of a quite remarkable man, little knowing, of course, that eventually he was to dominate my own career and life.

His iron will had been forged by smashing his way out of an underprivileged background. He was born in Canada of Irish parents but then returned to Belfast – a city with which he always had an intense love-hate relationship – to be brought up by his mother and grandmother after his parents' marriage broke up. It was breadline living with no extras or bathrooms. When he left school at fourteen and went to work in the shipyards, he was still wearing short trousers. It was there that he learned to take no notice of being a mild figure of fun. He was, in fact, almost the prototype seven-stone weakling who saw the advertisement inviting him to stop having the sand kicked into his face. Only in his case it wasn't an advertisement, it was a book in Smithfield's, the secondhand booksellers, about bodybuilding and physical education. Buster bought it on hire purchase and went away to change his life.

Weights were prohibitively expensive, so he made some from metal he stole from the shipyards. He fooled the security check at the gates by tying the weights to a piece of rope, putting the rope round his neck and then slipping the weights into his pockets or down his trouser legs. His legs would be bruised and his neck would be chafed but the collection of bodybuilding equipment back in his bedroom soon became so impressive that his grandmother lived in constant fear of the whole lot crashing through the floor into the kitchen. His next ambition was to own a set of chest-expanders he had seen in a shop window. They were far beyond the reach of his purse but the shopkeeper was so struck by Buster's almost paranoiac determination to build up his tiny frame that he said, 'If you can pull them out fully you can have them for nothing.' It was a challenge that Buster couldn't refuse. He borrowed another set of expanders from a friend, took them home and almost burst his lungs learning how to master them. Eventually he went back to the shop like some miniature champion bending down to pick up the gauntlet. The shopkeeper gathered his entire staff together to witness the test. Buster gripped the handles, took a huge breath and stretched the expanders right across his chest. The owner kept his part of the bargain, and Buster's growing armoury over the kitchen had increased by another few pounds.

He exercised his brain just as much as his body. He was a voracious reader of everything, but particularly medical, physical education and mechanical magazines. He also wrote articles for weightlifting and physical culture papers, even though his spelling at that stage suffered from having to have left school to go and earn his keep as soon as the law permitted. His grandmother used to recall how Buster would be sitting at the kitchen table and continually shouting to her in the yard, 'Granny, how do you spell so-and-so?' She used to rush into the house to reprimand him: 'Don't shout out things like that, son. The neighbours will think you're stupid.' She was ambitious for him, too, and used to worship him.

It was typical of Buster that he never totally mastered spelling. His brain and thoughts were always flashing way ahead of the word he was writing and, anyway, he didn't see much merit in mastering what he only regarded as the logistical matter of getting the letters in the right order. Life was about much more than that. He used to draw, as well, and became a very talented cartoonist. For a while, the *Daily Mirror* used some of his cartoons in Ireland. They were mostly political, rarely about sport. It was almost inevitable, with his background and the climate of the times, that he should have been extremely left-wing for a while. He drifted away from Marxism as he grew older and I don't think he ever became associated with any political movement. He was such an original thinker that he was a one-man party in himself.

There is no doubt that his enormous self-confidence as an adult came directly from his decision to take up bodybuilding. He was self-made in every sense of the phrase. When he had any extra money to spare he would buy himself an extra egg so that he could have two instead of one for a meal, which the family budget couldn't run to. He was very conscious that he needed the protein to build up his body, and the life he led as a teenager burned up calories at a fearful rate. Work started early in the shipyards and as soon as his shift was done there he would rush home and get to a gym for weight training every night. At one period, after getting soaked by rain when rushing between his work and his passion, he contracted pneumonia. It didn't deter him. Nothing deterred him. He became an international weightlifter, a weightlifting coach, a famous figure in the bodybuilding field, one of the best-developed men in that highly competitive business, a man respected throughout the world in the field of physical education, a successful businessman and the owner of an extremely cultivated mind who thought freely and lived a packed life with style.

His early days of extreme left-wing thinking and fiercely militant trades-unionism may seem incompatible with his later life, when he loved to acquire good paintings and drive fast, expensive cars. But it wasn't. He enjoyed his success and liked to be seen to be successful but he never forgot those early days or renounced his principles of humanitarianism.

His name, McShane, would have implied to most people in Northern Ireland that he was a Catholic, but he wasn't. There were even those who thought the nickname 'Buster' was a kind of smokescreen for a first name like Seamus or Patrick. But he was hiding nothing. He was christened Robert Terence and was promptly rechristened 'Buster' by his family as soon as he was old enough to totter around. Apparently he was both boisterous and clumsy and he had a terrible record of breaking everything from crockery to small but treasured family heirlooms. Buster he became, and Buster he remained to his mother, his grandmother, all his friends and, later, his wife. I never called him anything else.

In fact he was brought up as a Protestant and was sent to church regularly and took part in a lot of church activities. His talent for art was soon recruited to provide a new set of hymn numbers to be slipped into the frame each Sunday. But if they thought they were training a God-fearing churchwarden of the future, or even a lay preacher, they must have been sorely disappointed. Buster questioned everything from the Immaculate Conception to the Resurrection and came to the conclusion that neither made as much sense to him as the theory of evolution. Nor did he think that the religious differences between people who regularly worshipped the same God had done a great deal for the happiness of Northern Ireland. He became an atheist and remained one.

He was never discourteous to people of deep religious faith, but he could be quite violent in his scorn of those who tried to impose their views from a platform of piety. I recall waiting in his car for him one Saturday morning in Belfast when he went into a store to collect the inevitable armful of books and magazines for his weekend reading. On the street corner, wearing a placard bearing some such suggestion as 'The Wages of Sin is Death', a self-elected saver of souls was hammering out his message to all the passing sinners out doing their shopping. Buster glanced at him on his way back, got into the car and slammed the door in temper. 'Just look at that stupid bastard, standing there preaching. Why doesn't the fool get out and do something? Who's he influencing? No one.' He could never understand why a person could be demonstrative and ineffectual at the same time.

His faith, like his politics, was utterly practical. He was an enormously outgoing person who did not shy away from other people's problems. Nor did his success insulate him from those who had failed to fight their way out of the back streets. A casual meeting with a complete stranger at an auction sale, for example, was the start of something quite big. The man was looking for a cheap typewriter and filing cabinet to help a small organisation known, somewhat prosaically, as the 'Old People's Coal & Grocery Fund'. Buster gave him a few shillings towards it and then started asking questions. For years after that, every penny we collected at our talks and demonstrations about physical fitness went to that fund. Buster also started visiting old people all over the city and on both sides of the sectarian line. Quite often, a few days after his visits, a blanket or some other small comfort would arrive. Around Christmas, the fund would send out something like 150 hampers to needy cases, and Buster would comb through the list of gifts with a very critical eye. 'A bottle of lemonade isn't very nutritious,' he would say, and insist the committee changed it for a tin of condensed milk. He would have been mortified if there had ever been any publicity about this side of his nature. He was quite content to be known as a rebel. When the BBC produced an excellent television documentary on his life and work in Northern Ireland, he must have shocked many people by saying in it, 'I gave up religion at sixteen. I thought it was an unhealthy thing.' Buster, above all, wasn't a hypocrite.

For a while I used to be an atheist. You may well suspect that it was because of Buster's influence, but that is not so. His outlook only confirmed views that had been growing in me for a long time. They started, naively, with my mother's death, when I was consumed with bitterness because all the ministers who visited could do nothing for her. Those are no grounds to reject a faith but, as I grew older in a country where religion often concealed bigotry of the worst kind, I could only come to the conclusion that the loving God for whom they dressed up in their best clothes every Sunday did not exist. It was a considerable rejection because I, too, had been brought up according to a fairly strict Christian code. As Northern Ireland people will recognise from the school I went to, it was the Protestant code. Later, in lodgings in Belfast, I came under the influence of a Presbyterian family whose attitudes to the Sabbath were so strict and rigid that to file your nails or clean your shoes on a Sunday were sins to be condemned in the same breath as cruelty or culpable homicide. Out of respect for their habits I went to church regularly for almost two years. During that time I was rarely spoken to by another parishioner unless they were to say 'Good morning,' in reply to my 'Good morning.' I could not sing and nor could I understand the value of sermons which were either academic or abstract to a city whose people needed love and humanity to be preached in the simplest terms.

I am happy to say that in the years that followed, as we became quite well known in Belfast, Buster and I were made as welcome in the Protestant Shankill Road as in the Catholic Falls. If we were invited to speak in one, we made sure we received an invitation to speak in the other. That the same options were not open to everyone then only illustrates the great sadness of the division that separated our city for so long.

In those early years in Belfast, however, Buster and I had far more personal motives and ambitions on our minds. Mine was to develop into a good athlete; Buster's was to develop his business from a makeshift third-floor gymnasium into a health club. It was perhaps inevitable that we were on the kind of collision course that led to him suggesting that he should become my full-time coach. For eighteen months I had merely been one of the athletes using his weightlifting equipment and accommodation. Now as he was planning to move to new premises – once again on a top floor, but this time at least with some wallpaper and a changing room boasting the ultimate luxury of a mirror – he told me that he thought I was not getting the best out of my shotputting with the strength I was developing. Could he become my coach? I did not hesitate to say yes. He had this quite extraordinary ability to give you a surging confidence.

Our first session as athlete and coach was on a damp day in the depths of winter in Ormeau Park. The very first time I put the shot under his direction it hit the ground with a splosh and almost disappeared like a cannonball sinking into a rice pudding. Buster did not bat an eyelid. He removed a large, immaculate white handkerchief from his pocket, prised the shot out of the turf, carefully wiped it perfectly clean and handed it back to me for the next throw. Like all great coaches he could be an extreme bully, but when bullying was unnecessary, he could display remarkable gallantry.

The following year, after the Commonwealth Games in Perth, he invited me to join the business. My role was clearly defined from the start. I was to be the dogsbody factotum around the latest gym he had taken, this time in Upper Church Lane, Belfast, a location with real class: it had lino on the floor. It was to be a part-time appointment, which I could work in with my teaching job. Its first attraction was that I would no longer have to pay my weekly gym subscription, which had now risen to fifty pence a week. I was still thinking about this when Buster made up my mind for me by tearing up my membership card. I did some filing, some general office work and some health instruction in the gymnasium. Of course, I was now, under the quite ludicrous law laid down by the millionaires and noblemen of the International Olympic Committee, a professional. Within their terms of reference I was a cheat throughout the remainder of my athletic career. By their definition, I was a perjurer every time I stood there at subsequent Olympic Games and allowed the oath of amateurism to be taken solemnly in my name. I was 'investigated' several times, and on each occasion had no compunction at all about telling the first lie that came into my head. Of course I wasn't a professional. I was spending more out of my teaching salary of nine pounds a week on athletics than I could ever afford. Proportionately I was spending more to represent my country at sport than IOC President Avery Brundage was spending on his renowned collection of Chinese jade (which by the 1970s was valued at £35 million). I never had a penny to spare because I was spending it all on sport. Anyway, the anomalies of the definition of amateurism were so huge that, had I been undertaking the same sports instruction in a school or in the armed forces I would have been regarded as a true-blue amateur, because that's what the rule book said. When the rules are foolish, you are entitled to ignore them. This, by the way, is not what certain newspapers like to regard as a 'sensational revelation'. There is nothing sensational about it at all and nor am I revealing anything which anyone remotely connected with athletics hasn't known for years. If you wanted to make money in the late 1950s or early 1960s, the last thing you became was an Olympic competitor.

The situation didn't change when Buster invited me to join his staff full-time. I was now being offered precisely the career that both my father and my headmaster wanted for me when I came to leave school. I hesitated because I was enjoying teaching domestic science and I was quite good at it. But, as I improved as an athlete, certain other pressures were growing. I had the chance to go abroad on more and more overseas trips, and while the school principal could not have been kinder or more co-operative, the Ministry of Education were proving somewhat difficult. They were prepared to allow me leave of absence but without pay. I took their point, but there was the small problem of how I was going to eat or pay the rent. Buster's usual pragmatism settled my dilemma. 'Come and join me,' he said, 'and the problem won't be there any more.' I went and joined Buster.

They were days of supreme happiness. The gymnasium was becoming well known in the city, and more and more people were enrolling. As the clientele grew, so did the staff. I finished up in a team of four female instructors. There was Irene Miskimmon, who could have walked off with the Miss Ireland title any time she wanted, only she was too modest to go in for it. There was Hilary Rush, who was smaller and had an enormous sense of fun. And there was wee Jean Mitchell who never forgot to bring the cheroots along when we had saved up enough money to go out on the town for a night together. We worked increasingly long hours, sometimes from ten in the morning until nine in the evening, and I think I write the truth when I claim that in our years together we never had an angry word. Nor were there even any slightly resentful looks when I went away on my athletic trips. They were always happy for me to go and were delighted when I did well.

Altogether we had nine years in that gym. Eventually the lino gave way to carpets and sauna baths were built in, but it never lost its homely atmosphere. The only small panic I remember there was when the floor below us fell vacant and was taken over by a gentleman who insisted on transforming it into a strip club. This might have been very good for his bank balance but it didn't augur too well for ours. Many of our clients were eminently respectable and Buster reasoned that they wouldn't be too happy about being seen going in and out of a doorway which was now being frequented by rather unhappy looking men in traditionally dirty raincoats. He tried to get an injunction against the club but failed.

There is a sadly ironic end to the story. We finally moved out to go into palatial new premises in Upper Arthur Street. On a Sunday evening three months later, the old building was bombed out of existence. I went down to look at it the following morning and stood rather tearfully on the far pavement, remembering the happy times we had had there. The roof was blasted away and the floor of our gym was sagging down at forty-five degrees. We had left a little equipment there as a precaution against our new building being the target for a bomb attack. It was strewn around everywhere, and the vibration belts used for muscle toning were hanging down like ladies' garters that had been abandoned in a hurry.

A lady beside me on the pavement said, 'Isn't it desperate.' I was still sniffing a little and I said, 'Yes … and I used to work there.' The lady looked me up and down with what appeared to be surprise. 'There now,' she said, 'I didn't even know we'd ever had a strip club in Belfast.'

The dominating figure of all these years was Buster. It is inevitable that his name will recur again and again in this story, so it is perhaps important that I do not eulogise or paint a picture of a paragon. He had enormous magnetism and infectious enthusiasm, but modesty did not bother him overmuch and he could certainly be less than gentle on occasions.

Once, coming home from Australia, we were forced by fog to spend a couple of days in Calcutta, as it was then called. Although it was long after Partition, some of the old habits of the Raj still survived. We were booked into an old colonial-style hotel and Buster saw red every time he heard some elderly patron clicking his fingers and then saw half a dozen Indian waiters tumbling over one another to answer the call. Buster was always the champion of the less privileged, though we were soon to realise that the waiters were the lucky ones. It was impossible to walk through the streets at night without picking your way carefully through thousands of people huddled up in blankets or sheets on the pavements. I hated the place.

It was at about this time that Buster had started his art collection and it was now as impossible for him to pass an art gallery as it always had been for him to pass a bookshop. In one gallery in Calcutta he saw a picture of a man reading a newspaper at a pavement cafe. To me it was just another picture but he recognised the value of it immediately and this was confirmed when he turned it over and discovered the name of an artist who had recently won an important Italian award. At £40, it was a genuine bargain. Naturally Buster did not have anything as practical as money on him, so I had to go and cash some of my travellers' cheques and raise it for him. He went back and bought it. What fascinated me, even though I knew him well by then, was that he refused to let the gallery wrap it. It was large and valuable and awkward to carry through customs and on to airplanes, but Buster was determined that everyone should see him as a connoisseur and a good judge of art. It was an exhibitionist streak in him that he never lost. He carried it through the streets of the city. He carried it off the plane in London in such a gale that when the wind got under it he was almost lifted off his feet. But people around him were almost walking upside down to see what masterpiece he had bought and that, Buster loved.

That painting was almost the first really good piece he had in his collection and is now extremely valuable. Continually he was encouraging me to buy something of real value like that but I've never had any real appreciation of art and I always had the nagging thought that I was going to be cheated. Buster, meanwhile, was having to move house to find room for everything he was accumulating. He first built himself a bungalow, with lots of unusual brickwork, based on the then startlingly contemporary styles of the Commonwealth Village in Perth. Later he moved to a large, beautiful house in the suburbs of Belfast. He was always proud that it was no small contrast to his childhood home, which hadn't even had a bathroom.

When he came finally to build his ultimate dream of a health club it was, once more, a completely personal design. All the architect had to do was make the ideas professionally viable. Buster knew that the most advanced health clubs were in America, so that was where we went after the Tokyo Olympics. We must have visited between fifty and sixty, traipsing by way of Honolulu to Los Angeles and San Francisco and Washington and New York. Buster went into every one of them as though it were the Taj Mahal all over again, looking, peering, asking questions. Some of them were exclusively for women and he would be refused admittance. That was where I came in. I would be packed off to bring back a full report. I was still very reticent about that kind of business, and I was always in danger of falling victim to paying a full year's subscription before I could get out again. I became absolutely fed up with it, but Buster hammered his way onward, bursting through doors and demanding to know everything. The result was that, at the end of that trip, there was probably no man living who knew more about modern gymnasia. He was also subtly teaching me the business along the way. He never got tired. He was living confirmation that good health heightens the enjoyment of everything in life.

In everything he did he set his sights high. He could be hard on himself and those around him in times of failure. Just occasionally his quick, explosive temper showed through and though the following incident happened quite late in my athletic career this, perhaps, is the place to record it.

We were preparing for the big one, the Munich Olympics of 1972, and all was not going well. I had been pestered with Achilles tendon trouble, and was getting pain every time I ran. The days were running out and our nerve-ends were beginning to show. It just wasn't going the way we had planned.

One afternoon, out at the Queen's University track, I was putting the shot incredibly badly and with each successive throw was becoming more tense. 'I don't know what the hell you're doing,' snapped Buster, 'but you're certainly not doing it right.' That was all I needed. I thumped the shot down on the gravel and snapped back, 'Well, you're my coach. You tell me what I'm doing wrong.'

The next thing I knew I was lying flat on the ground. Buster had hit me. He'd struck me so hard that he knocked me clean off my feet and I lay there shocked and bewildered and desperately hurt, not from physical pain but because of what had happened between us. We were both acting totally out of character. For me to retaliate; for him to hit me. Those were things that just didn't happen between us.

I got to my feet, but I was so angry I couldn't talk to him. I walked away, right down to the far end of the track. There are few athletic grounds in the world with more beautiful surroundings than that of Queen's University but I saw nothing. Only red. Eventually I turned and went back, noticing thankfully on the way that at least there were no witnesses to what had just happened. News of incidents like that spread like a bushfire.

When I reached Buster he started to laugh. 'How the hell did you get down there on the track?' he said. 'Because you knocked me there,' I said. 'My father never did a thing like that to me, and you'll never do it again.' We finished the training session and went to the car. Buster suggested we have lunch somewhere. 'Take me home,' I said, and we drove in silence across the city. He pulled in to the kerb and I got out, slammed the door and ran into my flat, determined to take no telephone calls. I just had to sort out in my own mind whether I was going to continue in athletics or not. I knew that if I were to break with Buster I would get out of sport altogether. I would never work under another coach.

The telephone rang. I sat there and stared at it but it went on ringing. Whoever it was knew I was in, and the only person who could know that was Buster. I knew that it was only his desire for me to do well that had made him do that awful thing. But did mere ambition justify people treating one another like brutal sub-humans? The telephone continued to ring. I walked across and picked up the receiver. Buster's voice said, 'I'm sorry, P, I shouldn't have done it.' It was the only time he ever apologised to me in his life.

# 5

# Queen of the Workers

What was I to do? The year was 1960. I was still a teacher, and for months my friend Joan Wallace and I had saved for a holiday-of-a-lifetime on the Costa Brava. We'd been students together and now we were both teachers in Belfast – and on the money that pays, you don't just chuck it all overboard because you receive a letter inviting you to represent Great Britain in an athletics match against Hungary at the White City, London. I had been dying for the invitation but I was paying for the holiday and fate decreed that both things would happen on the same day. Had I known Buster then as I was to know him later he would have gone to the telephone, sorted it out in thirty seconds and told me what to do. Instead of which I was staying with my family in Lancashire and listening to my father's advice. 'There's nothing for it,' he said, 'you'll just have to decide between one or the other.' That settled it. I was determined to do both.

Even now the cheek of what I did makes me go cold. I went to a phone box and contacted Jack Crump, secretary of the British Amateur Athletic Board. 'Mr Crump,' I began, stumbling over how to explain my predicament, 'I've got this invitation to compete at the White City but I've got this holiday booked in—' Mr Crump cut me off very gently and explained that of course there was no complication at all. My friends simply went on ahead to Spain, I competed in London and flew out on a later plane to join them. Naturally my one-way ticket to Spain would be paid for by the Athletic Board who, unreasonably, were almost detaining me in London for their own benefit. Would I please have a very successful athletics meeting and a very happy holiday? I had never heard anything like it. This was star treatment. It appeared that I had arrived.

It was my first United Kingdom international selection, and there was no doubt who was responsible for it. Marea Hartman, the England women's team manager, had invited me to join her own club, the Spartan Ladies' Athletic Club of London, and while performing for them at Hurlingham, I had suddenly pulled out a shot-put of something like 39ft 11in. This was almost as good as anything achieved by the two best shot-putters in the country. Clearly I was now earmarked as someone to encourage and so, after the two comparatively quiet summers since the Cardiff Commonwealth Games, I was on the way. I performed quite well against Hungary, but it must say something about my temperament that I was as equally excited about the prospect of going on holiday to Spain that same evening.

I have travelled many thousands of miles all over the world since then but I don't think I have ever had a more adventurous journey. I was the classic innocent abroad. I went to London Airport straight from a reception in Park Lane and took my seat in the plane next to a very smooth-looking gentleman who insisted that there was absolutely nothing to this flying business at all. 'Just sit back there, relax and enjoy it,' he said. Unfortunately our plane passed through an area of mild turbulence, which caused my companion to lose his composure for a moment or two while he was spectacularly ill all over the place. We arrived in Barcelona about two o'clock the following morning.

The first thing I discovered was that the courier who was going to meet me hadn't turned up. The second thing was that my luggage had been left behind in London. The third was that I had not the faintest idea how far away Tossa de Mar was, or even in which direction it lay. The fourth was that I had no cash, only travellers' cheques, and none of the airport banks was open. The fifth was that I desperately wanted to visit the loo, but I'd been informed that all Spanish lavatories were custom-built to accommodate men and women simultaneously. They weren't getting me into one of those. So I sat there all night, shifting uneasily through a number of yoga positions, while they washed the floor under my feet.

Finally help arrived in the form of the next flight in from London. My luggage was on it, a courier was present and eventually they squeezed me into a taxi with three men who were also bound for the Costa Brava. Happily their physiological needs soon happened to coincide with my own. They stopped the taxi and must have been astonished to see Britain's newest international athlete break a world record to beat them to the toilet. By not much later than three o'clock that afternoon I was standing in High Street, Tossa, in all my Park Lane finery – a green blazer, a homemade cocktail dress of pink crepe, and a pair of stiletto, winklepicker shoes that were killling me. I staggered to the hotel, joined my friends, flopped out on the beach in the blazing sun and went out like a light. Naturally I would have burned to a frazzle had someone not shown mercy and covered me with beach towels. 'Mary P.,' I vowed when I woke up, 'if you're going to conquer anything you're going to have to start getting organised. What's more, if you can make an international team as a shot-putter, just think what you could do if you really got down to strict training.' It was probably the first time I'd ever realised my own potential.

Even so, the resolution to 'get organised' was easier said than achieved. Later that summer we went to the Continent again for matches against Germany and Poland. Now the completely haphazard approach I had taken to the Cardiff Games was gone. I wanted a disciplined existence, I wanted to dedicate myself to the business of winning, yet all I found was confusion. One afternoon I was getting down to some hard practice on a training ground when, one by one, almost every member of the male, English 'heavy mob' came by to have a look at my method. One said that I was doing this wrong, another said I was doing that wrong, almost no one suggested I was doing anything right at all. 'If I'm that bloody bad,' I asked myself, 'what on earth am I doing here?' I am sure they all meant well but they certainly didn't do much for my confidence.

I went to find a shoulder to weep on and it was lucky that the shoulder belonged to Denis Watts, one of the most gentle and understanding men in British athletics. Denis was national coach and, like myself, came from Liverpool. He knew that I had just begun training under Buster in Belfast, but that in no way altered his attitude when confronted by a crestfallen and rather tearful girl who badly needed her shattered ego to be pieced together right there and then. He talked to me a great deal and did much to sort me out at a critical time. Later when I returned to Northern Ireland, he continued his confidence-building programme by sending me lots of amusing little notes all designed to impress on me the fact that I had a great future in athletics, as long as I could believe in myself. His methods were in direct contrast to Buster's. Occasionally when I was over in Liverpool visiting relatives I would go and train with Denis at the Liverpool University track. If the day was cold he would bring a hot water bottle to training so that the shot I was to tuck between my cheek and neck would be warmed up for use. I owe him a great deal for pulling me through one of the great depressions of my life. It is trite to say that without believing in yourself you can achieve nothing, but in my case, it took an agonisingly long time for that simple fact to sink in.

The irony is that as soon as I had accepted this, another figure was to enter my life to remind me that there are widely contrasting degrees of self-confidence. When I first set eyes on Mary Bignal – soon to be Mary Rand and later, Mary Toomey – she was stepping out of a sports car outside the restaurant I was at with Doris and my father. She was escorted by a Siamese prince and looked as though she was about to pose for a glossy advertisement in *Vogue*. In fact she was arriving to compete in a British Pentathlon Championship, but that was how Mary liked to make her entrances everywhere. She was radiantly beautiful, had enormous style, apparently travelled everywhere with an entourage of admirers, was always surrounded by reporters, knew every top athlete in the world by their first name and, all in all, gave the impression that Hollywood was wherever she happened to be.

I watched her, mesmerised and fascinated, across the restaurant. She laughed a lot, was easy with everyone but, above all, seemed utterly blasé about the stir she was creating. I could think of no greater gulf between the way of life of two human beings than hers and mine. Watching her, knowing that I was shortly to be out there competing against her, almost made me a nervous wreck on the spot. I was back in that street in Tossa wearing all the wrong clothes all over again.

Mary was two years younger than me and, as I was to discover later, came from a very similar social background, but at that moment she was virtually everything I wanted to be. I had the feeling, there and then, that I was destined to live in this dazzling girl's shadow for the next few years, and so it proved to be. I neither had nor have any resentment about it. She was to become the greatest all-round woman athlete I have ever met and we were to build a deep and lasting friendship before it was all over.

I was to have one brief moment in the spotlight when to everyone's surprise, not least my own, I went to the European Championships of 1962 and finished fifth, well above my old heroine, Thelma Hopkins. These were only the second major Games in which I had competed and they were the first outside Britain. A fifth place in that highly competitive field was, by any standards, a good achievement, but to have finished so far ahead of Thelma in a pentathlon really did end the years in which I had played lady-in-waiting to the great star of Northern Ireland. But now I was to play lady-in-waiting to the greatest star in all Britain. It seemed to be my eternal role.

To say that Mary was the leading all-round sportswoman of my generation may imply that I am finding excuses for never having beaten her in a pentathlon. This isn't so. She would have emerged as a star at almost any branch of sport to which she applied her enormous talents. She was a beautiful swimmer and an outstanding hockey player. In South Africa on one occasion we were watching some local ladies give a demonstration on a trampoline. We were both invited to have a go. With some embarrassment I bounced around on it for a few moments and than made way for Mary. Mary's performance could have been televised. It was quite outstanding and I am sure the local ladies didn't believe her when she confessed afterwards that she had only ever been on a trampoline twice previously in her life. On another occasion she was invited to present the awards at one of the *News of the World*'s nationwide darts competitions. One of the attractions was a set of gold darts to be presented to the person who threw the first bull. Mary was to get the competition going by throwing the first dart. It was quite typical of her that she took careful aim, threw that first dart straight into the bull and won the prize for herself. Once, I stood with her on the side of a tennis court in America while her husband was taking lessons from a professional coach. All the while she was watching I could sense her impatience. She was itching to be playing herself. Eventually her chance came and she went on to the court to play as if she had just spent a month warming up with the Wightman Cup Team. The coach merely shook his head and said 'How does she do it?'

It typified her approach to every sport she touched. The secret, I think, was that she was without any kind of embarrassment in any situation. She would have attempted the pole vault had anyone allowed her and she would have done that well, too.

In some things I did envy her. I envied the fact that she achieved everything she did without ever having to train as hard as I did. I was never jealous of her easy manner with men, but I was envious of the number of admirers she had. Everywhere we went there always seemed to be a welcome committee awaiting her with flowers and presents and the promise of parties. She just took it all in her stride, assuming that this was the natural order of things. She had the priceless assets for the athlete of long, slender limbs, and even when the competition was at its toughest she remained supremely polished. In those early days she used to compete with a pearl ring on her engagement finger, rather as though she had just stepped out of a Dior gown to go out on the track. Perhaps she had. I remember one afternoon when she went out and bought ten dresses in a single shopping expedition.

I often wondered where all this supreme assurance and poise came from. She had certainly been adored by her family, but she had also gone for a while to Millfield, that remarkable school in Somerset that produced so many outstanding athletes and sportsmen. She also loved to hold the stage. I said to her once, 'If there was a single chair in a crowded room you would be bloody well sitting on it.' She laughed and denied it, but I was right. In her personal life, her liking to be the centre of attraction didn't bring her complete happiness, but during her phenomenal career in sport it was probably her greatest asset of all. It was a concealed arrogance that made her such a natural leader and supreme competitor.

It took me a long while to get over those early feelings that she was some kind of goddess among the plebs. They didn't wear off until we were thrown together as both teammates and roommates at the Tokyo Olympics of 1964. There is nothing to beat communal living to learn about a person's real character and I learned much about Mary in those weeks in the room we shared with Ann Packer and Pat Pryce. She was a total fanatic about tidiness and, as the dominant personality in those quarters, she made us live as neat and orderly a life as she did herself. Nothing was permitted to be out of place. To leave a sweater draped over a chair, as I was in the habit of doing, was almost an indictable offence. Everything had to be in its exact place, in our sections of the room as well as hers. She was exactly the same about her home life. She would not dream of going out until her home was in perfect order. Nor could she sit in a room, as I have a perhaps reprehensible capacity to do, with magazines strewn about and papers piled up on the table. Everything would have to be neat, in date order, in logical sequence and squared up with the edge of the table. I have read that Ian Fleming, the writer of the Bond books, had the same obsession. A psychologist would probably find interesting parallels there: they were both immensely successful, charismatic people, envied by millions. But I couldn't help feeling that Mary was making hard work of living. If anything, she was fussy to a fault. But she was a winner and, for her, perfection was no part-time aim.

This was a side to her that the press, who dogged her footsteps and logged her whirlwind romances and travels and marriages, didn't see. She was good 'copy' everywhere she went. But she was marvellously human, too. In South Africa, we stayed with Jean Ellis, and Jean came into our room late one evening to find me shrieking with laughter at the sight of Mary in a long Jane Eyre nightgown. All day long Mary had been enrapturing some rather solid South African gentlemen with skirts so short that nine-tenths of her thighs were exposed for public approval, and here she was going to her lonely bed wrapped up like a nun. Maybe it was only reprisal on my part. Our South African tour came just at the time when ultra-short skirts became fashionable, which meant that tights were coming in as fast as suspenders were going out. Mary, inevitably, was a leader in the new mode and expressed her horror one morning at the length of the skirt I proposed to wear that day. 'Good God,' she said, 'you're not going out in that. Get it turned up.' We turned it up to what Mary decreed was the correct length, only to discover that the suspenders to which I had remained resolutely loyal didn't exactly lend themselves to this kind of experiment. I spent the rest of the trip wearing Mary's cast-off tights. It was the same with our hair. Mine, until I grew it, required about as much attention as Kew Gardens in springtime. I needed perms and curlers and clips and rollers, whereas Mary washed hers every day and just shook it out and brushed it and looked a million dollars in five minutes flat. It is hard to see, perhaps, how we became such very close friends, but we did. The friendship was forged in Tokyo where Mary's pursuit of perfection ended with her bringing back to Britain a complete set of Olympic medals: a gold for her world record leap in the long jump, a silver for her second place in the pentathlon, and a bronze for her part in the 4 x 100m relay. I was very happy then to have been some assistance in the pentathlon.

Tokyo, as the phrase goes, was something else. In fact that is an apt description because I had never seen anything like it before or since. There were murmurings at the time that perhaps it was too early to hold an Olympic Games in a country which only thirty years before had been waging war against the world, but I have to be truthful and say that that thought did not stay with me very long. Tokyo was a beautiful, thrilling city: a combination of incredible modern bustle and gentle centuries-old courtesy. One hour you would be sitting in a taxi being driven at breakneck speeds down an eight-lane city street or fighting your way into an underground train that looked as though its destination was to be Wembley on Cup Final day. The next you would be sitting on cushions in a jeweller's shop where the business was being transacted as though tomorrow or perhaps next month would be quite soon enough to conclude a purchase. I remember going into one where I removed my shoes at the door, went in and sat down on a cushion on the floor and then went out again to find that my shoes had been moved around so that they were pointing towards the exit. It has often intrigued me how much a Japanese shoe-turner is paid for an honest week's work. There were ladies in smart Fifth Avenue clothes and ladies in kimonos. There were men who looked as though they had been dressed by some tailor in Savile Row, and others who were still wearing the traditional robes. The schoolchildren, with their immaculate white ankle socks, were a picture of health and contentedness. Perhaps this is an over-romantic picture, but I found Tokyo a heavenly place.

This was Asia acting as Olympic host for the first time. A record number of countries, 94, took part and between them sent 5,541 competitors. It was also my own first Olympics and I wept with sheer joy at the beautiful opening ceremony. Such emotions wore off, however, when Mary and I came into contact with our leading opponents in the pentathlon. Irina Press and Galina Bystrova, of the Soviet Union, did not exactly welcome us as long-lost or even new friends. They were undisputed favourites for the gold and silver medals, but they recognised in Mary a very dangerous rival. This may well explain their attitude to us which was to treat us with such arrogant condescension that we might well have been a couple of Mayfair debs who had strayed on to the track by mistake.

This was more Mary's problem than mine because she was in there with a chance while it was generally acknowledged that I had none. I hoped for a good placing but little more. For all that, one look at those formidable ladies was enough to make me determined to burst a lung to help Mary in her challenge, and it is one of the happiest memories of my life that I was able to do just that.

Mary was in marvellous form throughout those Games, and as we came to the final event of the pentathlon, the 200 metres, she at least had the chance to come between Press, who was certain to take the gold, and Bystrova, who had to run pretty well to take the silver. The draw decreed that, while Mary ran against Press in the second heat, I was to run against Bystrova in the first. As a runner, Bystrova was something of an unknown quantity, but we knew that if I could beat her then the silver would be Mary's. I ran as I had never run before. Coming down the final straight, I thought I would explode but I stayed there and beat her and, despite what you may read in the remaining pages of this book, few races in my life have given me more satisfaction. Mary took the silver medal. That deepened our friendship and it was that day that I lost all awe of her. Athletically we were still not equals, but as human beings we rubbed along pretty well, recognising that the other had something to offer. When I was doing the long jump, Mary would say, 'Why the bloody hell can't you get your bottom up?' When she came into my sphere I would say, 'Why the bloody hell don't you learn how to put the shot?' It was the one event of which she had very little idea, which just goes to prove, in pentathlon terms, how brilliant she was at everything else.

My final memory of Mary at those Tokyo Games was of her lying in bed in our room the night before her long jump final. She sang a couple of the little songs she used to sing every night to her daughter, Alison. I knew suddenly that she was too tense and nervous to go to sleep and the rest of us joined in until, eventually, we all dropped off. The next day Mary smashed the world record. That's how good she was.

My own placing in the Tokyo pentathlon was fourth, one outside the medal. I was very satisfied. It was as much as Buster thought I could do and better than I thought I could achieve. It was also as much as I would ever achieve while the star of Mary Rand, as she was known by then, shone so brightly in the firmament. All I could do was work harder and harder. Derek Clarke, for years a leading British decathlete, saw it all. In a letter to me much later he wrote, 'Mary Rand was Queen of the Naturals, Mary Peters, Queen of the Workers.' The only thing was that I hadn't really started working yet.

# 6

# The Runner-up

Although the pentathlon was part of the Olympic programme for women in the mid-sixties, it still hadn't been introduced into the Commonwealth Games. We were back to the old routine. Buster consulted all the charts of comparative performances and decided that I would now concentrate on the shot and go to the 1966 Games in Kingston, Jamaica, with one single target in mind: the gold medal. It was then he announced that to build up strength for this single objective I would undergo a body-building programme which, in theory, sounded unpleasant and which, in practice, proved to be hideously revolting. In short I was put on a diet which virtually amounted to forced feeding.

Already I was taking all the vitamin supplements, but now I was to undergo the agony of physically forcing food into myself. A typical single-day routine involved the following: for breakfast, a grapefruit, a bowl of cereal, at least three eggs and bacon followed by toast, marmalade and coffee. I arrived at the gym to start work at 10.00 a.m. where I would immediately have two pints of milk and two cartons of yoghurt. For lunch, between 12.30 p.m. and 1.00 p.m., I would go to the restaurant on the corner and have a full three-course meal, often followed by cheese and biscuits. Halfway through the afternoon there would be more milk and yoghurt. Mid-evening I would have a full protein dinner consisting of meat, fish or chicken followed by fruit, ice cream and coffee. Quite often I would then be forced to have sandwiches before I went to bed.

The additional vitamins I was taking were vitamins E and C, and the only relief was that I wasn't also being subjected to the B12 injections I had been having earlier.

Of course there was no compulsion; I could have quit at any time I pleased. But Buster was my coach and as long as I wished the arrangement to continue I was prepared to accept his training and diet schedules. Nor did I cheat. When he asked me what I'd had for breakfast I would tell him exactly. I couldn't lie to him, so instead I did exactly what he said, even though I found the whole process nauseating, particularly when it came to the milk and yoghurt routines mid-morning and mid-afternoon. I was already so full that it was sometimes almost impossible to get them down. To aid my digestion, which at times felt as though it was going through a series of 24-hour strikes, Buster arranged for me to have a rest in the afternoons. There was a large old safe in a nearby car showroom and he arranged for me to go there, complete with a lilo and blankets, so that I could lie down in complete seclusion. It did nothing for me at all. I always felt desperately overfull and, despite all the blankets, it was invariably too cold for me to drop off to sleep. I used to lie there in the murky darkness imagining that spiders were slowly wending their way down from the ceiling.

There were two other disadvantages. First, my food bills shot up astronomically. Buster paid for the milk and the yoghurt but all the other meals were paid for out of my own pocket. I came very close, literally, to eating my full salary every week. And second, soon came the problem that I no longer had any clothes at all that would fit me. I needed a completely new wardrobe. Nor was it the kind of wardrobe that you can buy off the peg. The combination of huge intakes of food, and the murderous weight training programme I was undergoing each evening meant that I was developing the kind of shape that would defeat any tailor. My upper arms and around the shoulders were developing so disproportionately to the rest of my body that my overall shape was beginning to look like that of Superman.

One afternoon, not long before leaving for Jamaica, I went out shopping with Buster's wife, Margaret, to buy the prettiest dress I could possibly find. It was probably the lowest point of my life. I tried on everything I liked. Nothing at all would zip up. If a dress fitted me round the neck and across the shoulders, then it hung out over my hips like a bell tent. If it fitted me round the hips, then there was no chance that it would ever reach round my shoulder blades. I bought nothing and went home in despair and cried myself to sleep. I adore lovely clothes.

I suppose I was the only athlete to turn up for the Commonwealth Games in West Indies wearing cast-off maternity clothes. Margaret looked out all the blouses and skirts she had stored away since her last confinement, and with a few alterations here and there we somehow got a wardrobe together. At least the blouses fitted me across the back and there was room to tuck them into the skirts.

There remained the problem of a light topcoat. At the very point when I had been feeling my lowest, I had seen a woman crossing a Belfast street wearing the most elegant white coat I had ever seen. It became almost an obsession for me – I wanted to go out and buy one exactly like it. It was hopeless. Eventually I found a white coat of sorts in the cheapest of chain stores, which more or less went round me. I bought it, but in a rage of temper one day said to Buster, 'I'm now having to go out and get the cheapest rubbish on the market because of what you're doing to me.' Buster was quite unmoved. He had decided on his course of action. My weight, in a matter of months, had soared up from my usual 10 stones 6 pounds to 13 stone 4. It wasn't fat, it was muscle. I hated every minute of the whole detestable operation.

The alternative would have been to have taken steroids. At the time, 1966, I knew nothing about steroids at all. Now everyone knows that their use was, rightly, universally condemned and banned. It was widely believed that their use, certainly in the vast quantities in which some athletes are supposed to take them, can cause sexual impotence. It was not because of this, however that I resolved not to take them at any point in my career in athletics. Nor, in my case, was it anything as highly principled as the fact that it was blatantly cheating. My mother's death from cancer had left me with a horror of introducing any element of an untested drug into my body. I feared that it could give me the same disease and I felt that, if steroids could achieve rapid muscular growth, they could also cause rapid cancer cell growth. This may have had no basis in scientific reasoning but it was enough to convince me to leave them alone.

It was around this time that a well-known British coach put the story round that I was a steroid-taker. He apparently refused to believe that I could put on almost an additional three stones in muscular weight in a single summer in any other way. Well, athletics can be a spiteful world and perhaps he couldn't think of any other reason why I was continually improving. I am not sure what his motive was but his allegations made me very angry.

By this stage I was something of an old hand on the circuit, but to a girl who had been brought up in the sheltered environment that I had, the news that greeted us as soon as we arrived in Kingston, Jamaica, came as a bit of a shock: we had to submit ourselves to 'sex verification' tests. And until we'd done so, we couldn't take part in the Games.

Obviously you cannot be a female athlete for very long before you discover you have certain problems to contend with which never bother men. Very early in my career, I met Dr Wilson Johnson, of Queen's University, Belfast. He was a kind and gentle man, and was extremely advanced in his field, so it was no problem at all for him to prescribe for us the contraceptive pill, which would permit us to go into a major athletics event without any fear of being inconvenienced by a period. I was so innocent at the time that the pill's other, intended, purpose had never occurred to me. I must be one of the very few takers who honestly believed it was discovered to help young ladies succeed in athletics.

I took the pill during particular stages of the athletic year in order to regulate menstruation during training spells or major competition. And while I appreciate that my doing so may seem to have been at odds with my fear of putting any kind of drug into my body, the difference between it and steroids was that the pill had been checked out for side effects over long periods of research, whereas steroids, at that time, hadn't been sufficiently investigated to determine fully the short- and long-term effects.

I, along with the other female athletes in the team, also received the very finest medical attention possible at the West Middlesex Hospital in London where Doctors Andrew and David (whose surnames I cannot mention) talked to us in such a down-to-earth yet expert manner that it filled us with confidence. Specialists in gynaecology and muscular troubles respectively, they did more for British women's athletics than a lot of people whose names were regularly seen in the newspapers. Before any major event, every athlete had the most exhaustive medical check-up, and if any treatment was required it would be provided on the spot. Team manager Marea Hartman was completely responsible for setting up this outstanding service and it proved to be a major development.

However, I digress.

I forget exactly which room of which building we were instructed to report to for the tests, but all of us from the British teams had been summoned together to prove our womanhood, and I must confess, there was a certain amount of embarrassment. Sex education has never been part of the curriculum at any of the schools I went to; we probably got around to the birds and the bees in biology classes, but that would have been the height of it. And now, there we all were, women of thirty-five and schoolgirls of sixteen, wearing our housecoats and standing in the corridor outside that forbidding room in Jamaica, waiting to be examined. We had to go in, one by one, in alphabetical order, so I knew I had a long wait.

We got away to a bad start. A doctor emerged and said in an overbrisk voice, 'If any of you have got knickers on, go and take them off.' Well, for God's sake we all had knickers on, and bras too, because this was the middle of the afternoon and streaking had not yet been invented. We all looked at one another somewhat sheepishly, and then went back to our rooms and returned starkers under our housecoats. This is where a woman like Marea Hartman proved her worth. Instead of getting all uptight on our behalf she proceeded to make a huge joke of the whole thing. She produced a cine camera – to this day I don't know whether it had any film in it – and proceeded to shoot us in extravagant poses. Some played Mata Hari, some Lady Hamilton and a few brave ones actually unknotted their housecoats and gave the camera a quick 'flash' in the dirty raincoat tradition. It all helped to break the ice while we sat there like battery hens awaiting our fate.

Eventually the names began to be called and, one by one, victims went in. The athletes did not, we noticed, emerge smiling. They flew out of the door and rushed straight back to their quarters. No one gave us a hint about the kind of procedure we might expect. Some looked distraught and many were clearly upset. What the hell went on in there? We just had to wait our turn and see. The wait was so long that all sorts of things began to play on my mind. What was all this about? What were they investigating? Why was everyone fleeing so hurriedly? Other questions began fill the mind: *What if there is something different about me? Am I normal?* I have to confess that, as I sat there in that bare corridor, the very sight of those dashing away without telling us what we had to expect made my heart beat a great deal faster.

At last my name was called. I went into a bare room which contained two female doctors, one examination couch and one large enamel bowl containing some white, cloudy antiseptic in which the doctors apparently washed their hands after each examination. What occurred next I can only describe as the most crude and degrading experience I have ever known in my life. I was ordered to lie on the couch and pull my knees up and the doctors then performed an intrusive examination. I left when it was over and, like everyone else who had fled that detestable room, I said nothing to anyone still waiting in the corridor as I made my way, shaken, back to my room.

That was the first of several such examinations. The next was at the European Championships in Budapest and, while it was scarcely more dignified, at least we knew what to expect. This time we went into an anteroom in pairs, removed our clothes, draped them over chairs and proceeded through another door at the far end of the room into an examination hall where no fewer than ten doctors were waiting to give us the once-over. It was so overwhelming that I can't recall whether they were all women, all men or a combination of both. All I do remember is that as we entered, we were clutching our passports. I can't remember where I held mine but I do know that, once again, it made us feel as though we were being auditioned for some pretty seamy strip-show. By now, all the reporters had cottoned on to what was happening and they were waiting outside the building to fire off some stories about our most embarrassing moments. To foil them, most of the British girls got together and we emerged singing that lovely tune more commonly associated with the 'Eton Boating Song' – 'Swing swing together, with your bodies between your knees …' – but with very different words.

Down the years the whole procedure was to become somewhat more sophisticated but, at the same time I felt, a little more sinister. By the

Mexico Olympics of 1968, they had ostensibly developed a method of determining sex by saliva tests and chromosome analysis. This was altogether more acceptable from the personal point of view but, before they started, I went to Marea Hartman to demand to know what would happen to any of our girls if they did fail a test. It was all very well to say that all this was being done in the name of fair play in sport, but there were serious social implications as well. Supposing a girl failed the test, would she be eliminated from the Games in a blaze of worldwide publicity? Suppose the examining doctors made a mistake? A life could be ruined in the very brief time it would take for the news to leak out.

As captain of the team, my suggestion was that all our girls should be protected by a plan to have them taken to an isolation ward of a hospital should the chromosome tests show up any irregularities. The announcement could then be made that she had contracted some contagious illness and we would then just pray that our word would be accepted. Happily I was worrying unnecessarily as far as the British team were concerned but I think my concern was justified when one of our overseas opponents failed to pass the test. And it may be significant that two of my opponents in those early days dropped out of international competition altogether when they knew they would have to submit themselves to independent examination.

At least, after Mexico, I had a certificate to 'prove my womanhood' but somehow I came to lose that vital piece of paper before the Munich Olympics. By then the examination process had become still more sophisticated. They removed a hair from your head to examine the follicle and this, apparently, told them all they wanted to know. Unfortunately it didn't always work with hair that had been bleached or permed and, once again, a number of girls had to go through agonies of suspense while they were recalled to take a saliva test as well.

I cannot recall those Commonwealth Games in Jamaica with any affection at all. I had limited myself to a single event, the shot, and set my sights on a single target, the gold medal. After all that agonising preparation I should have won it, but I didn't. My main rival there was Val Young, the New Zealander, and at a pre-Games meeting I beat her easily. I shot-put 56 ft, which was a full 3 feet more than Val, and it really should have given me the kind of psychological advantage that would make me invincible. Even now I cannot fully analyse what went wrong on the big day except to know that I was irritable and distracted and quite unable to get myself into a winning mood. The very last straw came when the day's programme went haywire and the shot competition started an hour later than scheduled. I desperately wanted to get on with it but I had to wander around instead. It was during that hour's wait that I lost the gold. My concentration went and the adrenalin seemed to dry up and when the time came I was quite incapable of pulling out the big one. I had to be content with the silver.

I was furious with myself at being so mentally weak. But my own annoyance was nothing compared with Buster's wrath. Far from sparing me any sympathy, he stormed out of the stadium without saying a single word to me. In his view I had let him, myself, and Northern Ireland down, and wasted a complete summer's work. I rang him at his hotel and he refused to come to the phone to talk. I left a message that I would like him there when I went up to receive my silver medal. He refused to come to that ceremony either. I then went to his hotel and once more he refused to see me. Eventually, of course, he couldn't avoid me any longer. I made the mistake of putting on an almost light-hearted pose. 'Ah, well,' I said, 'I expect there are a few people somewhere who still love me.' That made him even more livid and I walked into a force-ten dressing down. 'That's your trouble,' he said, 'you can take defeat too lightly.' It was the start of a long lecture about mental attitudes. The difference between us was that I was very disappointed but wanted to conceal it. Buster was very disappointed and didn't care who knew. Eventually I said to him, 'If you react like this again I shall finish with athletics altogether.' Unlike the occasion when he struck me in training, it did not provoke an apology. He said nothing, only glowered. He came to realise, in the end, that I was as upset as he was.

As usual, Buster was right. I had talent, I had strength and I trained religiously. But until I hardened my mental approach I was always going to be the bridesmaid, the runner-up, the silver medallist, the second best.

It was too late to work on a fundamental change of character in that season of 1966. There were still the European Championships to come and I almost felt doomed before I competed. My failure in Jamaica had a paralysing effect on me. At my best I should have given the formidable

Nadezhda Chizhova a very good fight, but my defences were down. She won the shot with 56ft 6in and I trailed in almost 8 feet behind her. The year was a write-off and I was beginning to wonder whether there were enough years left.

# 7

# Mexico: Myth and Reality

The pentathalon, by definition, is five times as strenuous as most events in women's athletics. I found it essential to work only in alternate years in competition. I did little on track in 1965, following the Tokyo Olympics, and little again in 1967, following my pretty disastrous Commonwealth Games in Jamaica. The year 1968 was probably the watershed of my life in sport. I began preparing for it on 21 November 1967. All over the world, my rivals for the Mexico Olympics were doing the same. Unlike a good number of them, in the American colleges and the Iron Curtain squads, I had to hold a job while I was training. Buster devised a set of gruelling training schedules for me, designed to turn me into an Olympic champion. This is an extract from one of them to give you a sense of what my week looked like:

> FRIDAY: Usual warm-up plus relax sprint arm movement and ankle rotations. Sprint starts giving 5ft. Long jump: four from four strides off board for maximum height; three from six strides off board; two from 8ft holding height intro to extend landing. Relaxed full run-up, jumping emphasis on technique not distance. Two or three relaxed running with just one 20-yard period around 80 yards out with 90 per cent acceleration holding relaxed slightly wider arm action.

SATURDAY: High jump with warm-up leading into crab's bend and hypering on to landing area plus vertical jumps to mark on handball net. Four four-stride jumps over 4ft 10in. 5ft 2in for concentrating on steady stride pattern with 6-7-8 count at take-off. Emphasis on fast 7 to counter fault of long stride hindering quadriceps' drive with late and low pelvis position. Be conscious of (a) a fair pause between jumps, control adrenalin flow and hold relaxation and (b) you will always tend to be close in at take-off and must observer this and related good continual arc. Increase bar by one inch and jump as in competition until 5ft 6in and really concentrate for three good clearances. This is more important than stabs at greater heights. On specific days I'll set it to 5ft 8in with a side bet ☻. Hurdle work as it has now developed. We want a sharper, more forward action of your lead arm and head following it. Lack of this is partly caused by too much tension in your mastoid and trapezius is hindering your lead leg to drive smoothly but quicker to the ground. Thus just a little more flexibility in the trailing leg's adductors allowing a more rapid whip-up of the knee will get you into the 13.4s now that the new 8-stride approach is eventually settling in. Shot repetition, free glides relaxed but lower than normal followed by four stands and two glides. Then six puts all measured. These you can follow some days with three stands. Really coming out after it, and three similar six-inch shortened glides.

SUNDAY: Build up as you feel best for long jump, utilising, of course, 10-stride marker and develop a count-in. Keep the shoulders relaxed. Allow yourself six full run-up jumps, but remember your preparations must see your best jump in the first three. After that I would like to see you do glides with a 12lb shot aiming for 45ft, finishing with six stands with 16. We then start striding and two starts, followed by two 50-yards from blocks, two 80s, one easy 120, followed by a time-trial 150 and with full recovery, three-quarters speed through 200 metres.

WEDNESDAY: High jump warm-up as before, only four jumps over 5ft 3in concentrating on fast quadricep thrust and hyper and left-flick with far-out take-off. Work on hurdles and starts, ending with three starts over two hurdles and then two and three over three. Finish off with long jump but don't fatigue on it. Work for just speed and height off board. Don't worry about distance but check last stride length. If you want to do shot keep it to three stands and six glides.

Remind me to review nutrition.

You might wonder what I was wasting my time at on Mondays, Tuesdays and Thursdays. The answer is that I was weight training according to schedules so complicated that they make the one above look like light relief!

Buster's training schedule meant that, by 1968, I was altogether a harder woman. But that was not enough. I did not win a medal at the Mexico Olympics. By now my greatest personal rival had departed the scene but new opponents had emerged. The departure of Mary Rand – who, after being stricken by injury had been forced to retire – saddened me more than I can describe. I have to examine my soul very carefully before putting that on record because I knew that, even under new training schedules and with my new attitude, I would always be hard-pressed to beat her in any competition. With Mary gone, I felt that nothing was beyond me, but for all that I took no pleasure in her retirement from athletics.

Mary had gone to live in America. She still wanted to represent Britain in the Olympics so she had to return to qualify. We met at Crystal Palace where I had taken a week off to train. Poor Mary was very miserable. It was a difficult period for her domestically, but she was also severely hampered by Achilles tendon trouble, which forced her to go every day for treatment. Already Ann Wilson and I had qualified for the British team so there was just one place left and it was being kept open until Mary had competed in an international invitation meeting at which the selectors could judge her form. On the day, Mary could not compete at all. Sue Scott, meanwhile, competed for England with real distinction. Still the selectors refused to name the third choice. This was perhaps hard on Sue, but La Rand was not a lady you just passed over because of an injury that might heal itself in days or weeks. Unfortunately this was not the case. They arranged a special fitness test for her and Mary broke down before it had hardly started. She tried to hurdle and couldn't. Mary

Rand's glittering athletic career was over. The great challenge to me from within was over and, if there was anyone who felt more awful about it than her in Great Britain, it was me. I would have loved to have beaten her, but I never did and an opponent's withdrawal is no triumph at all. I can honestly say that being under her shadow for almost seven years left no scars on me at all.

They made me captain of the British women's team for the Mexico Olympics. In retrospect I am sorry because it didn't help my athletics. Then, as now, I have no idea what an athletics captain's responsibilities are supposed to be. Once, captaining a British team in an international match, I actually went to discover what I was supposed to do and the answer was, 'Whatever you choose to do.' I appreciated that it was an honour, and that it was meant to boost my ego, but frankly it was nothing more than a damned nuisance. I made sure the girls had their sex tests and turned up at team meetings and received their mail and messages but, in fact, I did nothing that the average hotel porter couldn't do with far more efficiency. A team captain has no authority in matters of conduct or the exercising of discipline. Those are the duties of the team manager. Of course you can urge your compatriots to do their utmost, but they are going to do that anyway so I would suggest the position is somewhat supernumerary.

In this respect athletics is quite different to other sports where captains either dictate tactics during the battle or standards of social behaviour after it. Clearly a pentathlon performer cannot tell an 800m runner how to approach a race nor, in my case, would I care to assume the position where I had to tell a responsible colleague how to conduct her life after hours. There was certainly one British journalist of the time – a gentle and kindly man whose hobby was growing roses – who would have had readers believe that every Olympic/Commonwealth/European Games was nothing more than a quadrennial vice-racket promoted for no other reason than to allow between 5,000 and 15,000 athletes and officials to engage in adultery and seduction. Of course there is a grain of truth in that: there is as much sexual activity at a major Games as there is at any other congregation of so many people. Of course it went on. But I have never yet been to a Games which warranted the headlines he produced, such as 'Sin City' or 'Village of Vice'.

The only problem is that at an event like the Olympics it is much more difficult for a couple to get together in some kind of privacy than it is, say, at an annual congress of the National Union of Journalists, where the delegates are on expense accounts that give them unlimited use of their own private rooms. The chances of a male athlete getting into a female athlete's room in a Games Village were absolutely nil. We were guarded closely, whether we liked it or not. In the men's quarters, meanwhile, the competitors were mostly quartered four to a room. This, admittedly, did not rule out the possibility of Mr A getting together with Miss B, but it did, you'll probably agree, make it bloody difficult. Messrs C, D and E did tend to object.

There was, of course, the old elastic-band-on-the-door-handle trick, so placed to warn roommates that it would be indiscreet to enter, and I know of one room at one Games where the occupants kept a wallchart detailing the ladies who had allegedly submitted to their limited charms. I wasn't outraged at all. I just found it rather sad that there were still some men about who found it ego-boosting to embarrass a woman by listing her name in their pathetic scorebooks. In the 1870s it may well have impressed their colleagues. In the 1970s and beyond it implied immaturity. If two people had a happy relationship – and I don't pretend that quite a few haven't at international Games – they just didn't talk about it.

When I was competing, young female athletes were watched over carefully and wisely from the moment they reported until the moment they were delivered back to London Airport. The person responsible for this was the remarkable Marea Hartman, the woman who had persuaded me to join Spartan Ladies' Athletic Club. Marea, herself a county sprinter in the era when shorts came down to the knee, became team manager for the Women's AAA in 1950 and full England and British team manager in 1954, a position she held until 1978, making her one of the longest-serving and most influential sports administrators in twentieth-century British athletics. She is credited with the post-Second World War integration of British women athletes into full competition and parity with that of their male counterparts.

She was the most indefatigable person, man or woman, I have ever met. You could phone her at midnight and she would be working. You could phone her again at 6 a.m. and she would often be back at her desk. She loved a drink and could swear as eloquently as a drill sergeant, as I discovered one day on tour when she slipped in the shower, damaged her back and put her tongue to words that I had literally never heard before. But for sheer common sense in the handling and protection and encouragement of young athletes, she had no rival in the world. She thought young, acted young and accepted every succeeding generation of young athletes as though they were the most important charges ever to come into her keeping. I recall, on one of my earliest trips with her, slipping secretly into her room, pinning up her clothes with safety pins, and giving her an apple-pie bed. It seemed pretty hilarious at the time and I suppose Marea had to put up with that kind of juvenile humour from a long succession of girls for over more than twenty years. But never once did I see her show any annoyance.

I have many instances of how she won loyalty and established her authority. One night, when we had finished our competition in Belgrade, several of us wanted to go out on what was an unashamed pub crawl with a few of the BBC men. Marea's method was not to forbid us but to come with us. We returned at five o'clock the following morning and flopped into bed. Not Marea. To avoid having to make any complicated explanations to the official with whom she was sharing a room, she slipped in quietly, had a shower and went straight to work. It was always assumed that she and her girls had had a good night's sleep.

She had an anxious moment during the 1964 Tokyo Olympics, when Linda Knowles, the youngest member of the team, still hadn't reported back by ten o'clock at night. Two of us pulled on our tracksuits, borrowed bikes and went out to search for her. We found her chatting quite innocently to some members of the Swedish team and brought her back to our quarters. This incident received quite a deal of publicity in the British Press, but Marea's method of dealing with it was interesting. The following evening we were being entertained long and lavishly by the British Embassy. At ten o'clock precisely, a car arrived to collect Linda Knowles. 'Quite late enough for you, dear,' said Marea, making her point. The incident was closed and the big stick was never wielded. When we got back to London Airport, Linda's parents were there to thank Marea for what she had done.

Over the years, during which we became very close personal friends, only one thing amazed me about Marea: her complete incomprehension of even the simplest mechanical device. Loading a camera or using a record player was utterly beyond her. She must have been the only woman in Europe who possessed an ultra-modern automatic washing machine that she never used. 'I haven't the faintest idea how it works,' she used to say. 'I just bung my stuff in a bag, take it round to the launderette and eat fish and chips while it's being done.' On the other hand there are few women who have vaulted over a 10ft wall to get out of a stadium when everyone has gone and the place has been locked up. That's what she did on my first overseas trip with her and it was the start of a lifetime friendship, which I treasured greatly.

But I have been diverted along the road to the Mexico Olympics. Much controversy surrounded these Games, from the altitude at which they were staged, to US athletes John Carlos and Tommie Smith's act of solidarity with the Black Freedom Movement during the American national anthem, to the brutal crushing of a student demonstration in which hundreds of protestors were killed. Curiously we knew less about the shootings than people back in Britain. We were not allowed to leave the Village unescorted and we weren't getting newspapers from home.

The trip began inauspiciously for me when I glanced out of the aircraft window about an hour out of London and noticed some rather disturbing black smoke pouring out of one of the engines. We turned around, landed quite safely at Heathrow and then set out again some three hours later. For me things never really recovered from that false start. I strained an ankle some days before the start of the pentathlon, told no one in case it should be interpreted as an excuse and finished a disappointing ninth. Unless I look up the records now, I remember very little of how I fared in each event. For all the hard work I had done, these were never going to be my Games. Ingrid Becker won the event and since she finished 295 points ahead of me I could only offer genuine congratulations to a long-time opponent. For me it was back to the drawing board.

I was fortunate then and, indeed, through most of my career, in that no one really expected me to win. To go to an Olympic Games as a white-hot hope is an agonising experience, and I do wish that sportswriters would realise this before they brand anyone as 'favourite' to win a medal.

One person who suffered badly in Mexico was Lillian Board, who had been made favourite to win a 400m gold medal weeks before she left her home in Ealing. The pressures on her became so great that throughout the whole of those Games we very rarely saw her in the Olympic Village except at bedtimes. She went out with her father and close friends early most mornings and returned late at night simply to escape the constant hounding and interviews. In the end she won the silver medal but I shall always be convinced that the gold would have been hers had she not been the victim of a huge press build-up before her event.

An even more frightening example of this in Mexico concerned the 800m runner, Vera Nikolić, then of Yugoslavia, whose compatriots were so positive that she would win the gold they actually prepared a special issue of a postage stamp which was to be put on sale throughout the country the day after her triumph. Perhaps only another athlete can understand the fearful pressure that this placed on her. In the event, she did not even reach the final. She ran off the track during her semi-final and was so disturbed by the thought of the reaction back home that, later that day she tried to throw herself from a bridge. Fortunately she was seen and saved. I would like to think that the media learned the lesson of that near tragedy, but unfortunately they didn't.

# 8

# The Road to Munich

In the early spring of 1970, following a year's rest after the Mexico Olympics, I equalled the world indoor 60m hurdles record at Cosford. After the disappointments of Jamaica and Mexico, I was desperately looking for some encouragement to help me through the endless training necessary to prepare me for my next two big targets: the Commonwealth Games in Edinburgh that year, and the Munich Olympics that were coming up in 1972. The Cosford record, whatever it was, really did give me a boost when I badly needed one. Four years earlier I had begun to feel that time was running out and here was another Olympics gone with nothing more than pleasure and self-satisfaction to show for it.

Exactly one year to the day before the Edinburgh Games, I got down to training again and this time I was determined that it would be gold or bust. Anyway, I knew I had a chance. Mary Rand had departed and for the first time my own specialist event, the pentathlon, was to be included in a Commonwealth meeting, though they had made a few amendments to it. The hurdles were to be 100m instead of 80m, and both Buster and I thought this would be to my disadvantage, as it would mean a complete revision of my stride pattern. I'm notorious for my short strides and I thought this would mean a great problem fitting in the paces between the hurdles, but it was surprisingly simple. I had to change my starting leg and amend the run to the first hurdle but I became accustomed to that swiftly and was soon very confident. The year's rest and the Cosford record, and the easy way in which I had adapted to the new hurdles, all did a great deal for my confidence which had taken such a battering. In fact, even then, my horizon lifted from the immediate challenge of Edinburgh to the one beyond, Munich.

I had less success trying to change my high-jumping style to the straddle method, mainly because Northern Ireland still didn't have ideal conditions for me to work in. Instead of soft-landing pits, I was falling into sand and jarring every bone in my body. So I abandoned that, went back to the old half-Western-Roll-half-Mary-Peters style of jumping, and didn't look back. Another record came my way when I set a new points total for a British pentathlon. In winning the gold at Edinburgh, I set up a new record for both the United Kingdom and the Commonwealth with 5,148 points. I was delighted about that and I was naturally very happy to win the first gold of what was now becoming a long career.

Yet, for all that, I was overtaken by the same feeling that comes back to me now, as I try to recall my emotions in the Meadowbank Stadium that day. Any euphoria was very much kept in check by the thought that this was still a long way from an Olympic medal. I have no intention of disparaging achievements in the Commonwealth Games but, really, my own success had been quite unspectacular. I had to put up with a certain amount of gamesmanship and, being a member of the Northern Ireland team, I had other events on my mind as well. In fact in the space of three days I took part in all five pentathlon events, the heats and finals of the hurdles and the qualifying round and finals of the shot, which is somewhat strenuous. Yet the prevailing memories now are less of wild jubilation over the fact that I had won at last, than of stirring the crowd up to perform a slow handclap when the officials were dreadfully slow in getting the 200m under way, and of complaining bitterly when told that I would have to hang around the stadium because Prince Charles, as he was then, was going to present my medal and he hadn't arrived yet. I would like to claim that I don't know what was wrong with me that day, but I do know precisely. I was impatient for real success and Munich, still two years away, had become an obsession.

One of the happy outcomes of Edinburgh was that Mike Bull, a tall and sensitive young Belfast philosophy student, joined me under the coaching of Buster McShane. Mike had won the pole vault gold for

Northern Ireland and Buster had great ambitions to turn him into a decathlete as well. It was strange that such an outstanding coach and such an outstanding athlete had taken so long to come together in a provincial city, but I suspect Mike, like so many people, was very wary of Buster's methods and possibly his motives as well. Any reservations Mike had were soon gone. He was astounded at Buster's enormous knowledge. Mike's arrival was a fortunate day for me. Training can become a lonely, weary business and training together we revived one another's interest and enthusiasm.

We were working with a single objective in mind: the 1972 Olympics. What I needed, I knew, was a chance I had never yet had: of being able to get down to solid, full-time training, uninterrupted by work or any other distractions. Many of my Munich opponents, I knew, would take full-time training for granted and all I wanted, even if only for a short period, was an equal opportunity. My main activity in 1971 was to set out to see how it could be achieved. This brought me to the door of 10 Queen Street, Mayfair, the offices of the Winston Churchill Memorial Trust. Buster had already applied for a Churchill Scholarship to go to the United States and write a book about social behaviour. When he didn't get one, or even the interview that might lead to one, he reacted quite predictably in announcing that it was quite obvious that the trust had a personal vendetta against him and that they could go and get stuffed. Buster always reacted like that when he lost. It made him all the keener that I should apply for one, although in the very next breath he was saying it was perfectly obvious that if he hadn't succeeded then I had no chance at all. I knew, though, that a great number of British athletes and coaches, including Mike Bull, had been financed through America by the Churchill Trust so I applied for an interview and got it.

I've never greatly enjoyed interviews of this kind and this one was no exception. The interviewers included the inevitable man wearing a pair of half-moon spectacles, Lord Byers, whom I recognised too late and Colin Cowdrey, the cricketer, whom I recognised instantly. They seemed in some doubt for a while about which of the scholarship courses I was applying for. Was it Docks and Docking? Was it Sculpture? Was it Nursery School Teaching? 'No,' I said, 'It is Participation in Sport.' They didn't look very impressed. What objective did I have in mind? 'Well,' I said, 'I think I can win a gold medal in the Munich Olympics. If I could just get away from the tensions of Belfast for a while and settle down to regular hard training somewhere where the weather is good, I honestly think I've got a chance.' They weren't very impressed with that either. Wasn't I a bit long in the tooth to harbour ambitions like that? Hadn't I been in athletics rather too long? Didn't I think I was setting my sights just a little too high? 'No, no, no,' I replied, but I could see from their faces that they weren't very convinced. I was applying for an £800 grant, far less than had been handed out to other sportsmen and coaches in the past, and the discussion about it went on so long that there was one point where I was on the verge of telling them to forget the whole thing and apologising for troubling them. Eventually, and very sceptically, they agreed that I should go.

'How did you get on?' asked Buster.

'Dead easy,' I said, 'they begged me to take the money.'

I went to Pasadena, in California, to stay with my good friends Bill and Judy Pearl. Bill's name was well known to anyone who had followed bodybuilding, for he was twice a Mr Universe; once when he was quite young and again when he was forty-one years of age, which was a remarkable achievement in a highly competitive business. He was an extremely modest man who was totally dedicated not only to his own sport but to promoting good health among other people. He ran his own gymnasium and was up every morning at 4 a.m. to train there for three and a half hours before coming back to take Judy and me for breakfast and then getting down to his own day's work. This, among many other things, included running a fitness course for the locally stationed officials of the American Space Programme.

It was heaven. It was also three and a half months before the start of the Olympics and exactly the perfect time to go into full work. I had never known anything like it before. All I had to do was eat and sleep and train. The sun shone every day, the excellent track of the Pasadena City College was within walking distance down the road, there was Bill's gymnasium to work out in and, once a week, a friend of ours, John Forde, used to drive me to train on the UCLA Tartan track in Los Angeles. Everyone was kind and I phoned Buster with ecstatic reports about the progress I was making. I was so on top of the world that in Los Angeles

I indulged in some real showing off. I asked one athlete if she minded whether I trained with her and she said, 'You're Mary Peters, aren't you? I used to do the pentathlon myself.' I thought I would show her what a real pentathlete looked like. I stood quite still and put the shot 47ft. If it startled me, it startled that poor girl still more. I then proceeded to put it properly around 55ft, trying to look as though I did that sort of thing in training every day of the week. There had to be some retribution for that kind of meanness on my part, and when it came it knocked me sideways. Overnight I developed the dreaded Achilles tendon trouble. It began as a nagging pain and gradually got worse and worse until, in the end, I was at screaming pitch. I couldn't bear to touch either ankle with even a finger. I had overtrained.

I didn't know how to begin to tell Buster what had happened. In a couple of my phone calls back to Belfast I pretended that all was still going well but it was pointless trying to keep up the pretence. I phoned him one evening and sobbed my heart out. 'I can't stay any longer,' I said, 'my ankles are so sore that I simply can't run any longer.' I have never been more distressed in my sports career. For the first occasion in my life I had the time yet I couldn't do anything with it. Buster's reaction was typical. 'I shall be out on the next plane,' he said. In just under twenty-four hours he was in Pasadena.

Buster walked into the apartment and barely spared the time to go through the courtesies of saying hello to anyone. 'Get me your training shoes,' he said. I laid them all out on the table. 'Which ones have you been using most?' he demanded. I pointed to the pair I had used almost constantly. They fitted snugly round the back of the foot and had built-up heels. I had chosen them deliberately because I thought this design would take some of the strain off my legs. Buster examined them closely and then took them across the room and hurled them into the bin. 'Now,' he said, 'we'll go and do some running.'

He took me down to the track and made me run, gently, on the grass. It was excruciating agony, just like jabbing something into the exposed nerve of a tooth. I cried with the pain of it all the time and I cried the next day, and the next, and the day after that when Buster took me back, making me go through it again and again, building up the distance all the time.

Bill Pearl and his wife watched it all in silent amazement. They clearly saw Buster as a complete monster. They said nothing. And by the end of a week Buster was proved right. The fluid was moving away from the back of the foot and slowly the pain began to ease. It still hurt but I could live with it.

There was one other small problem to overcome. To reduce the inflammation in the leg, a doctor had prescribed some tablets without warning me that it would build up fluid in the body. In the space of ten days I put on one and a half stone in weight and became so bloated that if you pressed your finger against my body it would leave a deep indentation. I could only think that I must have been overeating because of my anxiety. Buster stopped that, too. I went on to a course of diuretics and in a few days was back to normal.

Physically I had lost valuable time in my preparation but mentally I am sure that that distressing period actually did some good. I was flooded with relief to know that I wasn't, after all, going to miss the Games and I was filled with a determination the like of which I had never known before. Buster and I flew home to Belfast together and within a couple of days I did a pentathlon, all in one evening, on the worn-out track at Queen's University. I achieved a good score and I knew that the Churchill Scholarship had paid off. Two years later, as a former Churchill Scholar, I was invited to present Lady Churchill with a bouquet on her birthday.

Two other things happened before the Olympics. Buster, as I have written before, knocked me down. And competing in the long jump at Crystal Palace, where I was keen to win a prize of a Philips cassette-recorder, I injured my ankle. It was exactly seven days before we were due to leave. Not until long afterwards did I realise how serious it had been. I was saved by Dr David who injected so accurately into the ligament that I barely thought about it again.

Thus it was, after some alarums and excursions, that I went into battle at the Munich Olympics.

# 9

# Survival of the Fittest

The really big occasion doesn't exactly bring out the most noble traits of the human character. I recognised that in myself, and I certainly saw it in other people even before we got into the stadium for the opening day's events in the pentathlon that Saturday, 2 September 1972. The official car due to take us across the zig-zagging mile from the Village didn't show up, so we tried hitching a lift in the cars of other pentathletes, all of whom were sitting there looking about as tense as I was. Not one of them would stop. I asked an Australian team manager if we could share a ride in their minibus, which had enough room for a small army. The answer was an adamant, 'No.' Charity really began at home that morning. So we had to go through the infernal torture of catching one camp bus down to the security gates and then changing into another that stopped and started all the way across the vast Munich complex with us swaying inside like rush-hour commuters. It was no worse than what millions of Londoners go through every morning, I suppose, but on a day when you are looking everywhere for good luck omens, it makes you begin to wonder whether Caesar is already beginning to turn his thumbs down.

It wasn't the first irritation. The other one was bigger. The previous evening, when the draw for the heats of the 100m hurdles had been announced, I was staggered to hear I had been placed in the second heat with the slower runners while my own colleague, Ann Wilson, was up there with the very fast runners in the first heat. Only a couple of weeks previously I had run a wind-assisted 13.1 secs in Edinburgh, which was faster than Ann, and here I was being done down. It wasn't just a matter of pride; it is vital to do well in the opening event of a pentathlon and it is essential to be there with the fastest opponents. The pace is hotter and they 'pull you through' to a better time.

Ann and I were not only teammates but friends, but that did not alter the fact that both Buster and I felt we had been tricked. I was very upset.

I had to get out of the Village and its claustrophobic atmosphere so Buster and I went into Munich for a quiet meal. Even this proved a disaster when the waiter rendered my kebabs inedible by pouring pure curry powder over the lot. At least the table proved useful for writing a fairly strongly worded letter of protest about the draw to Arthur Gold, the British manager. We demanded an inquiry and got it. The draw, in fact, had been made by computer and my Edinburgh time of 13.1 secs hadn't been fed into it. At least this convinced us that there hadn't been any dirty work at the crossroads, but I still felt it was unfair. When Arthur Gold asked me if he could tear up my written protest I said he couldn't. I, too, was in the mood for a little charity starting at home.

It all increased the strain and tension as we set out for the track at the unearthly hour of 7.45 a.m. The hurdles were due at 9.30 a.m., a ridiculous time to expect one's concentration to be totally set. It was hard to fight off the feeling that nothing was working out. The only consolation I could find was in the number pinned to my back – 111 – and the fact that it had been handed to me by a man named Gold. Three firsts and a gold medal would suit me well, I thought. Around me in the indoor warm-up area there were twenty-nine other female pentathletes assembled from all over the world who would settle for that too.

The sight, as we came down through the competitors' tunnel into the arena, was staggering. Already there were 25,000 spectators in their seats. Within an hour it was jammed to the eaves with 80,000 and by then my black mood had gone. All our fears about the importance of getting into the first heat, though theoretically justified at the time, had proved groundless. Heide Rosendahl, as expected, had won it in 13.34 secs but my time in the second heat was faster. Christine Bodner, the East German, set a terrific pace and I kept coming through and coming through on her heels to cross the line in 13.29 secs. It was a fifth of a second better than

I had ever run before without wind assistance. Christine's time of 13.25 secs and mine were both corrected to 13.30 secs which meant that we had both equalled the Olympic record. It was a jubilant start in the event in which most of the experts had expected me to yield a little ground. So after the hurdles, Bodner led with 966 points, I was just 6 points behind on 960 and the two girls I had always seen as my biggest rivals, Rosendahl and the world-record holder, Burglinde Pollak, were lying third and fourth behind me. Rosendahl had 953 points; Pollak, 927; and Ann Wilson was fifth with 916.

It filled me with enormous confidence and determination, and that was just as well because enough niggling incidents were happening out there to crack the concentration of a chess master. I do not report them here from any sense of outrage, but for the enlightenment of the reader.

One personal crisis was already over for, even before the hurdles, I had fallen foul of the German officials over the matter of my running shoes. Understandably, you have to submit your kit for inspection as soon as you get into the track area. They rummage through your bag, searching for things like two-way radios with which you might be contemplating having an illegal chat with your coach. I was able to satisfy them that I was perfectly 'clean' on that count, but as soon as I handed over my shoes for examination they shook their heads and told me flatly that I would not be permitted to wear them. They were a new type of shoe, manufactured just before the Games, which had a dozen short plastic wedges in the sole instead of the six conventional spikes. Not only had the manufacturers assured me they were perfectly legal but I knew full well that many athletes had already used them in competition in these very Games. Yet here were mine being rejected. It could have wrecked all my efforts before the first gun went because chances were remote that I would be able to borrow, at short notice, another pair that would fit my hardly dainty feet. Astonishingly I had brought a second pair, fitted with the normal spikes with me. I say astonishingly because it was the first time in all my career that I had taken a reserve pair of shoes to a starting line. To this day I don't know what persuaded me to do it, because I had no reason whatever to believe that the first pair would be unacceptable. Perhaps it was the sheer relief that helped me hurdle so well.

At that point it had never occurred to me that certain German officials were doing everything in their power to help their own favourite, Rosendahl, win. But there was soon clear evidence that that was precisely what they were up to.

As soon as the hurdles were over, we were herded out of one exit and back up through a series of tunnels under the stands to the point where we were due to be led out into the arena again for the shot. This was the event in which I had to score heavily and knew I could. I had been going well in recent training, with distances of 56ft and even 57ft, and I wanted to get at it quickly before the feeling of well-being inspired by the hurdles wore off. It was important, at least, that I was out there warming up, but again German officialdom intervened. We were kept hanging about in a bunch near the entrance, unable either to communicate with our coaches outside or to get out into the stadium to practise. Suddenly I became suspicious. I started counting. There should have been twenty-nine of us but there were only twenty-seven. And, sure enough, the two missing girls were the West Germans: Rosendahl and her colleague Karen Mack.

I went up to a German official and demanded, 'Where is Rosendahl?' He shrugged. In an even less ladylike voice I demanded again, 'Where – is – Rosendahl?' He shrugged again and still said nothing.

It was becoming a rather boring and one-sided conversation, but there were no prizes for politeness at this stage, so I almost screamed the question at him a third time. It was what might be described as a 'rhetorical query'. I knew damned well where she was. She and Karen Mack had been quietly slipped away to the neighbouring indoor warm-up area, and were working away while the rest of us were stiffening up mentally as well as physically. The Germans were beginning to look rather worried by now. Although I was helpless to do anything about it, their little plot was rumbled by Buster, Marea Hartman and British athletics coach John Le Masurier, who had all gone to the indoor area to meet us. Once they saw that only the two West Germans were there, they immediately guessed what was happening. Marea lodged a complaint and Rosendahl and Mack were sent back to join the rest of us.

The difference between shot-putting as an individual competition and shot-putting as one fifth of an Olympic pentathlon is the absolute necessity to eliminate error. You only have three attempts, and if your first put is a foul, you will have subjected yourself to extreme psychological pressure. The ideal technique is to get a safe one in first and then belt the other two for all you are worth. If you are still going for the safe one with your second throw, you have conceded a big advantage.

Despite all the *Goldfinger* ploys behind the scenes, I still had time for a thorough warm-up out in the stadium. It seemed as though half a lifetime had passed since the start of the hurdles but, in fact, it was less than an hour. I felt confident, and I certainly felt aggressive, and with the crowd now at its capacity and the sun already climbing high into the sky, I was ready to assert myself. In the hush, I went for the safe one. It was safe all right, but the result was a disappointing 49ft 3in. Disappointing, that is, compared with the distances I had been achieving in recent training.

The second one I really let go. When the figures came up on the track scoreboard at the metric equivalent of 53ft 1¾in I knew that it was the best I had ever achieved in a pentathlon. Even so, I felt faintly disappointed again. This was where I had to put some distance between myself and those I knew to be my real rivals. Rosendahl I knew all about, but Pollak I had never set eyes on before coming to Munich. I can remember the feeling of relief when she turned out to be somewhat smaller, physically, than she had appeared in her photographs, but for all that I had a genuine respect for her record and was apprehensive about her potential.

Before my third put, I heard one of the many photographers talking to me in English. For some reason I had assumed they were all Germans in the centre of the arena, but this was Peter Kemp of the Associated Press, and I was so cheered up by it that I said, 'Watch this, it's going to be a new British record.' It wasn't. My third and last throw hadn't improved on my second but I had no reason to be disheartened. That second throw had beaten the field.

It put me in the lead of the pentathlon with 1,920 points. Pollak, some 6in behind me in the shot, had now moved into second place with 1,879. Heide Rosendahl hadn't profited greatly from her extra warm-up time, for her best distance with the shot was 45ft 5½in. She was now lying third overall with 1,783 points, but I knew, West Germany knew, and everyone who knew anything about athletics anywhere in the world knew, that she still had her best events to come.

As we gathered up our belongings and left the track for lunch and the long wait for the single event of the afternoon, the high jump, I also knew that I had never been in a better mental state in any major competition. After all the upsets, the suspicions, the cat-and-mouse games of the previous few hours I should, by nature, have been a sack of nerves. Unaccountably the fuss over my placing in the second heat of the hurdles, the non-arrival of the car that was due to take us to the stadium, the near-disaster over my shoes, and the gamesmanship the Germans had employed to give their own competitors an unfair advantage had served only to put me in a militant mood and give me more confidence than I had known before. For one thing, I could see a marked change in the attitude of the German track officials towards me. That didn't do any harm. Furthermore, I had at last come face to face with Pollak, whom I'd never met in competition before. Throughout the year she had been steadily rising as the new young star in the firmament, and as we charted her achievements back in Belfast, we had grown more and more concerned. What is more, every magazine and newspaper photograph I had ever seen of her made her look like an Amazon, some towering Brunhilde. In the flesh she turned out to be quite moderately built, and the very sight of her broke down a big psychological barrier.

The wait for the high jump was interminable. We had finished the shot by midday and were not due back to resume the battle before five o'clock. The success of the morning, however, had worked wonders with my digestive juices. Unfortunately, having decided to stay at the stadium, we discovered there was no food for the athletes. We compromised with fruit and chocolate from a stall and joined Ted Chappell, the team physiotherapist, in the warm-up arena. Then for a couple of hours I lay down, utterly relaxed. When the call came and I gathered up a fresh set of clothes, it no longer felt like walking out into death row. I bounced out, eager for the fight, and the mood endured out there in the stadium as the sun went down and a small chill came into the air and the evening turned into something very close to fantasy.

My previous best personal performances in the high jump were 5ft 6in for the pentathlon and 5ft 10¼in for straight competition. I knew that 5ft 6in would not be good enough in this company, and my first four jumps, with the bar steadily going up to that mark from 5ft 1in, presented no problems. I was over, clear, each time with the new Fosbury flop technique that I had adopted the previous year. But then, at 5ft 7in, I ran into real trouble. Twice I tried and twice I felt the bar go off beneath me. It left me with just one attempt and a lot of unfulfilled ambition and it was then that an invisible, but very real, lifeline from the crowd saved me.

Coaches are barred from coming out on to the track or having any kind of verbal contact with competitors. But, there, fifty yards away in the lower part of the stand, was Buster. He was wearing, as always, the bright yellow anorak he used, so that I could pick him out immediately in the crowd. I never had to look far. Without fail, wherever I happened to be in the arena or whatever competition was in progress, Buster was at the closest possible point permitted by the rules. How he did it I shall never know, for I don't think he ever bought a ticket throughout the whole Olympics. Anyway a ticket placing him a hundred rows back at the far end of that gigantic grandstand would have been useless. Buster used his wits and his driving personality instead. He was a hustler, and although that Olympic stadium was under the greatest security ever flung over a sporting event, he hustled his way to any point he wanted. He was a well-built man, and when his face was set with those determined lines I suspect that any steward or attendant would have been unwise to stop him.

But there he was, exactly where and when I desperately needed him. He was standing on his seat pumping his arms to indicate that I must run harder into the bar and then performing a kind of exaggerated mark-time, rather like some guardsman, to demonstrate that I should get my knees up higher. At the previous Commonwealth Games, when I had got into a hopeless muddle with my run in the long jump, I had panicked. Now, when some small sense of panic was almost justified, I was quite calm. It can be quite uncanny, this relationship between coach and athlete, but his confidence flooded into me. He knew every thought and doubt that had been going through my mind, and it was suddenly as though his brain had supplanted mine. I ran in hard for that critical third jump at 5ft 7¼in, got my knees up higher and sailed over.

My chances would have perished then and there had I failed, but now the whole of my body was alive. Buster wanted to keep it that way, too. He gave me a thumbs-up and waved his arms, ordering me to keep sprinting up and down the track, warming up for every jump.

The bar went up to 5ft 8½in and I was over first time. It moved up to 5ft 9¼in, now only fractionally below the best height I had ever achieved.

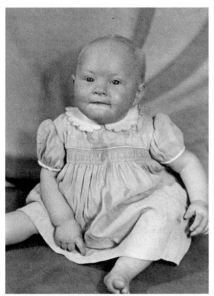

A baby sister for John.
I was born at the outbreak
of the Second World War.

In my school uniform for
Kingsthorne Road Primary School,
just before we moved to Ballymena.

A family holiday in Scarborough, 1946.
I was seven at the time and John was ten.

Victory in the high jump at Ballymena, 1951.
I went on to win the 'Junior Shield' for the best all-round athlete.

Clearing the high jump with Ulick O'Connor of the
*Daily Mirror* officiating, Trinity College Dublin, 1955.

Buster and Margaret McShane presenting me with a trophy on behalf of McShane Health Studios for being the first British woman to reach a 50 ft shot-put, February 1966.

Training with Buster for the Munich Games at the Pearl Gym in Pasadena, 1972.

On my way to my first gold medal: the long jump at the Edinburgh Commonwealth Games, 1970.

The winner's podium at the Edinburgh Commonwealth Games, 1970. This was my first time meeting the King (or the Prince of Wales as he was then).

The long jump at the Munich Olympic Games, 1972.
This was a vital jump on my way to gold.

The 200m at the Munich Olympics, 1972. To win my gold I had to run faster than I ever had before.

Trying to catch my breath after the 200m. I still didn't know if I had done enough …

… but I had won by one tenth of a second.

Malcom Brodie at the *Belfast Telegraph* was a great friend and mentor. I still have this article framed on my wall at home.

The homecoming parade, Royal Avenue, September, 1972. Police were trying to watch for threats, ticker tape was coming from the surrounding offices and happy smiling faces were everywhere.

This special moment was Buster's as much as it was mine.

Bubbles at the *Belfast Telegraph* offices. Little did I know the celebration would go on forever.

Again a minor crisis here, with two failures, but once more the third and final jump was a perfect one. It had a liberating effect which is impossible to describe. Nothing felt beyond me, and when they moved it up to 5ft 10in, I was over again, first time, to equal a personal record that had been achieved under very different circumstances. Not only that, it was this jump that killed off the opposition. No one else got over. I was now alone, leaping into the unknown.

There are many scenes which an athlete who has known some success will carry to the grave. For me, the scene that followed will remain the most vivid of all, for I came out of my intense concentration for a moment to realise an extraordinary thing: the great crowd were still in their seats, but there were now only two athletes still competing in the whole of that space-age colosseum. At the far end, Wolfgang Nordwig, a young engineer from Leipzig, was the sole survivor in the men's pole vault. He was climbing into the sky again and again, in pursuit of an Olympic record. At my end there was only Mary P., as alone on the stage as a singer left behind by the choir. The floodlights were on, and looking out from the almost Wagnerian setting I could see masses of waving Union Jacks and hear the crowd chanting my name again and again. It is not being modest to say it all felt like some dream, for there had been occasions in the past when I had completed a pentathlon high jump without a solitary spectator in sight and then, by the time I had showered and changed, had to clamber over a wall to get out of an already-locked stadium. Now some 50,000 people had stayed behind to see me and were shouting my name, just as they shouted the names of entire football teams at a Wembley Cup Final. Behind me, too, I knew that Buster and Marea were wildly urging me on. It was all so unreal that at times I felt disembodied, almost as though I were up there in the stands watching myself.

At the other end, Wolfgang Nordwig must have been experiencing much the same sensation for when I jumped, he stood aside and waited, and when he vaulted, I stood aside and watched him clear another mark and joined in with the great explosion of East German applause. Then it would be my turn again and I would settle down, shake all the other thoughts out of my head and begin to run.

I have never been so emotionally involved with a crowd. I so badly wanted to give them back some of the love and encouragement they were giving me, that I found myself doing incredible, extrovert things that had never entered my head before. I was coming out of the pit and then kicking up my heels like a foal. I was running down to the edge of the track to blow kisses to one particularly noisy group of British spectators. Every time, the tears welled up in my eyes until all I could see of them was a watery blur. I have seen the footage many times since, and each time, I simply cannot believe it is me. For all my extrovert antics as a front-garden skipper back in my childhood days in Liverpool, it was all completely out of character. It was long jumper Sheila Sherwood who said afterwards, 'Christ, after that you'll have no trouble getting on the *Morecambe & Wise Show*. You loved them all.'

Some day, when science knows even more about adrenalin, it may all be explained. For me, at the end of a day of enormous tension and physical strain, an overwhelming desire to give more and more for my coach and my team manager and those marvellous supporters who had come halfway across Europe was pushing me onwards and upwards.

The bar went up to 5ft 10¾in. Over first time. It moved on again to 5ft 11¼in, now 5½in higher than I had achieved only a year before. Again, up and over, first time.

It had to end somewhere, and it did, at 6ft 0½in. Even then, in that electrifying atmosphere, I almost made it with the second of my three final attempts. It was only the great long-drawn 'Oooh' when the bar fell for the third time that broke the spell. There were still two events and a bitter struggle to come on the morrow but I knew then, as I stood there, that I had been privileged to experience to the very depths of my emotions the meaning of two lines written by Thomas Osbert Mordaunt. 'One crowded hour of glorious life,' he said, 'is worth an age without a name.' By God, how right he was.

# 10

# The Long Wait

I was less tired than if I had done a day's Christmas shopping in Oxford Street. The euphoria of it all kept me up there in the clouds, and as I walked out of the stadium all I wanted to do was go back to the Village and watch the re-run of the day's other athletics on television. Buster and Marea were over the moon and they took me along to the PUMA shop for some athletics equipment.

When I finally saw the re-run, I can't say that much of what I was watching registered. The agony of waiting had not yet hit me, nor had the realisation that, not only was I within twenty-four hours of the greatest goal that an athlete can achieve, but I was also exactly the same time away from incalculable disappointment. Certainly I was ahead after three events, but the knowledge that Rosendahl's two favourite events – the long jump and the 200m – were yet to be tackled, came as a sobering reminder that chickens are not to be counted. Rosendahl had had a bad afternoon. Like me she had tried to adopt the flop method of high-jumping, but it had not worked out for her. She reverted to the old Corinthian style of the straddle and had achieved only 5ft 5in. Pollak, however, had used the flop technique as well and achieved a personal best of 5ft 9¼in. We were therefore going to bed with me leading on 2,969 points, Pollak second on 2,872 points and Rosendahl lying fifth with 2,668. Between Pollak and Rosendahl came Valentina Tikhomirova – with whom I was shortly destined to have what may be described as a 'small contretemps' – and the youthful Christine Bodner, who had been such an unconscious help in the hurdles. Tikhomirova was third with 2,744 points and Bodner fourth with 2,709. Both were fine athletes, but I still felt I could dismiss them from my mind. Pollak I could by no means discount as yet. She might be smaller than I had imagined from her photographs, but she was a dangerously wonderful performer. As for Rosendahl, I had nothing but respect. She was tough, she was hard, she was a brilliant long-jumper and a terrific sprinter. And she was West German. My own experience of that very afternoon had confirmed for me, if confirmation were needed, how a crowd can lift you up. She, of course, would thrive in front of an adoring mass who wanted nothing more than for her achievements to be rewarded by a rendering of their national anthem.

Buster had what seemed a million sheets of paper with ten million permutations scrawled across them: if Rosendahl did that, then this was what I must do in time or distance; if Rosendahl did this, then that was what I had to achieve. He had calculated everything. My only job was to jump and run. I wasn't going to win either of the second day's events, that I knew. What I had to do was keep in touch, maintain my overall lead. The figures started spinning round in my head and I absorbed less and less of what was appearing on the television screen.

There was a sharp tap on the window. A young man with a beard was peering in. He grinned, stuck his thumbs up and mouthed the words, 'Good luck'. It was long-distance runner David Bedford. I was almost a veteran by the time he had arrived in athletics, and had never exchanged a word with him. He had soon established a reputation of being a raving egocentric and, only that morning, had given an interview to a London newspaper advising every man, woman and child in the country to watch him the following day as he proposed to run the legs off the world in the 10,000m final. This kind of personal propaganda did not endear him to everyone, but I liked his gesture. He had his own pressures and problems at that moment, but he had time to concern himself with mine. I appreciated that very much.

We sat there for an hour or more before I could think about going to bed. I was very happy. I was tense but I wasn't nervous, which is where we came in at the prologue to these recollections. That long, that dreadfully long, lone night lay ahead. I tossed and I turned, and I turned and I tossed. I went back over every moment of that day and tried to imagine tomorrow. Sound sleep was impossible. I occasionally picked up *Time* magazine, but the words were meaningless. One figure kept roaring through my brain: 19.6. This was the distance Buster had said I needed to achieve in the long jump to be in with a chance of winning the gold. Even if Rosendahl came close to the world record in her long jump, and then went on to come first in the 200m (which was likely), the points would be in my favour and I could still prevail.

If my performance during the closing stages of the high jump the previous evening had been out of character I was, that Sunday morning, quite unrecognisable even to myself. The lasting criticism of me throughout my career had been that I had concerned myself too often with the welfare of the losers. I had been a ready shoulder to cry on. Now I was thinking of no one but myself. It is not with a great deal of pride that I now recall that during our warm-up on the outdoor track that morning I used Ann Wilson, my own team colleague, quite mercilessly for my own purposes. We were good friends and remain so, but she had not done well and she wasn't going to win a medal or get anywhere near one. All my generosity had gone, and since she was a very good long jumper I joined her in practice and, unbeknownst to her, got her to raise my own performance. I was beating her off short approaches and it boosted my confidence enormously. I simply didn't care what it did to her.

Back in the stadium, with the jumping about to start, there was another small incident which illustrates my mood and the general cut-throat atmosphere. Valentina Tikhomirova, the Russian athlete who had been European champion back in 1966, kept brushing against me every time she passed. You're not exactly cramped for space out there on the track, so I could only assume that she was doing it deliberately to unnerve and irritate me. Clearly she thought she was still in with a chance, particularly if she could drive me up the wall and make me lose concentration. It had to stop. The next time she did it, I drove an elbow into her ribs, quite violently, and kept walking as though nothing had happened. Out of the corner of my eye I could see her limp away. It never happened again and I knew I had won that little struggle of wills quite easily.

Again, as in the shot, you only get three attempts in the pentathlon long jump, so it is an enormous boost if you can get a big one in first time. I measured out my run of 112ft, which is eaten up in eighteen strides when you're travelling in the opposite direction, and put down Larry as my marker. Larry is a small leprechaun who'd been given to me by a friend at London Airport on the way out to the Games. The German officials either didn't like the look of him, or else suspected that the Irish little people really do have supernatural powers. They ordered me to move him and use a conventional marker instead. I sat him back on the grass where he still had a good view and proceeded to pull out, at the first attempt, the biggest jump of my life. It was certainly over 20ft, hugely past the 19ft 6in that Buster had calculated as being absolutely necessary. Unfortunately it was a foul. By the smallest fraction of an inch, I had overstepped the board.

Once more it was a crisis moment, but yet again the presence of Buster in his yellow anorak, forced back the wave of panic. He was on his feet in the stands, smiling, and his thumbs were up. It was the only gesture he made. It was just as well, for I was soon in need of every ounce of confidence I could get. To a great explosion of a roar from the crowd, which was already back at its capacity 80,000, Rosendahl hurdled herself into a phenomenal leap of 22ft 5in, a mere ¼in short of her world record. To produce it under this extreme pressure some thirty-nine hours into a pentathlon was a prodigious feat. It was certainly more than Buster had ever expected from her in his calculations and, of course, it drew her right back among the front runners in the overall fight. I was always going to give ground to her here, but to have to give that much didn't exactly commend itself to my nervous system.

My second jump was safe, in that I didn't overstep, but it wasn't long enough: 19ft 4¼in. The third one, by my personal standards, was a beauty, but it led to an agonised wait while the officials examined the board for a foul, then called up the chief judge from miles away for a final ruling. Eventually he stood up straight and signalled that it was legal. At 19ft 7½in, it was almost exactly what Buster had demanded of me, but the mathematics had been thrown out once more by Rosendahl's jump, which was fully 6in better than we'd anticipated.

Mercifully, Rosendahl couldn't improve on that in her remaining jumps. But in the meantime, Pollak had put the pressure on, too, with a jump of 20ft 4½in. It meant that the three of us were now almost deadlocked, with me just ahead with 3,871 points, Pollak closed up on 3,824 points and Rosendahl was right back in the running in third place with 3,750. There was only the 200m sprint to come.

It was a dangerous moment to start revealing one's admiration for opponents, but Heide Rosendahl deserved it. I had known her for five years and her career, at the highest level, had been pursued by ill-luck. She had been deprived of a medal at the European Games in Athens when the entire West German team withdrew for political reasons. At the Mexico Olympics, where she had been clear favourite to win the gold, she pulled a muscle warming up on the opening morning, and a year's intense preparation had been laid to waste in a second. In Mexico, as in Munich, I had asked, 'Where is Rosendahl?' Then it was her colleague Ingrid Becker who shrugged, gave an odd little smile and just said, 'She's out.' Becker knew that she could now win the gold herself and she did precisely that.

Now, four years later, here was Heide going for her life. It was almost as though all those years of frustration had driven her to that superhuman jump. To the mass of German spectators, it was charging the climax to the pentathlon with even more emotion. I could well have done without it. Between the events, John Le Masurier had been filling the West German coaches up with all sorts of fictitious details about the times and distances I was capable of, but the hour of kidology was over. Now a split second over 200m would decide it.

Towards the end of the long jump I heard someone urgently calling me from the photographers' trench alongside the track. It was another friend, Mel Watman, editor of the small but authoritative magazine, *Athletics Weekly*. He, like Buster, had done some lightning calculations after my final jump to work out what time I needed to achieve in the 200m to win the gold. He was in a high state of excitement, but I was terrified to turn round and talk to him. Some of the other girls were still jumping and I had the dreadful thought that I could still be disqualified for receiving trackside 'coaching'. I wasn't going to be caught like that. I was dying to talk to Mel, to know the best or the worst, but I stayed there until the last girl had jumped and was out of the pit.

Now came the most awful wait of all, and to make it worse I lost Buster. I assumed he would be waiting for me just outside the athletes' entrance, but he wasn't. For twenty minutes I stood on the grassy bank, watching car after bus pull away, taking my rivals back to rest and sleep. There was still no sign of Buster. He had gone away to search for a friend of ours, Bill Cook (Cookie), from Bermuda – a weightlifter and bodybuilder who had competed at the 1958 Commonwealth Games – but I didn't know that at the time. All I knew was that I was being surrounded by more and more autograph hunters, and people wanting to know how I considered my chances. Normally I am never abrupt with people like that. They mean well, and they are the people who keep athletics going, but at that moment I just couldn't cope. I found myself getting more and more worked up and distressed. The pressure was really telling. I had to get out so, without making any contact with Buster, I went back to the Village, ate some yoghurt very quickly and went to my room. One of the other athletes, Janet Simpson, asked me if I wanted to be alone. I didn't, so Janet stayed with me. I was in tears, sobbing because of emotions that I couldn't even define. I had missed Buster's assurances when I needed them most. I was worried that he would be angry with me for leaving the stadium without him. I was angry at the chaos at the very moment when I needed peace. Analysed at this distance they were all symptoms of fear. I was afraid that I wasn't going to run as well as I could. And, if I were still to win I had to run better than I had ever run in my life.

Several of my team colleagues came into my room to comfort me. They kept saying things like, 'What are you worried about? You're certain of a medal anyway.' I kept saying, 'Any medal's no good, it has to be the gold.' I could find no consolation at all in the thought that I only had to stay alive till teatime to become a medal winner. It was gold or nothing.

The wait was terrible. Another athlete, Pat Cropper, helped by leaving our quarters, going back to the stadium, and searching high and low until she'd found Buster, complete with Cookie, and telephoning back to my room that everything was okay. It was so okay that to this day I cannot remember leaving the Village and returning to the track. I must have been in a total daze because all I recall now is getting to the entrance and seeing Buster there. He ignored the subject of how we had missed one another after the long jump. It might never have happened. He was utterly calm, and all he kept saying, very softly, was, 'It's all right, P, we can do it.'

His calculations about the time I had to do agreed, frighteningly, with

Mel Watman's. It simply had to be the fastest I'd ever run. He didn't confuse me with figures and decimal points: I had to stay fairly close to Pollak but, more critically, I had to keep in touch with Rosendahl. Both, we knew, were going to beat me but what now was to decide it all was by how little, not how much. The respective fastest times we had ever done were 23.8 by Pollak; 23.1 by Rosendahl; and 24.2 by me.

Merely hearing Buster talk about it as though it were some abstract problem in a puzzle book had the usual calming influence. But, again, that was all undone. I warmed up in the indoor track so as to be ready exactly at the appointed time of 4.55 p.m. but was then informed I would not be running until 5.20. I must have looked like some poor wretch on the gallows who'd been told that he'd have to wait around for half an hour while Mr Pierrepoint had his breakfast. My mind was screaming, 'I can't go on like this any longer. I've got to go now, now, now.' But Buster said, 'Just go and lie over there,' and I did. My mind went totally blank until he came for me and led me across the road and into that pentathlon for the fifth and last time. He said, 'Right, P, this is it. Go.' It sounds like some rather predictable line from a film script now, but at the time it was rather apt.

I walked in and alongside the trench, past the hundreds of photographers and, behind them, the one hundred and twenty rows of journalists. I carried on round to the back straight where I tried a few starts and then opened up my stride for a few yards. I was aware now that, while there was no one on earth who could help me any more, at least my tension was being shared. The television cameras were all on this event and I knew that back home in Northern Ireland they would all be looking in: Catholics and Protestants, friends in the gym, fellow athletes and old school colleagues, Kenny McClelland, my first real coach, and Mr Woodman who, like me, had no Irish blood in him but loved the place to distraction. I couldn't let them down. I was running for them and Belfast now, and that was the last thought I had before turning and going to the starting line at the top end of the stadium with the left-hand curve just ahead and the finishing line away down there on the horizon.

I set my blocks and practised another start or two. It wasn't right. One of the pins clamping the blocks into the track was loose. I set it again. There were seven of us in this final heat and nobody spoke. I was in lane three with Bodner on the kerb, Pollak immediately to my left, Nedyalka Angelova of Bulgaria immediately on the right. Then moving outwards were Tikhomirova, who hadn't given me any more trouble since our 'accidental' collision, then Heide Rosendahl, then Karen Mack.

The pistol fired and we ran.

It is impossible for me to give an objective account of the race. There are certain athletes who claim that pressure heightens the perception to such a degree that they see everything as though it is happening in slow motion. I am not one of them. My recollections are of emotions, not sights. First came the surging relief that comes from knowing you have made a terrific start. I simply hurled myself into the bend and flew past Angelova, on my right, which was an enormous boost. Around 80m, I knew I was fractionally up on Pollak and was still within three metres of Rosendahl, who was going like the wind. But then, about 70m out, I paid for it. It was as though someone had thrown a switch and cut the power off. All the strength drained out of me and it suddenly felt as if my legs had turned to lead. I could sense my body getting more and more upright, which means disaster, and it was then, in the rising panic, that Buster's endless, driving coaching paid off. A million times in lonely training sessions I had heard him yell, 'Arms, arms,' and those words now flooded my brain. I pumped harder and harder with the arms until they were virtually dragging my legs behind them and thus it was, with the stadium swaying around me, that I covered those remaining metres and hit the line. I was absolutely out.

I knew, instinctively, that I had beaten Pollak. I was so close behind her that with each tenth of a second costing ten points she couldn't possibly catch me in the overall scoring. But what of Rosendahl? She had run supremely well. She had opened up a gap and kept it but was it enough to beat me out of the gold? Now only the scoreboard would tell.

I have written repeatedly of agonising waits. None was so agonising as this final one. I was standing there, engulfed by friends and rivals, staring at the scoreboard and waiting for the times that seemed stubbornly determined to remain the best kept secret of the year. Then Rosendahl's flashed up: 22.96 secs. It was a breathtaking effort, not only the fastest she had ever run but even faster than Buster had calculated for her in his most pessimistic moment. Now all that remained was for my own time to go up there in lights. When it came – 24.08 secs – my mind refused to understand it. For me, too, it was the fastest I had ever run, faster even than the 24.2 secs that I had seen as my absolute limit. But what did it mean? Had I won or lost? Were these two days and nights of physical effort and nervous exhaustion to end with the solemn playing of 'Deutschlandlied'? I couldn't work it out. I couldn't do the maths. Not even a simple subtraction.

Then someone came and put an arm round me. I turned and saw that it was Heide Rosendahl, and she had the answer written on her face. The gold medal was on its way to Belfast.

# 11

# The Aftermath

I eventually discovered that I had won my gold medal by one tenth of a second. My final total was 4,801 points, a new world and Olympic record. Heidi Rosendahl finished with 4,791 points, Burglinde Pollak with 4,768 and Ann Wilson with 4,279 points.

Once I realised that I had taken the gold, I ran towards the tunnel where, win or lose, I had arranged to meet Buster. I was besieged by reporters, but the only person I really wanted to see was Buster. When he arrived, I left the microphones hanging in mid-air and ran to him. We hugged for a long time, tears streaming down our faces. No one on earth could have understood the emotions we felt at that moment. They cannot be described. For a few seconds, no one else existed, but then we were both caught up again in the sheer chaos of it all. One voice, however, caught me totally unawares. 'Did you know, Mary,' said John Goodbody, the athletics writer of the *London Evening News*, 'that your father has been watching you all day?' Had it been Chairman Mao or a reincarnated Gandhi, I could not have been more surprised. I had last seen my father two and a half years earlier when he decided to live in Australia. I had last heard of him on holiday in Canada. I knew it couldn't be true. Buster, thinking quickly as always, showed a little apprehension. He took Goodbody aside and asked for a full description. It was as well to do that if you came from Northern Ireland. But the man described could have been no one but my father. Swearing everyone to secrecy, telling none of my aunts or uncles in case word got out, he had joined a party of Australian businessmen and come halfway round the world to see me win. That I could lose had apparently never occurred to him. I could almost understand his innocence. He had never seen me compete in a major championship before. I was desperate to run and find him then and there, but that is easier said than done when you are caught up in the tailwind of an Olympic victory.

For a start you do not just go and collect your medal. You have to be prepared for it as thoroughly as if you were appearing on the set of some American musical. On the way back along the track verge to meet the make-up artist and the hairdresser, I saw Arthur Gold in the stand. I unzipped the top of my tracksuit and thrust out the figures 111 which were still pinned to my front. It was his choice of omen, and he shared the joke, but it was the last unladylike gesture I was to be permitted for quite some time. In the make-up room, where they doll you up to appear before a television audience usually quoted as 400 million, it was tensely serious. In the hands of the male German hairdresser I felt like Madame de Pompadour getting ready for a night out. He drew my hair back tightly and used about a hundred pins and clips to weave it into the most elaborate style. I didn't like it, but felt a little timid about disturbing such a great artist at work. Buster, when he came down to see what was happening, had no such inhibitions. 'My God, P,' he said, 'what the hell have they done to your hair? Get those pins out right away.' We stood by the side of the track pulling out pin after pin and clip after clip until I was able to shake my hair free and feel myself again. The hairdresser was mortified at our wanton destruction, but Buster was right.

We had a long wait in that make-up room before the medal ceremony. Heide Rosendahl and Burglinde Pollak were there. We didn't talk, but Heide handed me a cigarette. I was almost relieved to see that she smoked as well. Somehow she was sharing my guilt. I urge young people not to start this stupid habit. We didn't know then how harmful to your health smoking is, and I can testify to the fact that I would have been a better athlete had I never smoked. But we are dealing in the truth here and the fact is that I got through an entire packet of cigarettes during the pentathlon. I guessed, looking at Heide, that she'd probably done the same. The strain of all that waiting hadn't been my exclusive problem.

Even now the waiting wasn't done with. I desperately wanted to dash away and see Daddy and fling my arms round all my friends, but the Germans had laid down strict instructions about the protocol of medal-presentation ceremonies. Nobody went anywhere until they were over.

But they certainly weren't going to stop me going out to the trackside to watch David Bedford's race. David, of course, had alerted the world to sit by their television sets and watch him win for Britain, and word of it must have reached 10 Downing Street. There, high up in the VIP box alongside German chancellor Willy Brandt and Princess Grace of Monaco, was British Prime Minister Edward Heath. Apparently he'd arrived just before my 200m. I was desperately disappointed when David didn't win his race. I suspect that that was what the prime minister had come to see, but at least he had had the consolation of witnessing one gold medal won for Britain. As it turned out, it was the only British athletics gold of the Games.

I was about to go back into the waiting room when someone said, 'Mr Heath would like to see you.' I went and found Buster because I wanted him to be there as well, and then Mr Heath came down the endless steps from the VIP gallery. He was very jolly, charming and kind and I rather got the impression he was surprised to have discovered that another Briton was competing that day. We all chatted away for a few minutes and I found myself telling him what had been uppermost in my mind all this time. 'At last,' I said, 'there's some good news for Northern Ireland.' He smiled and said, 'Yes, I just hope they don't celebrate too much in Belfast tonight.'

There was still another delay before the medal ceremony because the last lap of the walk was in progress. But, at last, the moment came and Heide, Burglinde and I were assembled in the correct order to walk out into the centre of the arena for the supreme moment of any athlete's life. After so many years spent preparing, I was very proud and very emotional to be walking out there to receive a medal for the people of Northern Ireland.

I felt certain the tears would be streaming down my face the moment Lord Exeter had slipped the medal collar over my head and they began to play 'God Save the Queen'. Doubtless they would have done but for the disturbance down on my left as we faced the flags. Poor Burglinde Pollak was gasping and sobbing and almost choking, and I was so concerned about her that my own tears held back throughout the unforgettable moments when the slow, solemn notes filled that towering stadium and the only movement seemed to be the Union Jack rising slowly to the masthead. These are the moments when your mind floods with visions of the green hills and familiar streets of home, and yet I stood there worrying about why Burglinde was crying. Was it because she hadn't won for East Germany, a country whose sporting system put such a high premium on winning? The language barrier prevented me from asking her, but Heide assured me, as we walked back across the track, that this wasn't so. Heide had found it hard to conceal her disappointment but Burglinde was simply overwhelmed, it seemed, at having won the bronze medal.

It was about then that the whole roof fell in. I wanted to race away and find my father, wherever he was, but that was impossible. I now fell into the hands of the communications industry whose competitive instincts make anything that happens out on the track seem as gentle as evensong. The BBC, ITV and ITN all wanted interviews at once, as did almost every radio interviewer. And all the while there was a somewhat officious and extremely agitated German trying to drag me away to a room down in the bowels of the stadium where the newspaper media pundits were waiting. 'You must come immediately,' he kept saying, but I'd had enough of being herded around like some prizewinning exhibit. Mark Andrews, of Independent Television News, turned on the German official and made the only intelligent suggestion put forward so far: 'We'll let the lady decide,' he said. I knew I could see all the English writers later, so I decided to do the television interviews first.

The ITV men had first use of the studio, if that is the right word for the cramped areas in which those armies of technicians and journalists and front men had to work. I was greeted by Dickie Davies, the *World of Sport* presenter, who was beaming and clutching two bottles of champagne. We drank one there and then, before the BBC interviews started. I was still being pursued by the German official who made a counter-attack, and another furious argument broke out. 'She's ours.' '*Nein*, she is not.' 'Yes, she is.' 'She is not. It is very rude what is happening here.' Certain other remarks followed this, which I have no intention of repeating here. Anyway, I was very relaxed. I'd just won a gold medal.

From the moment the BBC people took over the studio, I sensed that something curious was happening. Chris Brasher from the *Tonight* programme – who would go on to co-found the London Marathon in 1981 – was the interviewer, and he sat directly in front of me with Buster at my side. Suddenly, midway through the interview, I was astonished to see Buster getting up from his chair. I couldn't work it out. Chris and I talked for another few moments and then I noticed that someone else was taking Buster's seat in the chair beside me. I turned and came face to face with my father for the first time since he had immigrated to Australia.

Anyone who saw that reunion on television will have a better idea than I have about what went on. My father had sworn the whole family to secrecy about his visit to Munich. He just turned up, convinced his only daughter was going to win the gold medal, and introduced himself that morning to the BBC staff. Since the whole place was guarded like the Crown jewels, they asked him how on earth he had got into the TV offices. Apparently my father drew himself up to his full height and delivered himself of probably the most portentous sentence he has ever spoken: 'Young man, it is not for nothing that I have been in the insurance business all my life.'

It was wonderful to see him. I was very excited, but no more excited than my father who, it seems, had been telling everyone for months that I was going to win. Heavens was he proud, this man who, years before had taken us to sports stores in Northern Ireland to buy us equipment he really couldn't afford. In the end I felt quite sorry for Chris Brasher. Chris was an excellent interviewer of athletes because of his deep understanding of the sport, but this was an occasion in which he was hard-pressed to get a question in edgeways. My father just wouldn't stop talking.

Eventually it was over and my father, Buster and I placed ourselves at the disposal of the German official who, by now, had almost given up hope of ever getting us to the press conference. I was still carrying the other bottle of ITV's champagne, which we opened on the rostrum and shared with Heide and Burglinde. This helped because what followed was a terrible bore. Every question was ponderously translated into three languages, and by the time they'd finished that you'd forgotten what the questioner had asked. Then, when you had finished your answer, that too, was translated three times. It seemed a fairly pointless exercise when some of the questions were as profound as 'How old are you?' or 'Did you think you would win?' You soon learn that the good reporters very rarely ask questions at these kind of conferences. If they have an intelligent question, and you are prepared to give a reasonably intelligent answer, why should they waste it all filling the notebooks of those who just sit there and wait for it to fall into their laps?

By the time it was all over, I was raring to go on the evening's celebrations, but first the three medal winners had to go to a drug test. We'd had to take one the day before, and thankfully this one was somewhat more cursory, although, I thought, it was somewhat belated: the medals had already been awarded. It was soon established that no grave suspicion hung over anyone, so I went back and found Dickie Davies who had promised to run me back to the Village. The winding-down process is important because, suddenly, there is a huge void in your life. It is all over, for better or for worse, and now there is no demanding target consuming every waking second of your life. I wanted to get out on the town with my close friends, but it wasn't quite as easy as that. First of all my father, in his excitement, had lost his coat, his hat and his briefcase. Some German officials assured him that they would find them and return them to him tomorrow, but I knew that wouldn't satisfy him. 'I'm not leaving here until I've got them,' he said, and of course, he didn't. We found them in the end.

All I wanted to do then was slip into the Village, change into some evening clothes and leave. It wasn't that easy. The whole corridor was strewn with flowers and there were toilet paper garlands stretched from door handle to door handle all the way down to my room. When I finally got to my door, all the girls in the British team had written their congratulations around it on the wall. Inside there were still more flowers and the telegrams were beginning to pile up. Almost the first I opened was from William Whitelaw, the British minister in charge of affairs in Northern Ireland.

By the time we got away, it was time to drop my father back at the main station in Munich because he was staying an hour's train journey out of town. We then went to Buster's hotel and had a few drinks as a kind of net practice for the evening that lay ahead. By now, British runner Derek Ibbotson had arrived to drive us out to the chateau-like hotel the PUMA sports equipment people had taken over miles outside Munich. They had arranged a party, which compared pretty favourably with anything the Borgias used to set up for their more peaceful at-homes. There was enough champagne for swimmer Mark Spitz to have won seven gold medals in, and enormous amounts of food for anyone who felt inclined to eat. One thing impressed me enormously: they presented me with a watch. This would always have been a generous thing to do, but I only discovered late in the evening that with it being a Sunday, they had had to go into the city and beg a jeweller to open his store so that they could buy it. My memories of the event dim a little as the evening progressed, but I do recall a couple of things. Derek Ibbotson's daughter sat next to me at the dining table and kept pinching the chips off my plate. And at some point in the proceedings I was summoned to what appeared to be the only still-connected telephone in the place. It was in the kitchen, and sitting there, amid all the chaos and noise, I gave an interview to the *Belfast Telegraph*. What they printed the next morning, under the headline 'My Golden Day', was a most beautiful piece of writing which captured every emotion I had felt on that extraordinary day.

German novelist Thomas Mann once described Munich as the incandescent city, and his words fitted it exactly as we returned to the Village. It may have been 5 a.m.; or nearer 6 a.m., but the dawn was certainly breaking out there and bathing the city in a lovely glow. I slept for two, perhaps three hours, and awoke on top of the world. There was, in any case, no chance of sleeping any longer. All the girls in the British team were crowding into my room demanding to see my medal. They'd brought more champagne and soon began helping me open the hundreds of telegrams that had been stacked outside the door. These were from lifelong friends and people I'd never heard of. They were from rich people and poor people and business organisations and household names, and the cumulative effect was to make me wonder what the difference would have been had I won the silver instead of the gold. The sweat and the training and effort and the dedication and the sacrifice are precisely the same but Buster's uncompromising philosophy was right: there is no substitute for coming first. I had known enough moments of disappointment to know how to enjoy this one to the full.

Then two things happened that brought me back to earth.

# The Aftermath

In the evening I joined Marea Hartman and some of the British girls to attend a reception. I was in the mood for anything and everything … except what actually occurred. I had not been there very long before a gentleman of impeccable speech and manners approached me. It appeared that he was something to do with the British government. He informed me that the prime minister, Mr Heath, was giving a lunch party the following day and would be delighted if I would attend. He took the trouble to add that I would be sitting at the prime minister's right hand. It seemed that I was to be some kind of guest of honour.

I replied that I was very honoured and, of course, I would love to attend. Naturally I added that, since my coach, Buster McShane, had done as much to win my gold medal as I had, I presumed he would be receiving an invitation as well. The gentleman took the suggestion completely in his stride and said he would go and make sure that was in order. I went away and told Marea and Sandy Duncan, secretary of the British Olympic Association, about the invitation and then waited for the government's representative to return. Finally he did, looking, I felt, somewhat uneasy. 'Mr Heath is delighted to have you along to lunch,' he said, 'but is your coach an official member of the British Olympic party?'

I said, 'No, he isn't. He's my private coach.'

To which the reply was, 'Well, I'm awfully sorry about this, but this lunch is for members of the official party only.'

I then said, 'Well, would you kindly explain to Mr Heath that I shan't be there tomorrow.'

The gentleman was only nonplussed for a second. He said, 'Oh yes. I'll tell him you have a prior engagement.'

I answered, 'No, I would rather you tell him the truth.'

That, so far as I can remember, is the exact exchange of words in this rather unusual little episode. Prime ministers have far more important things to do with their time than listen to athletes asking if their coaches may accompany them to lunch. But after our conversation at the trackside in the Olympic Stadium the previous day – for which, given this latest development, I was very glad that Buster had been present – I have a small suspicion that Mr Heath never received the message exactly as I delivered it. Anyway I never went to the lunch and nor do I have too many regrets if I upset the seating arrangements.

As it happened there was soon something else to occupy my mind.

By the time I got back to my group, after the official refusal to allow Buster to attend the prime minister's lunch, I could feel a certain tension in the atmosphere. The light had gone out of the morning. My father and Buster had their heads together and were clearly arguing, and at my approach they broke off and went to the gents. When they returned I got hold of Buster and demanded to know what was going on. He said, 'I'll tell you later.' But that wasn't good enough. I wanted to know.

Buster looked at my father. My father looked at Buster. I stood my ground. Finally Buster said, 'All right, come over here.' We threaded our way through the little groups and the general buzz of the cocktail party and went on to the balcony outside. No one was there. Buster said, 'Look, a message has come through. It threatens that you will be shot and your flat will be blown up if you go back to Belfast.'

So that was what all the whispering had been about. That was the piece of paper Buster and my father had been looking at when I came back from my meeting with Mr Heath's representative. I didn't go cold or faint or any of the other things that happen in novels. I simply asked to see the message, but Buster wouldn't show it to me.

It was more than a year later before I finally found out the full contents of that message and the exact sequence of events that led up to me being told of the threat to my life. An anonymous caller from Belfast had telephoned the BBC in London and asked for this message to be passed on to me: 'Mary Peters is a Protestant and has won a medal for Britain. An attempt will be made on her life and it will be blamed on the IRA. Tell Mary Peters to say something about bringing the people together. I don't want to turn her into a martyr. Her home will be going up in the near future.'

Late on the evening of 4 September, that message had been relayed to the BBC's Olympic headquarters in Munich. A BBC official took it straight to the British Olympic Association offices where the president, Lord Rupert Nevill, was called in to handle the affair. As he later recalled, 'Naturally, we immediately alerted the Special Branch at Scotland Yard. But our first concern was to keep the whole thing out of the press, to keep it from Miss Peters and to play the whole thing down. I couldn't see that anything could be gained from Miss Peters knowing about it. I sent for

## The Aftermath

her father instead and explained everything to him. Obviously, security at this point was our responsibility but, at some point, the final decision about where she went after Munich was a family matter.'

They were probably doing what they thought best by bringing my father into it, but I was furious when I heard. They didn't know Daddy as well as I did. The row he and Buster had been having when I went back to join them was over my father insisting that I never went back to Belfast. He was very upset and emotional. Buster was completely calm. Out on the balcony he said, 'What are you going to do, P?' I said, 'This is a nutcase. There's no question about it. Of course I'm going back to Belfast.'

I am no simpleton. I knew that stranger things than this, with no warning at all, had happened in Northern Ireland. But I just didn't believe that anyone should want to kill me. What did upset me was the distressing effect it all had on my father. All at once the euphoria had gone and everything had gone flat. The whole British women's team was going out to another party that night but I couldn't face it. I made an excuse to Marea and instead joined a small group including Buster, Janet Simpson and her fiancé, and went to dinner in Munich's big revolving restaurant. I was conscious that I was quiet and off-colour, and to explain my mood I told Janet, in confidence, what had happened. As luck would have it, our return to the Village coincided exactly with the return of the other British girls from their party. Those who weren't due to compete for a couple of days, or had already completed their events, were in spectacular form. It was pretty obvious that it hadn't been a teetotal party. Sheila Sherwood and Delia Pascoe were dancing about and singing, and when we got into the lift they pressed every single button so that they could share at least a snatch of their song with every single floor on the way up to our quarters where yet another impromptu party immediately started.

All I wanted to do was get to my room, put the light out and sleep, but that was physically impossible. They tripped in and out of my room, demanding that I go and have a drink here or a coffee there and I became more and more depressed knowing that much of the reason for their high spirits was my win for our team and yet here I was, spoiling their evening. Janet tried to tell them I was tired, but they were irrepressible and that did no good at all. In the end I asked Sheila and Pat Cropper to come in and sit down and I told them what had happened. I begged them to say nothing to anyone.

They sobered up in the time it takes to flick a light switch. Both of them said, 'Don't go back. Come to live with us in England until you get yourself sorted out.' I told them I would be returning to Belfast. They said good night and I never heard another sound that night. Nor, in the months or years that followed, did those girls ever reveal a word of what I had told them.

It was about 1.00 a.m. when I got into bed. I was absolutely shattered. I had probably slept a total of about five or six hours over the three previous nights and a number of unusual things had happened over that period. I was asleep as soon as my head touched the pillow and I slept solidly and dreamlessly until 10.00 a.m.

What I didn't know until I woke up was that all hell had broken loose around me while I slept. At about 4.00 a.m., an Israeli wrestling coach named Moshe Weinberg had answered a knock at the door of his team's sleeping quarters at 31 Connollystrasse in the Village. Suddenly he shouted, tried to slam the door shut and was shot dead through the wood by a gunman from the Black September Organization, a Palestinian militant group. Behind him, Joseph Romano, Israel's best-known wrestler, reached for a knife. He was shot dead in the middle of the room. Nine members of the Israeli team were then taken hostage. The Olympic siege had begun.

Janet Simpson woke me up and said to come over to her room for a cup of coffee. We made it and went out on to the balcony. We looked down on to the most amazing scene I have ever witnessed – the entire Village was ringed by soldiers with automatic guns. It was as though World War Three had been declared during the night. We crossed the corridor and went into my room. The first thing we noticed was that all the piped music had been shut off, then that the streets of the village, normally thronged with people of every shape and colour, were almost deserted. And finally that out there, down the Connollystrasse, there were men crouching on every rooftop. Some had guns and some binoculars or radios. We must have been the last two people in Munich, even in Europe, to learn of the dreadful things that had happened that night in the Olympic Village.

## The Aftermath

It was a long, awful day. Most of the British girls were taken out of the Village for a ride around the local sights, but I went into town and joined Buster and a couple of other friends at the Diplomat Hotel. Someone bought a transistor radio, and through the afternoon we listened to the description of the scene back in the Village where the terrorists were still holding the rest of the Israelis hostage. After dinner I went back to the Village, and it was there I heard the news that the terrorists had been shot out on the airfield at Fürstenfeldbruck but the Israeli hostages were safe. Like most people I went to bed almost happy.

The next morning I awoke with a nervous rash on my legs. I knew what it was because I had suffered from it before, but I thought I would go across the Village to the team headquarters to check up with the doctor. As I was leaving, someone told me that the previous night's news had all been a mistake. The Israeli hostages were all dead. As it happened a memorial service was being held for them in the Olympic Stadium at that very moment. The Village was a ghost town. No one knew whether the Games would continue or not.

For the rest of that day I made plans to leave Munich. It had always been planned that I should return to Belfast before the end of the Games. There was much to be done back in Buster's gym and though, at one time, I would have liked to have stayed for the closing ceremony, there was now nothing to keep me. I knew the *Belfast Telegraph*, who naturally knew nothing of the charming message threatening to make life somewhat difficult for me if I came back, was planning some kind of an official reception. 'Can you come on Friday?' they asked. So I did.

The journey to Belfast took an unusual route, and for the first few hours I could not understand why. First we took one plane across to Frankfurt. Then we were whisked on to another plane at the very last minute to London. It seemed rather a roundabout route. In London, we came down the steps from the plane to quite a large reception of people I had never seen before, and were taken straight from the tarmac to the VIP room, where some welcome drinks appeared. We were just having a second drink when a man said to me, 'Were you conscious of what was happening as you got off the plane?' I didn't know what he was talking about. 'Well,' he said, 'I'm pleased about that, but every yard of the way you were surrounded by security men. In fact, there was a woman photographer there, and at the very best, all she could have got was a quick snap of the back of your head.'

It would be stupid to pretend that I had put the message from Belfast completely out of my mind. I hadn't. I didn't like it, but I was going back there anyway because it was my city, my home and the place I loved best. But it was fairly obvious that some people were taking the threat very seriously indeed. Our flight to Belfast was called, but nobody moved. Not in our party, anyway. A minute or two before the plane was about to take off, we were asked to collect our hand baggage. Then, in a rush, we were shepherded out to the plane, where Buster and I were the last to board. We were taken to seats right at the front and, again, it was not until we landed in Belfast that I learned that the placid-looking gentlemen sitting immediately behind us were from the Special Branch.

I understood their concern and I was grateful for it. There would have been a certain amount of criticism, I suppose, had I been shot. Anyway, they were taking no chances at this stage in the proceedings. It was a curious homecoming. The plane taxied up to the far end of the airport buildings and all the other passengers were asked to leave first from the rear exit. I found myself apologising to everyone for all this inconvenience. The whole airport, I discovered later, had been sealed off to the public except those who held special passes. Yet outside I could see that a red carpet had been laid out from the front steps of the aircraft and that a band was waiting. Jay Oliver, from the publicity department of the *Belfast Telegraph*, came aboard, introduced himself and told me what was going to happen next: 'When you go down those steps,' he said, 'someone will be waiting to give you a bouquet. Just say hello, collect the bouquet and keep walking. There's no time to talk to anyone and there's certainly no time for interviews. We've got a gold Rolls Royce waiting to drive you into the city.'

I did exactly as I was told. As I went down the steps, the band were playing 'Congratulations' and among those waiting at the bottom was Margaret, Buster's wife. We kept walking until we came to the gold Rolls Royce. 'From this point,' said Jay Oliver, 'there has had to be a small change of plans. We've had a man out all night putting posters on practically every lamp post between here and Belfast saying "Welcome Home, Mary". Unfortunately you won't see any of them. For security reasons we're going in by a different route.'

And so we did. We doubled back down country roads that I never knew existed, flying along between hedgerows at a breathtaking rate. When we got to the city, the first stop was at Buster's gymnasium. Outside, they'd hung up gymnastic rings in the form of the Olympic symbol. Inside, the members presented me with a radiogram and the staff gave me a gold bracelet, the first of many lovely gifts I was to receive over the next few days. The ever-thoughtful Jay Oliver whispered a piece of advice: 'Mary, this is the last time you're going to be near a loo for hours. It's going to get pretty hectic from here.' It's one of the things I love about Northern Ireland. Most of the people get their real priorities right.

Jay wasn't exaggerating. The Rolls was still waiting to take us down to the *Belfast Telegraph* office where there was lunch, a champagne reception and another presentation, this time in the form of a gold brooch shaped like the switchback roof of the Munich stadium. Then it was back out into the fresh air for the drive down Royal Avenue to City Hall.

Until that moment I had only seen anything remotely resembling a ticker-tape welcome in films about American war heroes returning to their home towns. Belfast, that afternoon, matched anything I had seen in the cinema. The confetti came down from the office buildings and up from the streets and there were thousands of people who all looked happy, but they were nothing like as happy as I was. We drove slowly along in a lorry with its sides stripped down and I leaned over the edge to let anyone see and touch the medal that Northern Ireland had brought away from the Olympics. It wasn't mine, it was ours. From time to time I noticed that the constable and several policemen who had been attached to our party weren't exactly looking relaxed about the security aspects of the arrangement. After all the precautions on aircraft, at airports and on the drive in to Belfast, it was somewhat contradictory, I suppose, to be driving along on an open vehicle. I've only thought of that since. At the time I simply didn't care.

At City Hall, they had opened the main doors so that we could walk through to another reception. A sentence like that would mean nothing at all in Bradford or Bristol or Baltimore or Brisbane or any other city you can think of beginning with the same letter. In Belfast, where they didn't open the main doors at all because of the Troubles, it was an historic moment. I made a speech there, which was quite emotional. It summed up everything I had felt driving along that great street of this great city which, for all its problems, is my eternal home.

So it went on. We went to the Europa Hotel, the tall white building near the station, which became so familiar to practically every reporter in Europe, for a press conference. The chef had baked a cake depicting the five events of the pentathlon. We went to Ulster Television where a studio assistant asked me to remove the bracelet I had just been given because it would flare under the arc lights. I only discovered the real reason halfway through our live interview when they suddenly produced yet another bracelet and presented it to me then and there. It seemed that every hour was Christmas day and it occurred to me that what I had said to Mr Heath was even truer than I'd thought: Belfast *had* been waiting for a happy day. The security people followed us out to Buster's home, where I was staying for the next few days, and then they withdrew. Their job was over. We were on our own. No one had been hurt. I hadn't needed the advice contained in that message to Munich advising me to 'say something about bringing the people together.' Bloody hell, I'd just been running my guts out for everybody, including myself. What more did he want?

That night we went to the Ulster Arts Club and a somewhat spidery entry in my diary records that I went to bed at 3 a.m.

We took the Europa's lovely cake to the Multiple Sclerosis Society and a lot of the bouquets out to Glencraig School, and by the Sunday, with the Olympics still going on in Munich, I was back at work. I really meant to see the closing ceremony on television the following night but someone insisted we all went out for yet another celebration and I missed the whole lot. 'To bed,' says the same diary, 'at 4 a.m.' It isn't the winning of an Olympic gold that tests the stamina, it's what happens afterwards.

Five days after that triumphal ride through the streets of Belfast I flew to Liverpool to join my father who was visiting relatives and friends before returning to Australia. Just as I was leaving, I received a telephone call from a member of the International Athletes' Club pleading with me to compete in a heavily-sponsored meeting at Crystal Palace, London, the following evening. Of course, it was nice to be asked, but I was a bit narked; the meeting had been planned for some months, but I hadn't

## The Aftermath

been invited to take part. Now, all at once, my name was in the headlines. As it happens, I'm a member of the International Athletes' Club, but that didn't commit me to dropping everything and running at their beck and call. I said I was going over to Liverpool to say goodbye to my father and that I couldn't make it. He pleaded with me on the telephone: 'In that case, would you just come down to Crystal Palace and make a public appearance? Don't run. Just come and show yourself to the crowd.' I weakened. I said, 'All right, I'll come if my father agrees to come with me.' I telephoned my father in Liverpool and he said he would join me. It turned out to be one of the more interesting trips of my life. In Liverpool there was a civic reception in the afternoon and a family party in the evening. We were going to look in at the Crystal Palace in between.

We left the reception and caught the 5.15 p.m. plane from Liverpool. We sat at the back so that we could slip off first, but somehow the IAC had got a message through that we were being met. We were let off first, but through the front door. For the second time in a week I was apologising to fellow passengers for the privileged treatment. As we went forward along the aisle, Daddy waved to absolutely everyone. It was like travelling with a US president.

A Rover was there to meet us and take us from Heathrow to Crystal Palace. As the crow flies it is only a short sprint on the Home Counties map, but as anyone who knows London's South Circular Road in the Friday night rush hour will confirm, it can feel like the proverbial slow boat to China. In any case, our timing was right. I had to be at the stadium by 7.25 p.m. and I had to be away again by 7.30 p.m. in order to make sure I'd catch the 8.45 p.m. plane back to Liverpool for the party with all those aunts and uncles and cousins. I had asked the airline if they could possibly hold the plane for us in case we were a little late. They said they could hold it for fifteen minutes, but not a moment more.

Ray Roseman, who was driving, did a marvellous job, but there was nothing he could do when we hit a solid jam of traffic at a roundabout just short of Crystal Palace. We couldn't move forwards, backwards or down any side road. It was then that I spotted a police car just ahead of us. I told Ray and my father to follow me if they could, jumped out of the Rover and dashed up to the police car in what must have looked like an action replay of my 200m final. It happened to be a little white two-seater sports job with two quite large policemen inside. I tapped on the passenger window. The passenger-side policeman wound it down and I was still gabbling away about my predicament when a great grin came over his face. 'Ah, Mary,' he said, 'jump in.' MGBs are not large, and I'm not built like a ballet dancer, but I squeezed in somehow and sat there on his lap with my arm round his neck.

We took off. There is no other description for it. Heaven knows how we got in and out of that traffic but suddenly we were at the gates of the stadium. There stood a large police inspector. My new friend wound down the window, cleared his throat and said, 'Actually, sir, Miss Peters here has a bit of a problem. You see ...' Police officers are wonderful. 'What are you waiting for then?' asked the inspector. Away we went again and they delivered me right at the top of a flight of stairs leading down into the arena, where Emlyn Jones, director of Crystal Palace, was waiting. I had two minutes to spare and in that time, to my delight, Ray Roseman and my father caught us up.

My father had my handbag in one hand and my coat in the other and, like that, we went out into the centre of the track to the microphone. I said a few words to the crowd, held up the medal from which I was now becoming inseparable and explained that we had to dash away. We got back into the Rover, headed back through the traffic jam and got to London Airport only five minutes after the scheduled time of our plane's departure. As good as their word, they had waited for us. Obviously we had had nothing to eat. In Liverpool we stopped the car at a fish and chip shop on the way from the airport to the party and arrived eating plaice and chips. I worked it out later that the time between my entering the Crystal Palace athletics track and leaving it was something well under four minutes.

# 12

# Life and Death

There is no doubt that the four months after the Olympics were even more exhausting than the four months before them. Beforehand I was at least getting the nine hours' sleep I had convinced myself I needed, but that was now impossible. I was lucky to get five hours, let alone six. I was travelling to England twice and sometimes three times a week. I was in constant demand to open things, auction things and say things and I was lucky enough to win a number of awards. I made more television appearances than any British politician during that period. Autograph hunters and well-wishers followed me everywhere I went.

Life was a whirlwind but I still had a full-time job to do at the gymnasium. There was also the small matter of answering all the letters I had received (there were at least seven thousand). A lovely girl called Harriet Duffin rang me up out of the blue one day and said she guessed I would have a lot of correspondence and that she'd be very happy to give me a hand. She typed almost every reply in her own spare time.

We became very close friends and I asked her to come over to London with me on one of my many trips. We were walking through Soho one evening when I happened to be wearing my very swish new black cape and hood. A gentleman who appeared to have certain diversions in mind stopped right in front of me, peered under the hood and announced his disappointment at what he saw. 'Now,' he said, turning to his companion, 'there's a real virgin for you.' 'That's no virgin' replied his mate, loftily. 'That's Mary Peters.'

So far as I can remember I heard only one disapproving voice in all that time. This was back in Belfast where the lord mayor, Sir William Christie, opened up City Hall again for a civic reception in my honour. People from every section of the community were there and I was invited to take myself along to Lunn's, the most expensive jewellers in the city, and choose myself a present from the people of Belfast. I had passed the glittering windows of Lunn's every day on my way to domestic science college and it had always seemed as remote as Tiffany's or Tahiti. Now there I was, going in without either a purse or a cheque book to choose the most gorgeous gold necklace.

Anyway, a television station rang me up half an hour before the City Hall reception began and asked if they could have a copy of the speech I was going to make in advance. I had to tell them that I never wrote out my speeches. I've always thought that is rather an overcautious way of going about things. It's almost certain that a previous speaker will take the very words you were going to say right out of your mouth or, if not, they will undoubtedly make several points that you will have to reply or refer to. I rather fancied my chances as an ad-libber, anyway, but at this reception I met my match when, across the room, accompanied by his wife, Eileen, came the Great Preacher himself. Towering of figure, commanding of voice, hair, chin, and with dog-collar gleaming, the Reverend Ian Paisley generously offered his congratulations. But then came the commercial. In that powerful County Antrim accent, which must have made sinners quake out in the street, he added, 'Mind you, Miss Peters, my only regret is that you should have seen fit to have done it on the Sabbath Day.'

It was later clearly explained to Mr Paisley, I gather, that I had not been in the position in Munich to rearrange the entire Olympics track and field programme so that the second day of the pentathlon should not fall on a Sunday. But that, I also gather, did not stop Mr Paisley repeating his disapproval of my abuse of the Sabbath when he went to work on his own church congregation the following Sunday. I wasn't actually there to hear it, but that's how the story went.

I liked Eileen Paisley. She appeared to be the quieter member of the family and was very sweet. She asked me for my autograph for her children and, since it was a weekday, I happily obliged.

At the City Hall event, the lord mayor told one story that brought tears to my eyes. Apparently one Belfast person became so excited watching the television transmission from Munich that he rushed out of the house, full of joy and inspiration, and decided to hurdle over his gate. Unfortunately he caught his foot in the top of it and fractured his leg.

One of the really memorable invitations I received came from 111 Squadron of the RAF, then stationed near Ipswich. They were absolutely over the moon about the fact that the number I'd worn in Munich had been the same as their squadron's and in late 1972, they asked Buster and me to fly over to East Anglia for a day as their guests. They wanted to do everything in supersonic style and planned to pick us up in a jet. This was scotched by a civil servant. They then asked the Royal Naval fliers near Belfast to fly us over. This, I gather, was scotched by the same civil servant. They weren't to be beaten. We eventually went over in a Comanche and had a glorious day. Out of deference to both the civil service and the RAF, they would only allow Buster and me to 'fly' in simulators, but it was great fun. Dinner in the mess that evening included a sweet named Pentathlon Mousse.

In London, of course, the award-of-the-year season was just starting, and I must say the critics and the panels and the adjudication committees were very kind to me. I don't regard any of these awards as having any greater value than the other, but the one which certainly has the biggest audience is the BBC *Sports Personality of the Year* show which, back then, went out live from the BBC Theatre in Shepherds Bush to many millions of viewers. The winner is genuinely a complete secret until the presenter announces it simultaneously to the winner and the country. Naturally I knew I was on the short list, but so were several others, including Richard Meade who had performed so brilliantly in the equestrian events in Munich. In fact the honour came to me and Northern Ireland, and I received the trophy from Princess Anne who had won it the previous year for her riding in the Badminton three-day event.

I was a little surprised at how nervous she seemed when she came on to the stage to present it, and it was partly because of this that I made the remark which I have been trying to live down ever since: 'Hasn't she kept it clean?' It seemed to lift the tension just a little and as soon as the live show was over, we chatted away like old friends. I realised then how entitled she is to feel somewhat apprehensive every time she speaks off the cuff in public. It doesn't matter what I say since I am responsible only to myself. But every word she utters is noted down and analysed for a double meaning.

We were joined on the stage by British boxer Henry Cooper, who was the loveliest man you could have met in two careers in sport. 'Good evening, Yer 'ighness,' said Henry, who could have afforded to set up eight elocution schools, but saw no earthly reason why he should pretend he wasn't brought up in the East End, 'I've just 'ad me car stolen.' Happily Our 'Enry got his gleaming new Mercedes back undamaged, but not before Princess Anne expressed her sympathy and recalled her own bad moment in motoring. Only a little while previously she had been stopped for exceeding the speed limit on a motorway and became the subject for enormous publicity in the press. 'I wouldn't have minded,' she said, 'if there hadn't been an item on the very same page in one of the newspapers about a driving offence which led to a person's death. That was worth only one paragraph, it seems, while I got half a page.' She was angry about that. I agreed with her then and I agree with her now.

Incidentally, a year later when it came my turn to hand the BBC trophy over to Jackie Stewart, the racing driver who had just retired, I said that he, too, shouldn't have much trouble keeping it clean as there were a couple of dusters in the box which had impressive little crests in their corners. It is astonishing how many people really believed that Buckingham Palace dusters bear royal insignia. They don't, of course. I was kidding. The only inscription those dusters bore was a very patriotic 'Made in England'.

Another major award was that given by the *Daily Express*. Gordon Banks, the England goalkeeper who had recently lost an eye in a car accident, was voted their Sportsman of the Year while I won Sportswoman of the Year. Unhappily, Gordon couldn't be present as he was still recuperating and the *Daily Express*, who were anxious to avoid a presentation lunch without either of the award-winners present, asked me to come over to London the previous night in case we should be grounded by fog in Belfast the following morning. They didn't stint on the hospitality. Margaret McShane and I were booked into a suite in

*Daily Express* Sportswoman of the Year, 1972.

'Hasn't she kept it clean?' Receiving the 1972 BBC Sports Personality of the Year from HRH The Princess Royal.

Pushing hard in the 100m hurdles, Christchurch, 1974. Mike Bull competed in those Games too. We were determined to win for Buster.

Gold at Christchurch, 1974; my final appearance in competitive athletics. On my right is Nigeria's Modupe Oshikeya, on my left is England's Ann Wilson.

Celebrating winning the 1964 NI Sports Personality of the Year with the Rolling Stones.

Me, Ann Packer and Mary Rand having our footprints recorded on a specially designed golden pathway at Crystal Palace, London, 1979.

Back to the Olympics ... this time with BBC Radio, 1976.
It was a lot less pressure than competing.

I was proud to have been chosen to carry the 2012 Olympic torch.
I later handed it over to Katie Kirk in the London Olympic stadium.

The official launch of the Track fund, Wellington Park Hotel, 1973. Our committee chair, Denis Wilson, is on the far left.

Out fundraising for the Track, March 1973. My goal was to replace the old, pot-holed track and support a new generation of athletes.

Enjoying the official opening of the Track, 1976. I frequently meet those who, as primary school children, spelled out my name.

With Seb Coe at the unveiling of the new Track statue, June 2013. Seb used to call me the Queen Mother when I was his team manager.

With 'Balloon Mary' and gold medallist Michael McKillop at a Spinathon fundraiser for the Trust, Olympia Leisure Centre, 2019.

Celebrating my 80th birthday, and our 'Race to a Million' campaign, with the 1999 Heineken Cup winners, Titanic Belfast, May 2019.

At my health club in Lisburn, 1997. I had 25 happy years here, keeping people fit and healthy.

Meeting Nelson Mandela in London, 1996. Mandela changed my life and I was inspired to go to South Africa to work in the townships.

the Savoy, which could have comfortably housed the entire Household Cavalry, horses included. There were two bedrooms, two bathrooms, a drawing room furnished with gorgeous drapes and antiques, a colour television and a telephone in each loo. The windows looked out over the Thames and the moment we arrived, a massive floral arrangement was brought in for us to enjoy during our very brief stay.

I was no longer the little girl checking in to the Cobden Hotel in Birmingham in her school uniform, but there were moments when I felt like it. 'Yos, modom?' demanded the lady at reception while she eyed my scruffy overnight PUMA bag as though it contained a full set of rusty surgical instruments. 'Peters,' I said. She consulted a list, which appeared to meet with her approval. 'Delighted to have you with us, madam,' she said in the sort of voice that she might just as well have used in the first place.

On the profusion of telephones in our suite, Margaret and I kept dialling things like 0, 9 and 1 in the vain hope we'd hear someone at the other end confess that they were actually room service. This was our own stupid fault because apparently the Savoy is wired up with a series of secret bells that, if pushed, will bring liveried servants running at any hour of the day or night. Since our requirements were no more demanding than two cups of coffee, we decided to give the staff a night off and go downstairs and get them ourselves. After going down and along for about half a mile we were courteously told that coffee would be served in our suite. By the time we got back they were just wheeling in a table covered by such acres of crisp white linen that, if we'd hung it out of the window, the entire Savoy would have taken off down the Thames and beaten the *Cutty Sark*'s record time to India. There's more to winning a gold medal, you may gather, than meets the eye.

The *Daily Express* lunch was a great success. I sat between Sir Max Aitken and Jocelyn Stevens – proprietor and managing director of the paper, respectively – with Jean Rook, the famous columnist, in close attendance. It was such high-powered company that I didn't like to confess how I'd spent half the morning. I'd been ringing secret bells all over the suite in an attempt to get back the shoes I'd put out for cleaning the night before. My shoes had got muddy when I stepped in a puddle at Belfast airport on the way over and my early upbringing insisted that I could not appear anywhere until they were shining again. My father always judged people by the state of their shoes, particularly around the heels.

Going down in the lift I knew the day was going to be a huge success. The lift boy said, 'How you doin', Mary?' and suddenly we were in a descending cube of Belfast. He came from the Shankill Road.

The *Daily Express* trophy certainly requires more cleaning than the BBC's. It is as big as a birdbath and massively impressive. When the meal and the speeches were over they wanted pictures of me holding it and it occurred to me that maybe this was what all those years of weight training had really been for. Their ace photographer sprang on to a window sill and stood there, legs straddled wide, camera glued to face, in the all-action pose of his honourable profession. It really was jolly unsporting of someone to shout at that moment, 'Hey, did you know your flies were open?' They weren't, of course, and nor did the subsequent pictures suffer from overexposure.

There was only one disappointment. I have a great affection for Gordon Banks and was sorry that he couldn't be there. I thought that, perhaps, I could to talk to him afterwards on the telephone so I asked his manager at Stoke City if he would be kind enough to give me the number. He did so on my solemn promise not to pass it on so that Gordon would not be disturbed by other calls. Unfortunately it was the wrong number anyway.

Around this time I went to an annual awards ceremony in Dublin, organised by the Texaco petrol company. It was one I attended regularly, usually accompanied by the late, great athletics supremo Les Jones. This particular year, however, Les was forced to withdraw at the last minute and sent a friend, Tom Clarke, who duly arrived, took one look at the assembled guests, including the then Taoiseach, Jack Lynch, and gasped, 'Les never told me it was black tie!'

It was gone 6.00 p.m. and all the shops were closed, but resourceful Tom begged to be excused, darted upstairs to his room and returned a short time later in full regalia, beaming. 'It's the head waiter's and it's still warm,' he told me. On closer inspection, he was wearing two belts and two pairs of socks as the head waiter's suit and shoes were two sizes bigger but we enjoyed a great night regardless.

I knew how he must have felt. Life was all so hectic then that, at one stage in the proceedings, I didn't have the time to go out and buy any new clothes for myself. I would work at the gym while Margaret would go to a store, pick out a selection of dresses and bring them back for me to choose from. I couldn't keep turning up in the same outfits, and the invitations were still pouring in.

One forty-eight-hour period around this time is a perfect example of the sort of thing I was doing: I flew Belfast—London to catch a plane immediately for Newcastle, did a television interview with sports presenter David Vine then caught the night railway sleeper back to London. I rolled off the sleeper, totally dazed, and got out to the airport. Flew London—Belfast and picked up a car at the airport to go out to Carrickfergus, a lovely little seaside place, to present the Town of the Year Award for the best-kept place in Northern Ireland. I then joined Buster to attend an afternoon meeting of artists, writers and actors and listen to Joseph Tomelty talk like an angel and then returned to Belfast for dinner with friends. And so, as a somewhat more distinguished diarist once said, to bed. Only with the alarm set for six o'clock the following morning to start the same routine all over again.

We flew over to London for yet another party and yet another presentation, this time as guests of the Sports Writers' Association who had elected me their Sportswoman of the Year. We danced and talked and drank a lot and were in no mood at all to go back to the hotel when the last waltz was over. So we drifted out into the night – myself, Buster, Margaret, and two friends, Deryck and Malcolm. We strolled around in the hope that there might still be somewhere open where we could get something to eat. It was about two o'clock in the morning and we were getting nowhere fast when we saw advice coming our way in the shape of an elegantly-dressed man. Given three guesses I might have identified him as a surgeon, or a banker, or someone rather superior in the Foreign Office. His accent matched his appearance exactly and he was extremely friendly when Buster begged his pardon for stopping him and asked him what London had to offer in the way of food at that time of night.

'Let me see, now,' he said, shouldering his umbrella and visibly concentrating. 'Bit of a problem, actually. There is a little place down there where you might get some greasy bacon and eggs, but I can't say I'd really recommend it.'

He thought again for several seconds and then his face suddenly lit up with inspiration. He looked at Margaret and me in our evening dresses and turned to Deryck who was linking arms with us. 'I've got a much better idea than that,' he said. 'Why don't you take these girls back to the hotel and **** 'em.'

With a cheery, 'Good morning,' he was gone as we stood there helpless with laughter. We seemed to laugh our way through all that autumn and winter. We had worked and we had won and every day was Christmas day. It was one of the happiest periods of my life.


It was not to last. In the early hours of the following Easter Tuesday morning, 24 April 1973, Buster had a drink with a friend in the first-floor bar of the Arts Club. When he left, he climbed into his Jaguar and drove out towards his home. Halfway there his car left the road and struck a stone wall. He died instantly.

It was early on that Tuesday morning that I found out. They rang me at about 7.30 a.m. to let me know but I wasn't at home. Holidays had always been rather lonely times for me in Belfast, having no family there, and I had gone to stay with Tom and Flora Craig, two good friends who, like me, originated from Liverpool. Somehow the police had traced me there. I took the call. Would I go immediately and see Margaret, Buster McShane's wife? Yes, of course I would, but why? And then they told me.

It must be difficult for anyone to recall immediate reactions to extreme shock but in my case, amid the confusion of thoughts, was the predominant one that it simply wasn't true. It couldn't be true. Buster was a survivor, a winner, a man who dictated his own fate, the epitome of life and living. I knew him to be an impulsive, aggressive driver but for all that he was a very good one, with the instant reactions of a very fit man. Anyway, he had promised to phone me himself that morning to see how my ankle was. We had trained together on the Friday and I had sprained it when I hit the stop board doing 52 feet, just as I'd bragged to him I would.

And what about yesterday, only yesterday? I'd been having a long-lie in at the Craigs when Buster had phoned and got me out of bed to watch a programme on television. It was the prototype of those superstars sports programmes from Florida where men like Rod Laver and Joe Frazier and Bob Seagren tried their hands at sprinting and swimming and bicycle racing. I had enjoyed it so much that I'd phoned Buster back and thanked him for letting me know it was on. 'Okay,' he'd said, 'I'll talk to you tomorrow.'

And now it was tomorrow. And as I stood there, comprehending at last what the police were asking me to do, I knew that this was no longer some nightmare, and that Buster was really dead. Buster's closest friend, Deryck Monteith, came to collect me in his car. On the way out to Margaret's we called at Buster's mother's home. We had to break the news to her because she hadn't heard of his death. Nor, yet, had Buster's children, for when we got there they were still asleep. So that terrible day began.

A number of slightly varying estimates have been made at the number of people who stood outside the crematorium hall on the day of Buster's funeral. The lowest is 10,000. There were no hymns, nor were there prayers. The music that day was The Clancy Brothers' rendering of 'I am a Freeborn Man' and B.J. Thomas's 'Raindrops Keep Fallin' on My Head'. The first was chosen because the words had special meaning for Buster and the second because it was a tune he liked. The address, a small masterpiece, was given by newsreader Larry McCoubrey, who had only recently narrated a film about Buster's life for BBC Northern Ireland. The wreath I sent was a precise circle of golden flowers with the inscription, 'My medal for you'.

There was neither time nor cause for me to think about what it would mean to my athletics career, but when eventually I did, it was to cave in beneath misery and decide there was no point carrying on. Then I asked myself what Buster would have done, and two weeks later I competed in a small meeting at Newham. There were hundreds of children there and they all queued up for autographs.

Children mean a great deal to me, particularly the children of Northern Ireland. I had a certain plan in mind that might in some way help them and I knew that Mary Peters, athlete, could achieve it more effectively than Mary Peters, mourner. Buster had wanted me to carry on until the Montreal Olympics in 1976, when he thought I would be at my very peak. I reasoned that I might do quite well in Montreal but that Burglinde Pollak would have been improving all the time and would probably beat me in the pentathlon.

But ten months away were the Commonwealth Games, to be held in

Christchurch, New Zealand. There I wouldn't be competing for Britain; I would be competing for Northern Ireland. Buster would have wanted that. So I decided to stay in training and go there for one reason only – to win a gold medal that I now wanted very badly indeed.

Then I would quit.

# 13

# When the Running Had to Stop

At a certain point in 1973, I realised that, if I wanted to win in New Zealand, I'd have to put the shutters up against any further public appearances and settle down to the really hard grind of training all over again. All the time I was doing it, one point was nagging me: I knew I'd left it too late. You cannot be casual about preparation for the big ones and, without Buster to control my life for me, I had this dreadful feeling that now, when I wanted to win so badly, I'd messed it all up.

I had never felt so lonely or unhappy before any big event, because every way I turned there were faces or situations that reminded me of Buster, and Buster was dead. There were many tears throughout that trip at moments when I found myself alone. There had been no one to drive me through those training schedules and now there was no one to tell me precisely what to do and when. More than that, there was just no Buster, roaring and laughing and slapping people and telling bawdy stories and belting through every day in overdrive. The world was a much emptier place.

It was the time to turn to friends. They knew, instinctively, how I was feeling. Mary Rand, now Mary Toomey, in whose shadow I had lived so long as an athlete, invited me to stay with her in California and train there, far away from the tensions and grey skies of Belfast, for a couple of weeks before going on to New Zealand.

Mary was by then on her third surname (like many other mutual friends, I had been somewhat shocked to pick up a Sunday newspaper one weekend and read that her marriage to Sidney Rand, the rower, had broken up). It was only later I was to discover that I had introduced her to her second husband. In 1967 we had both gone to Los Angeles as members of a Commonwealth team to compete against the United States. One night I went to a party given by several American decathletes at a glorious house they had overlooking the beach at Santa Monica. One of the athletes was Bill Toomey, soon to become the Olympic decathlon champion in Mexico. At a banquet after the match was over, Bill sought me out and asked me to bring Mary back to the beach house for another party. I introduced them, we all squeezed into Bill's sports car and, for my pains, Mary and I finished up having the only almighty row we have ever had.

I remember that, at some point in the proceedings, I drove to an all-night supermarket with an American 400m runner in search of anything that might be cooked up into a combination of dinner and breakfast. We came back loaded with hamburgers and eggs and, unfortunately, a king-size packet of potato crisps. We went into the kitchen where Bill and Mary were deep in conversation. Mary looked up and told me to go and get lost. I was so annoyed that I ripped open the crisp packet and emptied about a dollar's worth over her head. I was then led away to an armchair and ordered to behave myself and go to sleep. At sunrise, with the party still going on, I got up and made breakfast for everyone except Mary. It was the point of no return. She laughed and apologised, I laughed and apologised, and we agreed that our mutually appalling behaviour the previous evening may have been the result of what *Private Eye* magazine delicately refers to as 'overtiredness'. We'd certainly had a few drinks. Of such collisions are lasting friendships made apparently. Mary married Bill Toomey after the Mexico Olympics and on her way to California was photographed by the world's press at Amsterdam airport wearing, by way of disguise, the kind of wig you would associate with Louis XIV rather than one of the most beautiful girls ever to appear on an athletics track. She was never one to do anything by halves.

Now, in mid-December 1973, the Toomeys opened their home to me in America. Bill, in charge of physical education at the University of Irvine, was in training to take part in the latest American TV *Superstars* production. He was also coming to New Zealand as a representative of Chevron, the firm that had built the new running track in Christchurch, and was bringing Mary with him. For me it was a wonderful stroke of luck. I had been trying to keep to the training schedules that Buster had set me for the Olympics, but I needed personal contact, too, and Mary was an inspiration. In California she came out and tried to beat me at everything in our first training session, and was scarcely able to walk the next day. She also coached me in the long jump with such effect that I came very close to the 20ft mark, which I'd never previously achieved.

Immediately after Christmas, Mike Bull, the Northern Ireland pole-vaulter who had also been trained by Buster, arrived. Mike and I had made a pact that we would both win gold in New Zealand in Buster's honour, Mike in decathlon and me in pentathlon, to prove that Buster was the best multi-discipline coach in the Commonwealth – and one who was self taught.

For a while, we stayed with our friend John Forde, but then the weather turned bad. After three days of stair-rod rain we sloshed our way to a travel agent, changed all our schedules and caught the night plane to New Zealand. We were the first athletes to arrive in the Commonwealth Games Village, and were greeted by the kind of meals the Dorchester would be proud to serve.

I had never been to New Zealand before and found Christchurch full of surprises. It had streets as wide as New York, but it was still virtually a country town populated by friendly, worthy, sensitive people, who were used to living life at a leisurely pace. It was rather like going into one of those late Edwardian homes where the discipline was never questioned and no one ever seemed to do anything just for the hell of it. I was astonished, for example, to find a town packed with overseas visitors still shutting all its bars at ten o'clock in the evening. I was even more astonished to go into what appeared to be a very smart restaurant with some friends to find the head waiter wanted us to pay for our meal before we'd eaten it. No one seemed to eat in restaurants in the evenings, and maybe that kind of treatment was the reason.

But there were plenty of pluses too. Hundreds of local residents gave up their holidays to drive athletes and officials around, the food in the Village was so good that some competitors actually complained about being offered steak for breakfast as well as lunch and dinner, and the security was so tight that, for the first time in my memory, you could walk around in the Village without being thronged by hangers-on and autograph-hunters. One newspaper report claimed that this was because of the presence of the Northern Ireland team, but I regarded that as nonsense. Tragically, since Munich, all major sports events of this kind have had to be protected against all forms of terrorist attack or demonstration, and Christchurch did an incomparable job.

For all the milling thousands of people, and the few close friends I had there, these, for me, were still the lonely Games. Curious though it may sound, I found it hard, as a member of the Northern Ireland team, to be on chatty terms with members of the English and Scottish teams, even although we had been close colleagues in combined British sides. We were now rivals and I found it as difficult to say hello to them as they did to me. Perhaps Buster's philosophy was getting through at last. You had to be hard.

I was competing in four events: the hurdles, the high jump, the shot and the pentathlon, but in three of them I was doing little more than putting in an appearance. To diversify was to ask for trouble and all my thought and ambition was concentrated on the pentathlon. That was the one I wanted to win and I wanted the gold, if anything, more desperately than I had wanted the gold in Munich. It was scheduled for the first Friday of the Games, the day immediately after the opening ceremony.

Any thoughts that the waiting days and hours might drag were dispelled by the arrival of Deryck Monteith from Belfast. He had breezed in full of gossip and good cheer the previous Saturday, and the following day came out to watch us compete in a pre-Games meeting. He stood there all day in the blazing sun and it didn't surprise me, therefore, when he complained of feeling unwell in the evening. The next morning when he said he felt worse it became a little perturbing. Ex-Ireland rugger captains don't exactly cave in under the kind of ailments that a couple of aspirins and a large scotch will cure. He went back to his motel to rest, but when I phoned him later to see how he was, it was to be greeted with the news that he was seriously ill and that a doctor had been sent for. By the time I arrived at his motel the doctor had been and gone, diagnosing gastroenteritis. After watching Deryck stare speechlessly at the ceiling for four hours I sent for the doctor again. This time he diagnosed constipation. Early the following morning Deryck was on an operating table in hospital and undergoing surgery for a burst appendix.

It was typical of Deryck that he had no intention whatsoever of missing my last pentathlon, now only three days away. It was also typical of the tough attitudes of New Zealanders that they promised him he would be there provided he could prove to them that he could stand on his feet. I pleaded with the nurses not to let him do anything stupid, but they said keeping him in hospital would probably do him more harm than letting him out for the day. Anyway, the doctors were having bets among themselves about whether the stubborn Irish dentist could make it. With only twenty-four hours to go I wouldn't have risked 20p on Deryck's chances, but next morning he was out of bed at seven o'clock and walking up and down a corridor. The doctors were convinced and gave him parole. Happily Deryck's wife had two friends, Ross and Dorothy Lascelles, living in Christchurch. They borrowed a wheelchair and with the aid of that and a couple of sticks, Deryck got himself down to the Queen Elizabeth II Stadium. When I came out through the tunnel on to the track there were Deryck, Bill Cook (who had flown in from Bermuda), Mary Toomey and my father, all waving encouragement. My spirits rose considerably.

It would be wrong to pretend that I was at the same pitch of physical fitness that I had been at the start of the Munich Olympic pentathlon. For all that I felt well and in an aggressive mood and was suffering no ill-effects from the previous day, when a cold south wind straight up from Antarctica had cut through the stadium throughout the whole of the long opening ceremony. To avoid hanging about in the wind before the ceremony began we'd come to a quiet arrangement with the stadium foreman that I could go and sit in his hut until the march-past began. This plan came unstuck when we got there to find it occupied by a large, aggresive Alsatian. We shut the door on him and fled. Luckily, along with a couple of Isle of Man athletes, I found refuge in the large tent where the Maori dancers were changing, and we sat there on a rug until the ceremony began. It was viciously cold outside and we were only wearing flimsy dresses, but we smiled and waved our way round that track as though it were a glorious midsummer's day. It was essential, after all the grim publicity Northern Ireland had had throughout the world, that we showed ourselves to be a happy and united team.

Next morning, the wind had gone and it seemed like a perfect English June morning as we drove the six miles across town to the stadium, which was set in such rural surroundings that a herd of Friesian cows were munching away in a field only 300 yards from the shot-put circle.

But this was hardly the time to ruminate on the glories of nature. One hell of a day lay ahead because, for the first time in a major international event, the pentathlon was going to be decided in one day instead of two. There had been considerable wranglings about this decision. More than a year earlier I had written complaining about it, but had never received a reply. Taking this silence to mean 'no', I prepared myself mentally for a one-day competition and came to the conclusion that this would probably suit me better anyway. I was big and strong enough to reel the events off in quick succession and I wouldn't have to go through that dreadful torture of a sleepless night in between. Then, some two months before the Games I was surprised to receive a letter from John Le Masurier, the English coach, asking me to support a petition to have it changed to two days. This didn't suit my new outlook at all, so I replied that I wouldn't. Even so, when I arrived in Christchurch there were still moves afoot to press for the change. I must confess to getting somewhat bloody-minded about it. I was now reasonably experienced in the behind-the-scenes machinations of athletics. Our Irish team manager went to plead my case at a specially convened meeting and emerged with a smile that told me immediately that we had won the day. We were now committed to a programme which read: 10 a.m. hurdles; 11 a.m. shot; 1.30 p.m. high jump; 4 p.m. long jump; 5.30 p.m. 200 metres.

As the reigning Olympic champion, I was entitled to feel confident, but at the same time I was a little apprehensive, knowing that I had not prepared as thoroughly as these big occasions demand. I knew that the Canadian, Diane Jones, was a very big threat. At Munich, Diane had hit a hurdle in the opening event and had been taken to hospital to have several stitches put in the wound. That would have been curtains for some competitors, but she'd returned and put up such a courageous show in the four remaining events that she had still finished tenth overall. I met Diane soon after she'd arrived in Christchurch and, at the risk of sounding unsporting, was somewhat relieved to hear that, until quite recently she'd been suffering from an ankle injury. I knew that Ann Wilson, at her best, could be a real danger, and there was also Barbara Poulsen, the New Zealander. I had an uneasy feeling that a patriotic home crowd could do a great deal to lift her performance. One name that gave me not a moment's concern, however, was Modupe Oshikoya from Nigeria. I can't imagine why I should have had such a blind spot about her since she had not only competed at Munich but had finished a very creditable fourteenth. Yet I couldn't remember even seeing her there, and nor had I read about any of her performances in the athletics magazines. Had the pentathlon come later in the Games, I would probably have been more concerned, since it was at Christchurch that so many African athletes emerged in the very front rank of world-class performers. Perhaps my ignorance was just as well because, had I known of her capabilities, she would have given me a sleepless night. She was certainly about to give me a rather hard day.

I was fairly pleased with my time for the hurdles. It really is vital to get a good start and I was first away in my heat, led all the way and won it in 13.94 seconds. This was the same time as Ann Wilson achieved in her heat and far better than Diane Jones's 14.8, which lumbered her with a big points deficit right from the start. All was well with the world until I looked at the scoreboard again and saw that the unknown Oshikoya had just clocked a very disturbing 13.72 seconds. It still left me second overall after the hurdles, but it was distinctly bad news. I looked around to pick her out and there she was, looking calm and self-possessed. She wasn't big but she was beautifully built, and as she warmed up again she ran as effortlessly as a gazelle.

By late in the afternoon I felt instinctively that she could give me a great deal of trouble in the 200m, so it was more important than ever that I made it really tough for her in the shot. This was where I had to build up my points lead. Charlie Stewart, who was there reporting for the *Belfast Telegraph*, told his readers that I was looking very tense and nervous at the start of the shot and he was probably right. But the tension didn't appear to do anything but good. I improved with each of my three throws, building up from 44ft 4in to 49ft 2½in and then, finally 49ft 4½in. For the moment it pushed Oshikoya out of the picture, put Diane Jones right out of the reckoning and left me just ahead of Barbara Poulsen whose best throw was 48ft 7½in. We went away for the lunchtime rest with me leading the competition by seventy points from Poulsen.

The first afternoon event, the high jump, did little to change the position except to see Ann Wilson take over from Barbara Poulsen as a big rival. We started jumping at 5ft 1in and Oshikoya, Wilson and I all kept going clear up to 5ft 8½in. Then, at 5ft 9¾in we all failed. Each of us, therefore, added 974 points to our score with the long jump and 200 metres still to come.

Mercifully my first long jump was a respectable one of 19ft 0¾in because a long, disturbing wait while the victory ceremony for the 10,000 metres run took place did nothing at all for my concentration. My rhythm was completely gone when I tried to improve on it. In my second attempt, I slapped a foot right over the board for a no-jump and my third effort was simply pathetic. Oshikoya had pulled out a beauty and was still looking as cool as if she were just going off to a party. There was no Buster to turn to. Mary Toomey had been giving me the thumbs up and Deryck, Bill Cook and Charlie Stewart, the voice of Belfast, had all been giving me signals from the stand, but they will all know what I mean when I say it wasn't the same.

The points now flashing up on the board only confused me. I was still leading on points, but what did it mean in terms of yards and seconds in the final event? I went over to where all the Northern Ireland officials were scribbling away on scraps of paper. I knew by then that I wasn't going to be at Oshikoya's shoulder at the end of the 200m, but how much could I afford to be behind her? The consensus was that if I could hold her to an advantage of between seven and eight yards I would take the gold. I had a lead of 109 points overall and I was so heartened by the news that I can remember saying, 'I'll have to break a leg to lose.'

Well, I didn't break a leg, but I nearly burst my lungs. It was a murderously hard run, much harder than in Munich, coming as it did at the end of a single exhausting day's competition. I was away well but so was Oshikoya, and all I saw of her after the bend was her back which I dared not let pull too far away. It was a tremendous battle, but as we went over the line I reckoned I was between six and seven yards behind. The electronic devices confirmed it. Oshikoya's time was 24.15 secs, mine 25 secs dead. To beat me overall, Oshikoya needed to win by 1.2 seconds. I had done what I came for and the gold medal was mine.

Almost immediately I heard my name being called by a group of people and went across to the fence to discover who they were. They were the members of the Irish team who had been competing in the Commonwealth Paraplegic Games, as it was then known, in Dunedin only a few days before. They were on the first part of what was an exhaustingly long haul back from New Zealand to Belfast, yet they had insisted in getting off the plane at Christchurch to go to the stadium, so that they could see me competing for the last time. They were bubbling with fun and were so happy for me that it felt like a mini celebration of my gold, right there on the track.

My emotions had always been so close to the surface that I was surprised how calm I felt as I walked out across the track to receive my medal from Sir Alexander Ross. I was being realistic, not defeatist, when I knew that that was the last prize I would ever win as an athlete. All my mental preparation had been concentrated on the pentathlon and I knew that it was beyond me to key myself up again sufficiently to win any of the other events for which I had entered. Anyway I had subconsciously allowed myself the luxury of thinking that, if I justified the long journey with the gold on the opening day, then I could ease off and just enjoy the rest of the Games. It is not the way to win. My chances in the shot flickered briefly when I got in the best put in the qualifying rounds, but the old hunger had gone.

Athletics, like all forms of highly competitive sport, can become small, insular worlds at times, so it is good to be brought back to reality, which for me happened only a few hours later. After all the interviews and the champagne I went back to the Village and as I was coming out of the dining room I met a little girl wearing Scottish national dress. Derek Murray, our assistant manager, lifted her up, discovered her name was Nicola and then said, 'This is Mary Peters and that's the gold medal she's just won.' Nicola looked at the medal and then at me. 'Well,' she said, 'I've got forty-five of those at home.'

Two days before the Games ended there was another shock, this time with no humour about it at all. I was taking some friends out to lunch when Irish athlete Maeve Kyle stopped me and asked if I knew which flight Mary Toomey had left on that morning to return to America. I wasn't sure and asked why she wanted to know. 'There's been a plane crash,' said Maeve, 'but at the moment we don't know anything more than that.' Two flights had taken off from New Zealand for America that day and one of them, the Pan American, had crashed at Pago Pago with what was reported to be a heavy loss of life. Several London newspapers had open lines to their reporters in Christchurch and the reporters were frantically trying to get the two respective passenger lists. For two hours I was quite speechless. Before leaving America for New Zealand, Mary's, daughter, Samantha, had continually said, 'You will be safe, Mummy, won't you?' and Mary had laughed and reassured her in that carefree way she had about everything. After two hours the news came through. Mary Toomey had left from Auckland that morning by Air New Zealand. I just don't know what I would have done had the answer been otherwise.

The Games closed on a Saturday before almost the whole British Royal family and 34,000 other people. The whole stadium had justifiably erupted when Filbert Bayi, from Tanzania, broke the world 1500m record, but for me the main recollection of that final afternoon in athletics was of the totally unfair conditions under which the female high jumpers had to compete. I was one of them, but on this occasion I was not concerned for myself because I knew I wasn't going to win it.

I had struck up a great friendship with the very youngest competitor, the Australian Debbie McCawley, and she was only one of those consistently being hampered by other athletes, who were either running on the track or waiting around to do so. I thought I had seen nearly everything there was to see during a long career in sport, but the lack of consideration shown that afternoon by some athletes to others simply amazed me. Again and again the high jumpers had to break off because of people standing in their line of approach, or actual track events passing in front of them, or metallic announcements coming over the loudspeakers just as they were running in with total concentration. It was hopeless. I protested very strongly about it and I hoped it was the last time we would ever see organisers trying to combine an important field event with track events on a final day. There were many excellent aspects of the Games organisation in Christchurch, but that certainly wasn't one of them.

My annoyance may well have been a blessing in disguise. It certainly prevented me from becoming over-nostalgic, maudlin even, about the fact that this was the last time I would walk out into an athletics arena with that familiar half-nervous, half-elated feeling that you never lose before big competition. Down all the years, I had nearly always had that optimistic feeling that this was going to be the day when it all came right, but now there was some inner conviction that another medal was beyond me. I was really only competing because I knew that Buster would have wanted me to. I spent most of the competition chatting to Debbie McCawley. At 5ft 8in, well below what I had achieved in Munich only fifteen months earlier, I knocked the bar off. I knocked it off a second time. When I knocked it off the third time, the announcer solemnly announced that my career was over.

I could hardly wait to get away and nor was there to be any coming back. I gathered up my clothes, hurried across to the steps that went underground to the locker rooms, looked briefly up into the panorama of faces in the great cantilever stand, waved once and was gone. It was over, just like that. Had Buster lived, I would probably have continued for another three years until the 1976 Olympic Games in Canada, but I knew that without him there was little chance to do so with success. It had to be a clean break.

There was one final honour to come in that arena. Mike Bull – who had also done as he'd vowed, and won gold – had carried the Northern Ireland flag at the opening ceremony. I was to carry it at a closing ceremony, which was to prove less informal than sheerly chaotic. Only the previous evening, one of our Ulster boxers, the flyweight Davy Larmour, had won a gold medal. When the guard of honour came to haul the Ulster flag up to the masthead, the rope had jammed and it refused to budge. I was determined to make up for that by seeing to it that our flag was now the highest in the closing parade. I went and found the biggest man at the Games, the twenty-stone Canadian shot-putter, Bruce Pirnie. I climbed on to his shoulders and he carried me right round the track with the flag held high above my head.

Larceny isn't normally my game, but I badly wanted that flag as a final souvenir. Towards the end of our circuit, I pulled it down and gave it to one of our badminton players, Dorothy Cunningham. I asked her to try and sneak it back to the Village for me, as I would clearly be a prime suspect once the officials had discovered it was missing. Dorothy kindly agreed to try and I forgot all about it until I returned to the Village where the all-night farewell celebrations were just beginning. Marea Hartman invited us over to the English women's quarters for champagne and, as I was leaving their block, I suddenly caught sight of Dorothy, still clutching that flag. She was flanked by two police officers. I dashed across to start the explanations when one of the officers beat me to it by saying, somewhat gravely, 'I wonder if you would ask all the Northern Ireland ladies to gather in one room, please.'

I had an awful feeling that on my very last day I had caused real trouble for all the team. When we were gathered together the officer said, 'I am sorry to have to say this, girls, but would you be kind enough to go and search your luggage. You see, there's been a bomb scare.' The man must have thought I was mad for I suddenly heard myself saying loudly, 'Thank Christ for that.'

It was a hoax. There were no bombs at my last of the Friendly Games. We sang and danced and drank and laughed the night away and when the sun came up I was Mary Peters, the *former* athlete. I still have the flag at my home in Belfast.

# 14

# Back to the Olympics

Three years later, in 1976, I went to the Olympic Games in Montreal. After three Games as a competitor, it was my first Olympics as an onlooker. I had neither planned nor expected to be there, but as it was, I once again found myself behind the scenes, only this time it was as a complete rookie in the commentary box, working for BBC Radio.

The opportunity had arrived out of the blue via a telephone call from the then BBC Head of Sport, the great Cliff Morgan, with whom I enjoyed a long and enduring friendship. His wife, Pat Ewing, was Head of Radio and they were a formidable duo, Pat especially. Staff would jump to attention when she came into view. Pat thought I could do a job behind the microphone, and who was I to argue, so after the voice tests were completed, I found myself on a plane to Montreal, seated alongside one of the greatest broadcasters of them all, Terry Wogan.

Terry was to be an anchor man back in the studio in London for the Games television coverage and was being flown out on a familiarisation exercise. Much to Terry's chagrin, however, the licence payers' money didn't stretch to the pampered first-class treatment he was used to, and he had to settle for a seat in steerage with me. He was great company, both on the flight and for the duration of his stay.

Our first assignment was to commentate on the wrestling, which I had never seen before! I was surrounded by a host of international broadcasters, all jabbering away, noisily and excitedly, and I hadn't a clue.

'Help me here,' I pleaded with Terry.

'Don't ask me,' he replied, 'all I know is they do it on a mat.'

Eventually, like the wrestlers, I got to grips and, for a first attempt at describing an unfamiliar sport, I must have given a good account of myself ... or maybe not, because they sent me next to cover the gymnastics, which I did know a thing or two about.

Unfortunately, I didn't get to commentate on what was, for most people, the most memorable moment of the Montreal Games: when the iconic Romanian gymnast Nadia Comăneci achieved, on the uneven bars, the first perfect 10 in Olympic history. I didn't see Nadia in competition, but was fortunate to watch her in training one day and the sheer hard work and dedication she displayed for a 14-year-old left me full of admiration. She went on to record another six perfect 10s in her career, three more on the uneven bars and three on the beam, winning four gold medals, a silver and a bronze. Yet her feat in performing that first perfect 10 had been, quite literally, unbelievable: it turned out the Olympic scoreboard manufacturer did not think a 10 was possible and therefore had not programmed the scoreboard beyond 9.99. Instead, Nadia's score was displayed as 1.00.

It was exciting and interesting to see other sports at that level, outside the bubble of competition I'd been in during my previous Olympics. But I must admit, I also felt very strange not to be donning a vest and shorts.

The thoughts that whirled around in my head, as we journeyed to the Games were would I be thrilled or would I be envious of the athletes taking part while I could only watch on? Of course, I wanted the GB competitors I was commentating on to be successful and give me a good story to tell. But I must admit, at that first Games since my retirement, I did experience feelings of envy, which, I suppose was natural, having been ultra-competitive throughout my career. Those soon dissipated, though, as part of the process of becoming immersed in my new role.

And there were some perks too. Instead of the spartan Olympic Village accommodation I was used to, the Beeb had installed us in a five-star hotel, which was pure luxury by comparison. We enjoyed great companionship and many fun evenings with the broadcasters from around the world who were staying there. And yet, I still missed the camaraderie of the Village.

There were amusing moments, too.

## Back to the Olympics

Like when the Beeb asked me if I could persuade my pal Daley Thompson to do an interview that he wasn't particularly keen on.

'So, what are you going to give him?' I enquired.

I didn't mean money as that was forbidden for amateurs, which all Olympians were at that time, and the Beeb were sticklers for the rules. They were stumped, so I suggested they give him a bottle of champagne. An assistant was despatched to find one, but being a Sunday, the shops in Canada were closed and he returned empty handed. However, I knew Daley was going out to dinner that night with his aunt and the swimmer Sharron Davies.

'OK', I said, 'Tell him to order a bottle on us.'

He did the interview and a few days later, a bill arrived at the BBC's Montreal broadcasting centre – for $160, a ransom back then. Daley had only ordered a bottle of Dom Perignon, the rascal!

I encountered only one other UK female broadcaster in Montreal, the 1960 swimming gold medallist, Anita Lonsbrough, who also wrote for *The Times* and *Telegraph*. But I never considered myself a trailblazer in the field, now happily populated with many, many more gifted females (none more so than our own Ruth Gorman at Ulster Television, who came to interview me in my garden while on work experience at the *Belfast Telegraph* on the occasion of my 70th birthday and has blossomed since then). And I know that I was fortunate to work with some of broadcasting's greats over the years, including another great friend and ally, the wonderful Des Lynam who provided invaluable advice and encouragement. Audiences loved him and I could instantly see why.

In the end, pursuing a career in the media did not really occur to me. Commentating was a difficult field to master, and I saw the Montreal experience as an airlock, a transition, a rite of passage even, call it what you will, from which I emerged, ready to throw myself into other challenges.

In 1980, I was appointed as one of the four Great Britain athletics team managers for that summer's Moscow Olympics. As ever, I had neither sought nor expected to be offered the role. By this stage, Marea Hartman, who had held the position, was entering her sixties and had been in the post for around 40 years. David Shaw, the chief executive of British Athletics, felt he wanted someone younger in the role, so he called me out of the blue to offer me the job. I was coming forty-one.

I had been good friends with Marea and worried our relationship might be affected if I took her place, but we spoke and it wasn't an issue. We remained good friends until her passing in 1994.

With that settled, I was thrilled to be asked and had no hesitation about accepting. I saw it as a natural progression from my athletic career and I was happy to be measured up for the blazer.

The other team managers were Nick Whitehead, who had been a sprinter in the sixties and held the lead role; Lynn Davies, the 1964 Olympic long jump gold medallist; and Margaret Oakley, whose background was sports administration.

All the various sports at the Olympics take their own team managers. Some would only have one, but as athletics is the biggest, the workload required the four of us and even then we would be on our feet most days from six in the morning until midnight. And it wasn't as if we were doing it for the money. Us four managers were paid $5 a day in living expenses!

Unlike football managers, we weren't involved in training or tactics, but the level of responsibility was much the same. We dealt with issues as they arose, and if the matter was deemed serious, we would refer it upward to Nick. Our job was to make sure the athletes were where they should be in the right place at the right time and in the right gear. Due to nerves or focussing on their events, some of them would forget all three. I would count the first athlete on to the coach at the Village and the last one off at the stadium. We shepherded them to and from their events, and if a disqualification or appeal occurred, we would file the paperwork and pay the administration fee. Thankfully, there were few unsurmountable problems.

I was team manager again at the 1984 Los Angeles Olympics, and over those two Games, I dealt with such diverse personalities as Daley Thompson, Seb Coe, Steve Ovett, Tessa Sanderson, Fatima Whitbread and Zola Budd, and all the hype, baggage and sometimes controversy that enveloped them. And while that alone was stressful – really, it was like herding kittens – due to the global political backdrop of the time, the Moscow Games gave me a real baptism of fire.

Ahead of the Games, US President Jimmy Carter declared that the United States would boycott the event in response to Russia's 1979 invasion of Afghanistan, and sixty-five other countries joined the boycott. The pressure on GB to withdraw from the Olympics stepped up when Prime Minister Margaret Thatcher declared that the team should not go. However, any final decision over whether to participate was left in the hands of the sports governing bodies and the individual athletes themselves.

I wasn't privy to the decision making of the UK athletics chiefs in the lead up to the Games but they deliberated and quickly decided we would go. Some team officials felt that I should seek a meeting and speak to Mrs Thatcher, but I declined as clearly her mind was made up. As she once famously said, 'The lady is not for turning.' It was then suggested that they should have Mrs Thatcher speak to someone like the then seventeen-year-old swimmer, Sharron Davies. 'She's too young to have an opinion,' someone scoffed, to which I replied, 'If she is old enough to represent her country, she is old enough to have an opinion.' Again, a meeting never took place.

For my part, I simply could not contemplate competitors being denied the chance to compete after all the hard work and sacrifice they had channelled into reaching their peak. I tried to imagine how I would have felt if world events in which I had no part, and over which I had no control, had forced me to miss the Munich Olympics and denied me my gold medal. What was to be gained from depriving these athletes of the chance to win medals of their own?

When the 2020 Tokyo Olympics were cancelled during the Covid pandemic, I was asked if the one-year delay would make that much difference to the athletes' preparation. 'Seismic,' was my answer. The cancellation changed the course of Olympic history in terms of medal winners, no doubt about that. Every athlete's preparation is focussed entirely on that moment in time when you go for gold. I can honestly say that had my event in Munich been put back by even an unscheduled day, I would not have won gold. The margins are that fine.

And so, we went.

Because we travelled to the Games against the wishes of the politicians, it was decided that the team would not take part in the opening ceremony but be represented by a solitary flag bearer, the general secretary of the British Olympic Association, Dick Palmer, who carried the Olympic flag.

This was also the flag raised for the British medal winners in place of the Union Flag, and the Olympic anthem was played instead of 'God Save the Queen' for the five gold medallists.

Not all the GB sports flew the flag (metaphorically) in Moscow, however. In the event, the British associations that completely boycotted the Games were those that governed equestrian sports, shooting, yachting and, to my deep regret, hockey. The GB hockey team had two players from Northern Ireland, Jenny Given (now Redpath) and Violet McBride. I watched a much less accomplished Zimbabwe team win the women's hockey gold in Moscow and couldn't help thinking Jenny and Violet should have been on that podium, or at least been afforded the opportunity. It was tough on them, as I saw first-hand when I returned home from the Games. I know they think about what might have been to this day.

It was a difficult time for everyone. The uncertainty surrounding participation in the Games was far from ideal preparation and made everyone's jobs even harder. And if we thought negotiating the political minefield to get to Moscow was difficult, our work as team managers was only just beginning. We had barely unpacked our suitcases when the GB Head of Delegation threatened to send Daley Thompson home.

Daley had given one of his typical, irreverent interviews to the press, topping it off by declaring, when asked about his ambition in life, that he would like to have babies with Princess Anne! The top brass had apoplexy over the front-page headlines back home but I managed to smooth things over by assuring them that Princess Anne – who, after all was a friend of mine, and who also knew Daley – would have been amused. That was Daley. Unconventional does not begin to describe him, but I knew how to manage him and I've loved him from the moment we met.

I have been the butt of his humour, too. He turned up at a very posh afternoon tea we were staging at the Europa Hotel as part of the celebrations for the 50th anniversary of my gold medal. He was on his best behaviour until an interviewer poked a microphone under his nose and asked what had stood out about me when we first met. 'Her big boobs,' he grinned.

Over the past fifty years he has attended every one of my Trust events (more on that later) and always in his tracksuit. Daley doesn't do formal.

Once, when we were on a speaking engagement on a cruise ship, he refused to sit at the top table as it would have meant wearing a dinner jacket – instead he ate his meals with his children. 'Adidas pay me to wear these,' he said, pointing at his tracksuit. 'I get nothing for wearing a dinner jacket.'

It was on that cruise that I discovered his kids had never seen TV footage of his incredible athletics achievements, including his golds, until they popped up on screen on the stage where he was speaking. 'Is that Dad?' they asked me, mesmerised.

Many much less successful athletes then Daley would have had their reels on a constant loop. Not Daley, He was, and is, so laid back about his achievements. Despite this, I am pleased to say something of Daley rubbed off on his son: in 2022, Elliot Thompson was crowned decathlon champion at the UK Championships, 46 years after his famous dad first won it. Indeed, Elliot has also competed at my track in Belfast.

It was after Daley's decathlon gold medal win in Moscow that he said something so profound it has resonated with me in the decades since. Asked if he felt his gold was devalued by the absence of the Americans, he shrugged: 'Nope. I beat everyone who turned up.' That sums up the essence of competition for me. Never mind all the background noise. If you're not in, you can't win.

Much of the media focus and hype in Moscow centred on the supposed rivalry between Seb Coe and Steve Ovett. In truth, they barely knew one another and had rarely directly competed. Each was expected to win gold in their respective events, Coe in the 800 metres, Ovett in the 1500.

The nation had been whipped up into frenzy ahead of their first meeting in the 800m final, with households across the country divided over their particular favourite; Coe, with the boy-next-door looks and a perceived posh background (in fact, he went to a comprehensive school), and Ovett, the more aloof, working-class hero.

I had been collecting athletes from Moscow airport on the night of the final so only just made it back to the village to see Steve beat Seb to the 800 gold. The entire team were in shock as Seb had been expected to win easily. On top of the disappointment was the realisation that to win gold he now had to beat Steve in the 1500 final, Steve's specialist event.

Seb's world looked to have caved in on him as I went to greet him on his return to the Village, via a side entrance to avoid the media and the backslappers. I gave him a hug and a peck on the cheek to which his father and coach, Peter, brusquely responded, 'Don't kiss an idiot.' So I kissed him, too!

Seb's night didn't get any better when he discovered he had lost his tracksuit. It is one of the untold stories of the Moscow Olympics that he climbed onto the podium to collect the silver medal he didn't want while wearing a tracksuit he had borrowed from me.

As history relates, it all came good for Seb a few days later when he turned the tables on Steve in the 1500, showing how unpredictability is the spice of sport.

Seb and I somehow bonded over the years to become great friends as I followed his career in politics and then as a leading figure in the British Olympic Association, delivering the 2012 Games to London.

The Games went well for us as a team – GB won 21 medals, including 5 gold for Allan Wells (men's 100 metres), Steve Ovett (men's 800 metres), Seb Coe (men's 1500 metres), Daley Thompson (men's decathlon) and Duncan Goodhew (men's 100m breaststroke) – though we had to deal with disappointment, too. Tessa Sanderson's ambitions suffered a severe setback when she failed to qualify for the javelin final. It was suspected Tessa had been the victim of dirty tricks: when a Russian rival was throwing, the gates of the stadium were allegedly opened in order to provide her with wind assistance.

We signed off those eventful Moscow Games in style after Lynn Davies, the long jumper, and I were asked to do a BBC interview, reflecting on events. 'Only if you give us a case of champagne,' we demanded, half joking. Somehow, in a city of shortages and few luxuries, they produced one and back we went to the village to celebrate with the team at a farewell party. Seb was nowhere to be seen, so I sent one of the other athletes to fetch him from his room. 'He was in bed,' she reported back, 'and I am so disappointed … he was wearing pyjamas.'

Soon, it was time to go home, and as I sat in the airport I got speaking to our own Hugh Russell, a Northern Ireland boxer who had won bronze in the flyweight division. As an amateur, he had also won bronze at the 1978 Commonwealth Games and would go on to hold the British bantamweight title in 1983, and the British flyweight title from 1984 to

1985. Hugh hadn't been able to spend his daily roubles allowance and was preparing to fly home with a fistful. 'Those are no good at home,' I told him. 'They will be worthless, you had better spend them here in the duty free.' So Hugh bought a camera.

He is now, as well as my favourite boxer, an award-winning photographer with the *Irish News* newspaper and I like to think my advice may have inadvertently steered him towards his brilliant photographic profession.

Looking back, I think the Russians performed a superb organisational feat in the circumstances. And, on a personal level, I felt immense satisfaction in knowing I had worked hard for our athletes and could not have done more. We were right to go – no one remembers now who didn't turn up.

At the end of it all, I returned home exhausted. I felt I had competed for each every one of them and shared their emotions, win or lose. And I was ready to do it all again four years later.

Three months before the start of the 1984 Summer Olympics in Los Angeles, the Soviet Union retaliated for the widespread boycotting of the Moscow Olympics by declaring it would not participate in the 1984 Games. But even with that, the rollercoaster ride that was my first experience of GB Olympic team management at Moscow in 1980 meant I still felt mentally ready for all eventualities.

Yet no one had predicted the seismic impact of the sudden parachute landing into our ranks of a slight, shy young South African girl called Zola Budd.

Zola had become an overnight sensation in her native South Africa earlier that year when, aged just 17, she broke the world 5000m record in a time of 15:01.83. This she did, amazingly, while running barefoot. Her time was not officially recognised by the International Athletics Federation due to South Africa's exclusion from international athletics competition (due to apartheid), and with her country also banned from the Olympics, there was no expectation Zola would be competing in the Games anytime soon.

All that changed with the intervention of the *Daily Mail* newspaper.

Incredible as it may now seem, the *Daily Mail* was responsible for Zola's GB recruitment, using her grandfather's British nationality to secure her UK citizenship and a passport. The whole matter was rushed through the Home Office with indecent haste, in a way I don't believe would happen now – similarly qualified people sometimes have to wait years for their official documentation, as I know from conducting citizenship ceremonies at Hillsborough Castle in my later role as Lord-Lieutenant of Belfast. But the newspaper clearly used its influence with its friends in high places, and with the Games fast approaching, whisked Zola from her homeland to Guildford in Surrey, from where she embarked on a series of appearances in events around the UK, including one at my own track in Belfast – again, more on that later – that attracted thousands.

Zola was box office gold, but her arrival also stirred up a hornet's nest. On the one hand, anti-apartheid groups protested loudly at the preferential treatment Zola had been given to get around the Olympic ban on South African athletes. Others saw Zola's presence as depriving a GB athlete of the chance to compete at the Olympics. I must admit, I considered her inclusion very irregular, but not to the extent of bearing animosity towards her. After all, it was my job and duty to attend to the needs and wellbeing of all our athletes.

And having been selected, it was heartening to see her teammates welcome her into the fold. I was especially pleased to see Tessa Sanderson, who was vehemently opposed to apartheid, make a point of presenting Zola with a teddy bear mascot on their arrival in Los Angeles. It was a simple act of kindness that meant a lot and spoke volumes of Tessa as a person.

My first direct contact with Zola came when I accompanied her to her first press conference of the Games – her first exposure to a hostile American media who were rooting for her rival on the track, the home-grown favourite Mary Decker. Zola's previous experience of the media was only with the supportive *Daily Mail*. In fact, she'd had to be discouraged from accepting payment for exclusive articles, forbidden under the strict amateur rules at the time. She was shy and nervous and asked how she should approach the inquisition.

'No one has ever seen you smile,' I said. 'When you walk into that room, a thousand flash bulbs are going to go off. Just keep smiling for those cameras and believe me, those journalists will warm to you.'

It didn't last. Days later one of the most controversial and hotly disputed incidents in Olympic history occurred.

The media hype around Zola meant the eyes of the world were on her 3000 metre final duel with world champion Decker, but it would end badly for them both. Budd and Decker were normally front runners, so were unused to running in a group. Their inexperience of the pack situation they found themselves in that day first led to a collision at the 1700m mark as Decker came into contact with Budd, knocking Zola slightly off balance. Both seemed to regain their composure and stride but with no daylight between them, they collided again, this time with more serious consequences for both.

Their second coming together caused Zola to lose her balance, stumbling into the path of Decker, knocking the latter off the track and out of the race. Zola continued, despite being in pain, with blood streaming from an ankle injury caused by Decker's running shoe spikes (the incident had happened very quickly and it was only through the video replay that it became clear that Zola had been spiked from behind and had stumbled, impeding Mary). Zola finished seventh to Romania's Maricica Puică, who is much less remembered than the furore that ensued.

I was hovering near the area where the athletes left the track at the conclusion of the race and it fell to me to take Zola for medical treatment to her badly spiked foot, then for a drug test. Normally, it is the first three who are routinely tested, with one other chosen at random, and this time it just happened to be Zola, but you do wonder in the circumstances if she had been singled out.

She passed the test and I then accompanied her back to the Village in the allocated transport. We sat together and Zola appeared to me to be traumatised. She spent most of the time looking out of the window and answering questions only briefly. She was a very shy girl and never very communicative and I felt she was deeply shocked. I was told later that there had been so many threats to her life that we had had a helicopter escort on that journey back to the Village. Those threats came from all quarters: Americans aggrieved at her role in denying Decker gold; anti-apartheid opponents; fellow South Africans, unhappy that she had chosen to run for GB; and people back home, angry that she was, in their view, depriving a British-born athlete of selection.

It was all so bewildering and overwhelming for her.

On arrival at team headquarters I suggested she have a shower and change before I took her to meet her *Daily Mail* minder, John Bryant, and her mother who were staying in a nearby hotel. While I waited, I received a phone call from a journalist to say that Zola had been disqualified from the event and, after a short time, another call from the same source to say that she had been reinstated – our overall team manager Nick Whitehead had protested her innocence and won the appeal. I told Zola on her return, but she made no reaction at all to the news. We then made our way to the back gate of the village to meet up with John Bryant.

It was all too much for her. Despite her entourage, I saw then how vulnerable and alone Zola felt. She was just a shy little girl, out of her depth and drowning in all the hostility surrounding her. The following day, the decision was made by our Head of Delegation to fly her home, primarily for her safety and mental well-being. Having closely observed Zola as the latest controversy to envelope her unfolded, I felt it was the right thing to do.

Even then, we feared a media scrum at the airport when, by sheer coincidence, it transpired Zola had been booked on to the same flight to London as Prince Philip, but she managed to slip on board quietly and without incident.

Zola went on to marry and, ironically, live in the US where she had endured such trauma and, eventually, she was reconciled with Mary Decker, making a documentary together called *The Fall*. Despite my reservations about the manner of her inclusion in the team, I felt sorry for Zola in a situation that wasn't of her making.

I would hate to feel that I had failed any athlete, and I don't believe I ever did. Many years later, when the Black Lives Matter movement began and sportspeople were taking the knee, I phoned Tessa Sanderson, who had been especially kind to Zola, to ask her if she had ever, during my management, felt victimised or excluded because of the colour of her skin. It was reassuring to hear she had never felt that way as I simply could not contemplate any athlete being treated differently from another for whatever reason but, above all, on the grounds of race or colour. We were all in it together.

I was with Tessa in the lead-up to her event in Los Angeles, where she took the gold medal to become the first British woman to win a throwing event at the Olympics. It was wonderful to see her win after her disappointment in Moscow four years before. I accompanied her to the stadium and she was so hyped up. She was carrying a small rubber ball which she hurled against a wall with such force as she waited for her final to begin. Some athletes, like Tessa that day, are hard to control in those situations. You want them to be hyped up but not so much as to run out of adrenalin too soon. They need to peak at just the right time.

We were so precise in Los Angeles that one of my jobs was to take the bus every morning from the Village at UCLA to the stadium and log the journey time. It could range between forty minutes and two hours, so we always made sure our athletes were on board at least two hours before their competition was about to begin. If they arrived early, we had a physio's room underneath the stadium where they could bed down and rest.

That meticulous approach worked as it produced 37 medals, including gold again for Daley Thompson (decathlon); Seb Coe (1500m); Tessa Sanderson (javelin); Malcolm Cooper (shooting); and Steve Redgrave, Andy Holmes, Adrian Ellison, Martin Cross and Richard Budgett (rowers).

There was just one real heartstopping moment related to my role as manager and it had to do with the hated 'sex verification' tests – made all the more embarrassing as competitors now had to wear a badge to prove they had been successfully tested. I had instructed one of the team doctors to ensure all the female athletes had undergone their mandatory tests, but the javelin thrower Fatima Whitbread had somehow been overlooked. On the morning Fatima was due to begin her qualifying event, her adoptive mum, Margaret, approached me and questioned why Fatima had not been tested like the others. I was dumbstruck. Without that badge and paperwork, Fatima would not be allowed to compete.

I jumped immediately on a shuttle bus into the city and persuaded an International Amateur Athletics Federation doctor I knew to sign a letter that would allow Fatima to compete and take the test later, which to my relief, was accepted. She took part, later passed her test, and went on to win a bronze medal.

I still shudder to think about the consequences otherwise. Fatima would not have won her medal and that would have been down to me.

I may have delegated the testing checks to a doctor but, ultimately, the responsibility rested with me.

There was just no handbook for managing the situations we were plunged into in Moscow and LA, we simply dealt with what was put in front of us. What I took most from my time in the role was the lessons in crisis management that stand to me to this day.

I decided to step down from the British Olympic management team after LA. It was truly an honour to have been asked to serve, but I had commitments back home, and I also felt it was time for someone younger to step up (though in the end they appointed someone older!).

But while LA marked the end of my official Olympic team involvement, it was not my last Olympics. I attended Seoul in 1988 for New Zealand radio, and was a spectator at Barcelona in 1992, Atlanta 1996, Sydney 2000 and Athens 2004.

I eventually did pass the torch, quite literally, to a younger bearer during the opening ceremony at London 2012 when, as one of 12 past gold medallists, I handed one of the torches that lit the flame to Katie Kirk, from Holywood, County Down, one of my Trust-supported athletes.

I even had a Tube station temporarily named after me for the duration of the 2012 Games, as did all the previous UK gold medal winners. After the Games, it went back to being Wood Green, but the road outside remains Mary Peters Drive, leading, appropriately to Lillian Board Way, after my 1968 Mexico Olympics teammate who was taken, so young, by cancer, a month after her twenty-second birthday.

Again, it was an immense honour to be involved but all my pride was reserved for Katie who will remember the moment forever.

The three Northern Ireland Knights of the Garter:
Alan Henry Brooke, 3rd Viscount Brookeborough is on the left;
James Hamilton, His Grace, the 5th Duke of Abercorn, is on the right.

Outside Buckingham Palace with my MBE, 1973.

With my CBE after the Buckingham Palace investiture, 1990.

Invested as a Dame Commander (DBE), 2000.

Being made a member of the Order of the Companions of Honour (CH) by Prince William, Windsor Castle, 2015.

Greeting Her Majesty the Queen when I was Lord-Lieutenant, Crumlin Road Gaol, Belfast, 2014.

With representatives from my Trust meeting the Duke and Duchess of Cambridge at the Empire Music Hall, Belfast, 2019. HRH Prince William had just announced that I was to receive the Order of the Garter honour.

With HRH The Princess Royal, our patron, and Adrian Moorhouse at the Sports Writers' Association Golden Jubilee Ball, 1998.

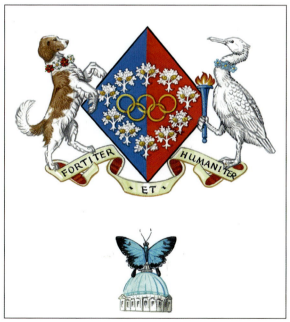

My heraldic shield, which is displayed in my stall at St George's Chapel Windsor.

At a citizenship ceremony when I was Lord-Lieutenant for the County Borough of Belfast Hillsborough Castle, *c.* 2011.

Taking part in a parachute jump to raise money for my Trust, Newtownards Airfield, 1974.

Willing to try anything: me, age eighty, abseiling at Belfast Castle, 2019.

The official launch of the Mary Peters Trust with children from Pond Park Primary School, Harbour Commissioners offices, 2008.

On Sunday 28 April 2013, accompanied by Belfast Lord Mayor Gavin Robinson, I herded sheep through the city centre. This was to mark me being granted the Freedom of the City of Belfast, which took place on 8 May.

Given ten extra years to live.
Home after having my open heart surgery, 2018.

With my niece Vanessa and her husband, Grant, at Baronscourt,
hosted by the Duke of Abercorn, 2019.

# 15

# Building for the Future

The bombscare in Christchurch and the death threat I had received in Munich were not the only up close and personal incidents I had faced as a result of the Troubles. The worst had occurred on 23 March 1973, a little over a month before Buster's death.

It had been a hectic week. I had worked in the gym every day and been out every night and I was very tired. I went home, locked the door and awarded myself the ultimate luxury of doing absolutely nothing at all. My flat then was so arranged that, by leaving the door open between the living room and the adjoining bedroom, and swinging the television set round, I could lie in bed and watch TV. I have no idea what programme was on that night. All I know is that I was so tired I was dozing, jerking awake, and then dozing off again. It must have been around eleven o'clock when I decided I had to make the effort to get out of bed and switch the set off. I did so and then, by some habit, which I still have today, I went to the window and drew back the blinds a little to see what kind of night it was outside.

The horror I saw there was so dreadful that for a few moments I could not take it in. A soldier was lying in the pathway. There were armed troops in my garden and police both there and in the garden next door. Immediately outside was an ambulance with its light flashing. And in the dim light behind and around there seemed to be hundreds of watching faces. They weren't moving, just watching. This, at first, was the thing that struck me as being the most horrible of all. But

I stayed at the window myself and, as I did so, three stretchers were brought out and placed in the ambulance.

The crowd hardly diminished. I went back into the bedroom and switched on the radio. Eventually, around midnight, a local news station began putting out a bulletin. They reported a multiple shooting in Cedar Avenue and began to fill in the first details of a crime so gruesome that within a matter of hours it was putting Belfast back in the headlines all over the world. Four soldiers, all sergeants, had been lured back to the house with the promise of a party but instead had been shot dead. Three had died instantly; the fourth had managed to crawl to the front door and out on to the path. Where, in the name of anyone's god, was it all going to end?

I didn't live in the avenue the bulletin named, but it was just round the corner. There could not have been two such incidents as this in a single night. It then struck me that I had heard not a single sound. Had the television been turned up loudly? No it had not. Had I been dozing? Yes, but hardly sleeping soundly. And how much noise did exploding guns make? I didn't know. Yet I had heard nothing at all. Not a sound.

Eventually I went back to bed. I was hardly a novice to the violence of Belfast, which I had seen at close and long range before. But I was not unshockable. I slept fitfully between then and dawn and when I woke it was with a feeling of misery and absolute despair. Then a more personal reaction set in. There were still soldiers in front of my house and occasionally they spoke to the early morning passers-by on their way to work. Then I heard one say, 'You know who lives here?' He mentioned my name. From that moment I stayed away from the front window. I dressed quickly but why I don't know. I knew less than the average radio listener about what had happened in the house next door to where I was now standing, yet I knew I would be pursued. It was one of the lesser rewards for having competed in the Olympic Games. What could I conceivably add to the objective coverage of so terrible a night? Nothing. But I knew that it would be hard to persuade certain branches of the media that that was the case.

I had to go to work. Eventually, at around 9.30 a.m., I left the house, trying to cover my face as I went down the path. I got halfway across the road to the bus stop when I heard someone shout, 'Well, have you got your medal with you today?' There was a BBC television crew on the far pavement, and within a few seconds of arriving at the bus stop they were behind me. There was a gentle tap on my shoulder. I knew they had a job to do and I am always sympathetic to any professionals who are answerable to bosses who sit back in the warm comfort of base and make the decisions. But on this occasion I pleaded with them. I suppose they had good reason not to believe me when I said I had seen and heard nothing, but I said, 'Please, please don't implicate me in all this.' Perhaps it is quite possible to be very cool about these things in Surbiton or even Chicago, but Belfast in the seventies was a slightly different story.

I do not know whether that BBC crew shot any footage of me or not, but I was terribly upset. I got to the gymnasium, where I was now among people I knew, and I broke down and cried for the first time since I had drawn back the curtains and witnessed that gruesome scene. I then phoned the BBC and asked them not to use anything about the fact that I lived next door. It was shortly after this that we all removed the street numbers from our doors or gateposts.

Later that day a number of newspapers phoned for interviews. There was nothing I could possibly tell them and I refused to speak to them. Buster spoke to them instead and begged them not to mention that I lived next door. He cancelled an engagement for me that evening, took me home in his car and waited with me until I felt prepared to go inside. It was not that I felt any particular danger. I knew only that I had to get over the ordeal of spending the coming night in that flat alone. One totally insignificant detail has puzzled me ever since. When that neighbouring room was finally cleared of its horrendous evidence, a single unshaded electric light was left on in the centre of the ceiling. One year later, to the day, it was still alight. I had no idea that light bulbs at that time could survive so long.

This, of course, was not my first encounter with Belfast violence. In July 1972, on the night of dreadful Bloody Friday, I learned a lesson about the stupidity of bravado by leading two waitresses from a restaurant straight into crossfire. And on the night of the Abercorn Restaurant bombings in March that same year, I phoned Crystal Palace in London to cancel my visit to a weekend get-together of pentathletes. I just didn't want to go. It wasn't that by staying in Belfast I could do anything, but someone, I thought, had to stand fast. Someone had to do something normal in this absurdly abnormal city. It was the weekend after the killings next door that we decided to redouble our efforts to build a new running track for the youth of Belfast.

It was a complete distortion of the truth to portray the average young Belfast teenager of the mid- and late-seventies as a street-corner psychotic, pelting rocks into over-tolerant ranks of British soldiers. I don't know from where successive TV crews managed to round them up. Maybe it was the same ones every time. What, of course, was terrible for every Belfast teenager was that they simply could not lead a normal life. By simple things I mean going to cinemas, theatres or to a football match, going out on dates or training for sport. If the Munich victory gave me any privilege to value above all others, it was the opportunity to draw attention to the abysmal standards of athletics training facilities in my home town. There were practically none. If someone had told an East German or Australian or Canadian athletics official that Belfast did not have a single usable artificial surface running track, they would have looked at you and assumed you were suffering from shell-shock. They are as common round the world now as tennis courts. But not only did we not have one in Belfast, we did not have one in the whole of Ulster, and nor was there one anywhere in the whole of Ireland either. There had been one owned by Queen's University Belfast, located some three miles out of the city centre at the south end of the Malone Playing Fields, but virtually over one winter it cracked and erupted and soon became dangerous for training and out of the question for competition. The kindly Queen's University had allowed me at least to train there for Munich and now I had the chance to give something back.

It began with a telephone call to Munich the day after my win, from the wonderful, late, great Malcolm Brodie, then sports editor of the *Belfast Telegraph*. Malcolm was a supportive friend and confidante until his passing in 2013, aged eighty-six. He was a pale, dynamic character who had no provincial hang-ups. He could pop up in Moscow one day, Paris the next and Rio the following week if there was any big soccer being played there. 'Listen, Mary,' he said. 'We want to set up a fund to commemorate your victory. Don't know where the hell it's all coming from, but the first suggestion from the Northern Ireland Women's AAA is that it's a scholarship deal. You know, pick out the most promising youngsters and get them over to England for a few weeks' training and coaching away from all the tensions here.'

Instant answer, 'Good idea, but no.'

Why did we always have to send people to England? Couldn't we do something for ourselves for once? Couldn't we organise something that certainly hundreds, probably thousands, could enjoy each year in our own town? A track for Belfast that would provide future generations with facilities to train and compete, facilities that I never had access to. Here was our chance to stand fast, not to run.

There was another point. In twenty years in athletics in Northern Ireland, I had never known any argument in any dressing room or committee room that had been caused by religious or political differences. Why should we be modest about that? Looking round, it seemed a damned good achievement. That was what I wanted.

Buster agreed. So did the *Belfast Telegraph*. It was a dream, but reality quickly set in as, amid the euphoria, it hadn't dawned on me that I would need to raise the money needed myself! From that moment, the track almost became an obsession.

The first step was to set up a fundraising committee, which then launched a Track Appeal, championed and campaigned by Malcolm through the pages of the *Belfast Telegraph*. By the time I got home, the newspaper had already printed thousands of flags saying 'Support the Mary Peters Track Fund'.

The site was no problem. The old Queen's University track offered the perfect location. It was set among hills and trees, and had banking round it to make it a natural amphitheatre. Down below ran the River Lagan. Denis Wilson from the university, who chaired our committee, negotiated the purchase for a nominal pound. All we had to do was persuade the educational authorities to let us make a start. In fact, they were delighted. The track had fallen into disrepair and they had already put aside £15,000 to repair the surface, but that, I knew, would barely look after the back straight. Yes, they would be delighted to add their £15,000 to our fund and agree that in future all sections of the community would have free access to the track.

Our committee, made up of representation from the university, the

Sports Council and the NI athletics governing body, was keen to see the new track provide first-rate training facilities, as well as being capable of staging international athletics meetings. Indeed, the committee was more interested in encouraging participation than in simply developing a prestigious complex to be used only on a very limited number of occasions each year. Thus the athletes of Northern Ireland would gain a first-rate athletic track in an easily accessible area on the outskirts of Belfast, the general public would have a place to train, coach and jog, and the university would gain a facility on its property. Win-win.

But where to start?

The first sum we thought we would have to raise was £60,000, but ambition and inflation almost doubled that within a matter of months. We might as well build in as many training facilities as possible while we were about it, and we certainly had to bring it up to the standard where, at last, major track teams would come and visit us from abroad. So the final target became £100,000.

All my grand career plans, underpinned by my medal win, were put on hold as I began knocking on doors and holding out collection buckets. It was, quite literally, beg steal and borrow. Somewhat cynically, I thought of Avery Brundage and his £35 million collection of Chinese jade. Or of the money that went up in smoke every night in Belfast. We could have worked miracles with only a fraction of that.

Even so we had our own excitement as envelopes came in bearing 25p from a pensioner here, 10p from a schoolchild there. That really was money. I'd never been involved in fundraising before and, anyway, I was completely rubbish about cash, which came from never having had enough to get concerned about. It was a long time before I realised that, although I was dashing madly about picking up cheques – sometimes £5, sometimes £25, from youth clubs and Women's Institutes and Rotary Clubs and schools – it was going to take an awful long time to raise £100,000 that way.

We then had a breakthrough in getting publicity in England for the track. In the space of a week I appeared on the BBC2 programme *Voices of Sport*, in which I was able to talk about what we were trying to do, and then we received a sympathetic half-page about the project in the *Daily Mail*. The paper was hardly off the presses before I received a call from

Geoffrey Wolfe, chairman of Wolf Electric Tools in West London. He said he would like to help. He gave £1,000.

That was but one of many, many contributions from *Daily Mail* readers, but it really gave us the encouragement that we needed. What I now wanted was the same kind of reaction in Ireland. Already I had been to see Secretary of State for Northern Ireland William Whitelaw, who had not only been one of the first to send me a telegram in Munich, but had given a party for me at Stormont Castle on my return. He was a fearfully busy man, under enormous pressure, but by enlisting the help of Denis Howell, MP, then out of office as Minister of Sport but soon to return in the 1974 election, and also ringing a friend of mine who happened to be Mrs Whitelaw's personal secretary, I got the meeting.

Mr Whitelaw was charm itself. He received me in a chintzy, comfortable room in Stormont and had his secretary there taking notes. I had taken along several jagged-edged samples of the broken track we were trying to replace. Almost his first words were, 'Your track cannot be a memorial to Buster McShane.' I thought he must have been misinformed about something. I explained that I just wanted a track, the name of it didn't matter, and that since most governments in most countries would have provided one anyway, and since enormous sums of money were being spent on repairing the destruction in Belfast, it did occur to me that the government had some responsibility. He said he would talk to the appropriate authority, the Ministry of Education. And so he did.

On 15 November 1973, the Northern Ireland Office issued a press release simultaneously in Belfast and London. It began, 'Lord Belstead, Parliamentary Under Secretary of State for Northern Ireland, today announced that the Ministry of Education is to make a major contribution to the Mary Peters Track Fund. Following a meeting with the organisers of the Fund, the minister said the government was prepared to contribute £1 for every £1 subscribed by the public … It is expected that this could result in a total government contribution in the order of £30,000.'

It was a jubilant moment. All we had to do was raise £30,000 and it would be matched by government funding. No pressure then. And it was never easy. Every time we believed we had met our target, the price went up. The more things change, the more they stay the same. We had an oil price crisis then, too, and since the material to be used to lay the track was oil based, we faced frequent cost rises.

Favours were called in from old friends and contacts.

We launched a new big appeal in Northern Ireland, and by March of the following year a £5,000 contribution from John Moores, the boss of Littlewoods Pools and of Everton Football Club fame, took us to the halfway mark of £50,000. And on Easter Monday, 19 April 1976, my dream finally came to fruition. As part of the opening ceremony that sunlit evening, we had schoolchildren line up in the centre of the Track to spell out my name in giant letters. To this day, I meet people who will tell me 'I was A' or 'I was P'.

In its early days, the Track regularly hosted meetings that attracted many of the top British and international athletes of the era to Belfast. These were staged by the late Les Jones of the NI Amateur Athletics Association, a brilliant organiser who used his contacts and persuasive powers to give local audiences a chance to marvel at athletes they only ever saw on television. Les put on events that featured greats like Ed Moses, John Walker, Steve Ovett, Steve Cram, Zola Budd, Shirley Strong, Fatima Whitbread and Tessa Sanderson. Ironically, though, I never myself competed on the track that bears my name as I had retired by the time it was up and running. I had, of course, trained on the old potholed surface I was determined to replace.

Wear and tear over the years meant that, by the mid-eighties, repairs and an upgrade were required again, way beyond the means of the volunteer committee who had taken on the running of the track – a task they had performed admirably. Thankfully, Belfast City Council came to the rescue, taking ownership of the Track and transferring management responsibilities to Athletics NI, the governing body for sport in Northern Ireland.

That new era saw the Track extended from six lanes to eight to keep it up to international standards and help attract showpiece events like the World Transplant Games, World Police and Fire Games and World Dwarf Games, which also gave a massive boost to the tourism economy with visitors and competitors coming from around the globe. It has been wonderful to see the Track evolve as a place for everyone. After all, it was built with community money for the community. And while the days of gold standard international meetings are no longer feasible – due to the eye-watering sums in appearance money the top athletes now command – it continues to serve its purpose in providing a focus for young people to develop for the betterment of themselves and society, taking me back to the original purpose I had in mind when I took the telephone call from Malcolm on that fateful night in Munich long ago.

There isn't a day I go there that the Track isn't a hive of activity. As well as the athletes in training, we have mother and baby groups doing laps with their prams, joggers and BMX riders on the woodland trails, dog walkers and people who just want to relax on a bench and take it all in. I am also pleased to see that it is in daily use by local schools and clubs, even if the children in attendance are sometimes not that impressed to see me!

Like the little boy who, as I passed by one day, was asked by his teacher, 'Do you know who this is?' 'Yes,' he replied. 'You won a medal in the olden days.' Or the other little boy who examined my medal and asked, 'Is it made of chocolate?' The highlight, though, has to be the little girl who on meeting me asked her mother, 'Is that lady named after this track?'

Presiding over it all is a life-size statue of me in my Munich running gear. It was erected in 2012, but not as Belfast City Council had envisaged. I had gone to a meeting with them, along with the sculptor, John Sherlock, and asked to see the design they had commissioned. I was surprised to see it was going to be a bust, me from the waist up, and I protested, 'You can't put me on a pedestal without legs; my legs did all the work!' So a full length statute was ordered and I then asked where it would be placed.

'Inside the perimeter fence,' I was told.

'This isn't Long Kesh,' I replied, referring to the former internment camp near Lisburn. 'I don't want to be behind the wire!'

Instead, I chose the location where the statue now stands on a podium, overlooking the track where I see passers-by taking selfies all the time, most recently my dear friend and fellow gold medallist, Dame Kelly Holmes, who posted her pictures to her 106,000 Instagram followers.

I love the place, and it's where I chose to pay a fitting tribute to my late coach – a summer seat dedicated to his memory.

'To Buster McShane,' the inscription reads, 'a man who made an average athlete into an Olympic champion.'

# 16

# The Mary Peters Trust

There are three things in my life of which I am proudest: my gold medal success, my Track and my Trust, and the three are inextricably linked as the first led to the establishment of the other two.

I have always been of the belief that I wanted to see my legacy in action, up close and personal. I wanted to create something that would not only give me a focus but would help others on their own sporting journeys. The Mary Peters Track went a long way towards achieving that goal, but I knew there was more that could be done. Hence the foundation of the Mary Peters Trust, initially known as the Ulster Sports and Recreation Trust, in 1975.

I was just coming to the end of my fundraising for the Track and was looking forward to a break from shaking collection buckets under people's noses, when the idea of a trust was first mooted by a Coleraine businessman friend, Dr John Moore.

The mission statement was simple. We needed something in place to help Northern Ireland's most talented young sportspeople take the first steps on the ladder to success in their fields, something similar to the Winston Churchill Fellowship that had enabled me to go to California in the build-up to the Munich Olympics. That award had made such a difference to me – I could train in the sunshine, away from working every day and from the Troubles back home, where my only training facilities were on the old, potholed track we would later regenerate.

John felt we should establish a similar scheme in Northern Ireland to aid our up-and-coming sporting talent – something that would not only provide them with funding towards equipment and travel cost, but put programmes in place to give them access to a team of experts that would aid their development, from medical to mentoring. I agreed to become the figurehead but, because my name was already linked to a charity, the Track committee, the new body became the Ulster Sports and Recreation Trust. Once again, I found myself doing the rounds of factories, schools, Women's Institutes and various events as the whole fundraising process began anew.

Our original set-up was amateur in every sense of the word. The then Sports Council lent a hand by seconding one of their staff, Robin Mitchell, to be our voluntary secretary, taking minutes and looking after the accounts (we didn't get a full-time staffer until 2016), and for years we lived a somewhat nomadic existence, sharing office space at Sport NI. We would later move to rented premises on Elmwood Avenue in Belfast, before relocating in 2023 to the Track, which I have always seen as our natural home.

The first four award recipients were given, between them, a grand total of £625 – a far cry from the £80,000 we now distribute annually. Two of those first recipients were from athletics, one was from judo and the last was a young swimmer called Ian Corry. I had known him from competing in the 1974 Commonwealth Games in Christchurch when he was just 14. I'd first met him at the airport when we were departing for New Zealand. His mum was there to wave him off and was very worried about him going on such a long journey on his own at that age. I reassured her, 'Don't worry. I will be his mum for the next month.' I kept my word and followed Ian's progress as he went on to become a noted surgeon who actually performed knee surgery on me many years later. As I climbed on to his operating table, I couldn't resist warning him, 'Remember, it's your mother you are about to operate on here.'

The Trust grew at a steady pace through our own fundraising efforts and donations coming in, but we were mainly below the radar of the general public's consciousness. That all changed completely by chance as a result of an encounter at a speaking engagement at a Rotary Club in Hillsborough, shortly after the sad death of our superstar footballer

George Best in 2005. After I had addressed the gathering, the floor was thrown open for a question and answer session when a man stood up and said, 'You won't like this question, but I am going to ask anyway. Have you thought about what will happen when you die? I mean, George Best has an airport named after him and his own charity foundation. What will you leave?' I replied that I hadn't given the matter much thought, but I had my Track and my career achievements that I'd hoped to be remembered by. A seed had been planted, though. I returned home that night, turning over in my head what the man had said.

The Track by then was established and being run by Belfast City Council, and I had the Trust, albeit not in my name. Above all, unlike the unfortunate George who never lived to see his name commemorated, I wanted mine to be a living legacy, something else I could put my name to in a meaningful way while I was still here. In 2008, at a meeting of the Trust committee, I proposed changing the name to the Mary Peters Trust and it was unanimously agreed.

From that moment, the dynamic changed. My profile was still high at that time and a year later, in 2009, I was appointed Lord-Lieutenant of Belfast, which helped in my role as the public face of the Trust. I was someone people could relate to, and that led to more and bigger donations coming in from companies, organisations and individuals keen to see talented young people given a sporting chance.

As older committee members stepped down, we in turn recruited new faces with fresh ideas who became more proactive on the fundraising front. The Trust today is run by a team of volunteer directors, each with their own skill set, and is administered by two fantastic staffers, Gillian Hetherington and Cathryn Gibson. From our modest beginnings, we became an extremely well-equipped organisation, able to help more and more young athletes each year.

We have helped over 4,000 young sportspeople so far – people like Graeme McDowell, Darren Clarke, David Humphreys, Paddy Barnes, Michael Conlan and Janet Gray. We have aided two Olympic champions – Jim Kirkwood, who is now treasurer of the Trust, and Stephen Martin, chair of the NI Commonwealth Games committee, who both won hockey gold with Great Britain in Seoul in 1988 – and our alumni also includes Paralympic gold medallists Kelly Gallagher, Michael

McKillop and Bethany Firth, as well as numerous World, European, Commonwealth, UK and Irish champions. And while the total amount of money given is hard to quantify with grants rising over the years (from an individual average of £150 initially to around £750 now), the overall figure would be well over a million.

The support we have had in Northern Ireland and beyond has been truly humbling. Our own Northern Ireland public have always been most generous in giving their support for the work we do, and many stars from the world of sport and entertainment have given their knowledge, talent and energy down the years. We have had many famous names from sport and the arts lend their support by making personal appearances as we handed out our funding awards to our young athletes. Tim Rice, Henry Cooper, Torvill and Dean, Sue Barker, Daley Thompson, Steve Redgrave, and Tessa Sanderson all gave their time freely, willingly posing for pictures with youngsters who still treasure the memories.

Princess Anne, with whom I have been friends since our first encounter on stage at the 1972 BBC Sports Personality of the Year Awards, has been a patron and prominent supporter of the Trust over the years, succeeding our original patron, Lord Grey of Naunton, who was the last Governor of Northern Ireland.

Her Royal Highness Princess Anne is the most hard-working member of the royal family, always especially keen and willing to help people in sport. In 2019 she was chief guest and speaker as we launched 'Race To A Million' – a campaign to raise a million pounds for the Trust to invest in supporting our young athletes. The campaign was to mark my 80th birthday in 2019, but such was the generosity of the public that we reached the target ahead of time – we celebrated with a huge party in the Titanic Building in Belfast. It was fortunate I was not born a year later, for within months the Covid pandemic had struck and all events were put on hold.

Thankfully, by Christmas 2022, lockdown restrictions had eased, and we were able to proceed with celebrations for the 50th anniversary of my Munich gold medal. A gala sporting evening was organised in Belfast's Europa Hotel. Again, Princess Anne kindly agreed to attend, and she quite literally took centre stage as chief guest, taking part, for the first time ever, in an informal question and answer session, conducted by

Northern Ireland's own national BBC sports presenter Holly Hamilton. The event was also attended by Olympic legends like Tessa Sanderson, Katherine Grainger, Joslyn Hoyte-Smith and Christine Ohuruogu, a host of local sporting talent, and Sir Jeffrey Archer acted as auctioneer.

We were all the more indebted to Princess Anne considering she had attended another engagement earlier in the day to bestow city status upon Bangor, fifteen miles away. That typifies her sense of duty. Before carrying out an engagement, the Princess will insist on knowing who she is going to meet and will often speak to as many as one hundred people. She possesses fantastic recall as well, often relating the story of the one-armed golfer she met at a Hillsborough Castle reception. He had lost an arm to bone cancer and she asked him why he had taken up golf. 'It's the only sport I need only one glove to play,' he replied to her great amusement.

However, had she arrived five minutes earlier at the Europa the day of our sporting gala, there would have been a different story to tell over the royal Christmas dinner table.

We thought we had prepared for every eventuality in welcoming our royal visitor to the event. The guest list had been vetted by the Royal Household, a meet and greet itinerary agreed, seating arrangements checked, security in place, traffic stopped and the street outside sealed as the royal limousine approached. But just at that moment, as VIP dinner guests gathered in the foyer to form a guard of honour for the grand entrance and I waited to accompany Her Royal Highness up the ornate staircase to the function room, a rather inebriated straggler from an earlier office Christmas party appeared, swaying on the top step. Whoops! All hearts below stopped as he tipped over the edge, tumbled down the staircase, rolled across the foyer floor, collided with the beautifully decorated Christmas tree and promptly deposited his Christmas lunch on the pile carpet!

All credit to the horrified Europa staff who swung into action like F1 mechanics at a pit stop. They quickly righted the tree, spirited away the tipsy reveller and vacuumed the carpet in double quick time so that no-one who hadn't witnessed the incident, not least Princess Anne, would have known it had ever happened!

Despite this somewhat inauspicious start, the event was a great success, raising over £60,000, all of which went to aid the development of future

NI sporting generations. That money, and the money raised by the many fundraising events over the years, will help grow our young talent for generations to come. And since we are a charity, every penny raised goes towards supporting our athletes.

I'm very proud of what we have achieved, how far we have come, and of the difference we have made to so many. For me, it has been an honour to see the tremendous achievements of our young athletes – those we have helped in some small way, or inspired to think big and reach for the stars.

I consider myself blessed to have been a part of that. It is what I mean by a living legacy.

How rewarding it has been.

# 17

# Life After Gold

People often ask how big a wrench it was, deciding to retire from competitive athletics after the Commonwealth Games, but in truth, it wasn't difficult. I was nearly 35, I had been lucky to win gold in Christchurch, I'd lost my coach and mentor, and I'd just had enough.

I'll admit the transition was difficult to start with – my life had changed beyond recognition. I had no clue what I was going to do. I had no plan and there were some long, lonely days to fill the vacuum of not training. But for the first time in more than twenty years I had *time*. I had time to clear the three-foot-high weeds out of my garden. I had time to make cushion covers. I had time to cook a proper meal instead of opening tins. I had time to invite people in to have dinner with me and time to go and visit friends I had neglected for years. Until that point, time was something that only other people had. My own life had been an unending rush from work to track to training to meeting, with just a few minutes in between to snatch a meal or a shower. There was certainly never time for a holiday because holidays were something you saved up to go away to the Commonwealth or the European or the Olympic Games.

Time is the most luxurious commodity there is and I luxuriated in it, not by wasting it but in using it in different ways. And, at the risk of sounding like the Dickens character Mr Micawber, I always believed something would turn up and invariably, it did.

After the New Zealand Commonwealth there were so many things I wanted to do with my new freedom from training and athletics that, reluctantly, I decided to give up working at the McShane Health Club. I had enjoyed many happy years there, but suddenly a new world was opening. I came back from those final Commonwealth Games to a mountain of invitations and I wanted, selfishly perhaps, to be free to accept them. There was an invitation to go to Canada to appear in two television programmes. There were invitations to make a public appearance here, to open something there, to advertise this, endorse that, try my hand as an 'expert' commentator with the BBC and London Weekend athletic reporting teams on television. I didn't exactly see myself as a package-deal 'personality for hire', but some of the offers promised me the freedom I wanted to enjoy.

And I thought I had earned some of them. Almost every year I had travelled further than any other British athlete. I had competed in more pentathlons than any other woman athlete in the world. So I threw in my job and trusted to luck. I wanted to earn just enough money to keep my head above water and leave myself time to continue my activities in Belfast. Money for personal possessions or luxuries didn't worry me greatly. It rarely does worry people who have never had any.

When I had quit teaching, I had given away all rights to pensions and superannuation, so Buster and I jointly bought a large house in Belfast which was designed to give me some kind of assured income if I were ever to reach old age. Obviously nothing was assured in Belfast at that time, so while I'd lived in the house myself for many years, the other three flats it contained remained empty (you could never be quite sure in those days who your tenants are likely to be). Nor did the value of property exactly increase, and I found myself living in a house of no value at all. It was also tainted by the horrific memory of the dreadful murders of the three soldiers at the property next door. So it wasn't a difficult decision to sell up, even though I made only £500 from the sale (once the mortgage was paid off and what was left from the sale price had been shared with Buster's widow, Margaret).

Someone once said that money isn't everything, but it's certainly handy when you need to buy something. I discovered that when I saw the house of my dreams, the cottage by the river that has been my palace for nearly fifty years. It came on the market in late 1975 and, once seen, I set my heart on it.

The price was £18,000, modest for a property even then, but I didn't need a mansion. Problem was, there were other interested bidders. I still felt I was well placed as several years before I'd done an advert for a local building society, the Gateway. As payment, they'd opened an account for me containing £200 for future use. When the time came, I naturally approached them to apply for a mortgage to buy the cottage. And they turned me down flat!

'You don't have a job, you're single and have no prospects,' they said.

My dream was slipping away until my then financial advisor quietly approached the Gateway and suggested it would not be a good look for them to be seen to be rejecting the Olympic gold medallist who had previously endorsed them. Did they really need those kind of headlines?

Thankfully, they relented and the cottage was mine. I moved in before Christmas in 1975.

I encountered similar hurdles when, the following year, I finally decided to set up my own health club. I'd always thought about doing it, and I had even identified premises in Lisburn, a two-storey building in a town that didn't have a gym and was close to my home, which made it perfect. It was a rental and needed a lot of conversion work. I also needed a lot of costly gym equipment, a sauna and jacuzzi. So, another sizeable loan was required, and this time I approached the Bank of Ireland who raised the same concerns Gateway had. Plus, they pointed out, I had no previous business experience. Again, my financial advisor worked his persuasive magic and we were able to convince the bank it was a viable proposition and their money would be safe with me, and so it proved for the next twenty-five years.

It wasn't easy. After the legendary Olympian, multiple Dutch gold medallist Fanny Blankers-Koen, cut the tape, I found myself plunged into a gruelling spiral of twelve-hour days while juggling my other time-consuming roles at the Trust, the Track and the Sports Council, as GB Olympic team manager (twice) and at countless speaking engagements and personal appearances. I was very hands on even though I had five young members of staff working various shifts as people had signed up expecting my personal touch.

It was tough, but rewarding, and there were fun moments. I laughed when one of my first members, Sadie, registered an 8 stone weight loss in a year. 'I'm not doing this to get fit,' she insisted when I congratulated her. 'I just want them to be able to get my coffin down the stairs!'

On occasions, too, I would nip out for an errand and find members I'd been working out with minutes before now busily tucking in at the fish and chip shop down the street.

Eventually, though, like athletics, I'd had enough and after twenty-five years wanted to do something else. I was tired of the long days and nights. More gyms were opening up with more up-to-date equipment and, faced with the prospect of reinvesting in new equipment or returning the building to its original state, I sold the business for £15,000. Today it is a music shop.

As you will have gathered from my early days post-retirement, having no visible means of support was a problem!

That was why for a while I agreed to do things like advertising certain products on television or paid speaking: I was earning my keep, not just 'cashing in' as so many sportsmen and sportswomen are accused of doing. Though some of the events I took part in I did for no fee. Like the occasion when the organisers of an elite social affair in London said, 'Of course we can't pay you a fee for coming over from Belfast, but we'd be happy to fix you up with a little Yves St Laurent number if you'd come and draw the prizes.'

As the filthy-rich so often do they forgot all about the little number until I reminded them. This provoked nervous coughs and a grudging invitation to go and choose some small memento from the great House of St Laurent. I selected a £20 royal blue silk blouse and a £60 taffeta green skirt and wore both that evening to the great occasion. 'Did you get something?' asked the organiser. 'Yes,' I said, 'I'm wearing it.' 'All of it?' he cried. 'Yes,' I replied. 'Isn't it beautiful?' and I gave him one of those smiles with which one confidence trickster instantly recognises another.

I found that in the wake of the Munich win I was asked to do a lot of public appearances. Over the years, I have spoken at so many events and fundraisers that I have honestly lost count – though some will stick forever in my mind. In 1974, following my last competitive event in New Zealand, I was invited to speak at an occasion hosted by the Murray

Halberg Trust – a trust similar to my own, in the name of the famous Kiwi 1500m runner. Halberg had a paralysed left arm from a rugby injury he received when he was seventeen years old. He went on to become one of New Zealand's greatest athletes, winning Olympic and Empire Games gold medals and setting several world records. There were 800 people in attendance at the event, but I didn't know anyone and was extremely nervous. As I waited to take the stage, the Bishop of Auckland, who was beside me, said that I looked relaxed. 'Just feel my knees,' I joked. 'Oh no,' he replied. 'Not on a Tuesday, thank you!'

On another day, while signing autographs for a group of schoolchildren at Newham AC in east London, one of the throng stood on my foot and nearly crushed my toes. 'Ouch,' I said, to which one of them instantly replied, 'You must have athlete's foot!' Another little boy handed me a ragged scrap of paper to sign and I asked if he didn't have anything better? 'Don't worry,' he assured me. 'I will copy it on to another piece when I get home.'

Some of the speaking I did was at private functions, some was televised. And, having begun my radio commentating career at the 1976 Olympics, I found to my surprise that I quite enjoyed the challenge. I was working for the BBC the night in Glasgow 1980 when Derry's favourite fighting son, Charlie Nash, took on Scotland's Jim Watt for the world lightweight title. I love boxing. Our boxers have always been our most successful medal winners at Olympic and Commonwealth Games and I have been proud to serve as a steward on the British Boxing Board of Control. That particular night I was commentating alongside the legendary Henry Carpenter, though I'm sure he was less than impressed with my ringside manner – I was supposed to be impartial but as the fight hotted up, I found myself shouting, live on radio, 'Come on, Charlie!'. My exhortations didn't help. Charlie lost, but it was a great night all the same.

Throughout it all, I have tried to act as an ambassador for sport and I like to think I have managed to do some good. Probably the most rewarding and satisfying experience arose unexpectedly on a visit to London in 1996 when I was invited by then Prime Minister John Major to a reception for sportspeople at St James's Palace. It was there that I met Nelson Mandela (you can tell how overcome I am by the experience by the way I am holding his hand in the official photograph). I was invited to South Africa to coach young people in some deprived township areas. I visited Soweto, Alexandra and Khayelitsha and found all the children I engaged with all desperate to be involved in sport. I was so inspired I returned home and began fundraising for them. I made marmalade and knitted dishcloths, things like that, and sold them, eventually raising £10,000 towards the building of Paarl School Primary.

Mandela was the most heart-warming man – he seemed to hold no resentment whatsoever for the thirty years he was imprisoned in shockingly harsh and inhumane conditions. I'd seen first-hand the terrible effects of the prison regime at the notorious Robben Island when, in 1990, I met Mluleki George, president of the National Sports Council. He had a permanent crick in his neck and I asked if he had been in an accident. Imagine my horror when he told me how, in Robben Island, he and other prisoners were tortured by being buried in sand up to their necks, with their heads covered in honey so ants could eat it, and that in his case, they had eaten all the way through to the nerves in his neck. It was horrifying. Mluleki survived that ordeal, only to be taken in 2021 by the Covid pandemic.

Perhaps more importantly in terms of being an ambassador for sport, after finishing competing, I came to serve on the Sports Council of Northern Ireland, now Sport NI. Some of my happiest and fulfilling times came as a result of that role, thanks to the presence and example of fellow board member, the late Don Shearer, a wonderful man.

Don was a former British Olympic footballer and Ireland international cricketer. Coming from a background as a shirt factory worker in Derry, he had no airs or graces and knew exactly the challenges faced by the amateur sportspeople whose lot we were striving to make better. As a footballer for the Corinthians club in London, Don would travel each weekend by train from Derry to Belfast, take the overnight ferry to Liverpool and on by train to London; then after the game, he would make the same journey in reverse. He was only late once. What young footballer nowadays would contemplate such a commitment?

Don also demonstrated the qualities that voluntary board members should aspire to. Sporting bodies have always attracted time servers, seekers of reflected glory and seats at the top table, but Don was the antithesis of the green blazer brigade. He attended every meeting and did his homework ahead of them so that he was well briefed on the topics to be discussed. He always offered wise counsel when it came to decision making. I learned a lot from him.

Yes, there were perks and events we regularly attended and, as the Sports Council was government funded, for the first time in my life, post-competition, I wasn't expected to fundraise for the privilege. But there were also challenges, not least in 1980 when Thatcher's government decided to dispense with us in a round of budget cuts. Sport was vulnerable as Mrs T seemed to consider it frivolous. And the writing was on the wall when, on one of her first visits to Northern Ireland, she noted, as she was being driven from the airport to Belfast, the number of new leisure centres springing up. 'We are spending too much money here,' she'd reportedly observed.

Those leisure centres were the legacy of the previous Labour government's Minister of State Lord Melchett who, admirably, saw sport and leisure as a means of giving young people a focus and alternative to becoming involved in the mayhem engulfing us at that time. But Mrs T saw only the cost on the national balance sheet and the monetary saving to be made from axing the Sports Council.

One of the toughest tasks of my life was accompanying the then chair, Jack Allen, to sadly tell the staff at the House of Sport, near my Track on the Malone Road, that their jobs were no more. One in particular took the news especially hard and rounded on me, saying, 'It's OK for you. You can go back to your health club and earn money there.' I replied that at least I had come to tell them face to face. Others couldn't look them in the eye and had stayed away.

We thought that was it – the end of the Sports Council. And then, remarkably and unexpectedly, we were given an eleventh-hour reprieve when our representations to government, which we felt had fallen on deaf ears, were taken up by local newspapers, the *Belfast Telegraph* and *News Letter*, who penned stirring editorials underlining the importance of sport to the normalisation of a troubled society and the role of the Sports Council in furthering that. To our astonishment, the bean counters listened and relented and we were saved.

That, in turn, allowed us to press ahead with one of our success stories: the Ulster Games of the 1980s.

Northern Ireland had become a sporting desert at the time with sportspeople and teams from other countries reluctant to visit, so we came up with idea of the Ulster Games, which would encompass all of the main sports and, with support from local business sponsors, attract competitors to come here.

A great idea, but even then we faced challenges. For instance, I wanted to have safety measures in place for our visitors. I was particularly concerned about a group of fourteen-year-old swimmers who were coming. Had I been one of their parents, I would have wanted to know they would be safe and well taken care of, so I raised my concerns at a board meeting. These didn't appear to be shared around the table and the attitude seemed to be, 'Don't worry, everything will be all right.' I stood firm and threatened to walk out and away from the Sports Council if my worries were not addressed. I wasn't aware of any particular threat and had no reason to think anyone would come to harm, but I was also conscious that any event showing Northern Ireland in a positive light could be a target for disruption, so I just wanted to be sure. As a result, the police were approached and assurances given that our visitors would be afforded ample but discreet protection.

On another occasion, when the Ulster Games were due to take place in Antrim during a particularly febrile period of the Troubles, we understandably experienced difficulty attracting entries from outside. Thankfully British Airways and the local council came to our rescue with a support package. To publicise this, I had to appear on national television and appeal to athletes who were having second thoughts: 'If you turn up at any airport and tell British Airways that I sent you, you will be given a free flight to Belfast,' I urged. And it worked.

The Ulster Games, now defunct, can be classed a success story for the Sports Council and Northern Ireland as they served their purpose in providing a sporting oasis until normality returned. Some may now take for granted major sporting events like the Giro d'Italia and golf's Open Championship coming here but it wasn't always thus and, though it was a struggle at times, I take satisfaction that we on the Sports Council held the line.

On a lighter note, we once hosted a dinner for our Special Olympics team at Belfast City Hall. The council staff had gone the extra mile to decorate the hall for them, even tying helium balloons to every chair. Of course, the youngsters untied the balloons, which took off for the ceiling amid great mirth – but not for the poor council workers who had to clamber up scaffolding to fetch them down.

Like those balloons, I was never deflated while doing my bit for sport.

# 18

# Fame on the Small Screen

My gold medal opened many doors for me, not least to television studios up and down the land.

For a decade after Munich, I was TV gold, appearing on screen alongside favourites as diverse as the heartthrob Omar Sharif and Noel Edmonds' comedy character, Mr Blobby – surely the only time you will see them namechecked in the same sentence!

Often, I had to pinch myself and wonder how on earth I came to be sitting under the lights alongside these household names. Me? A former domestic science teacher from a small town in Northern Ireland, suddenly thrust into the spotlight, rubbing shoulders with iconic TV and movie stars.

That was especially true when I found myself on the *Russell Harty Show*, perched between Omar Sharif and Diana Dors. Diana was fabulously glamorous and charming, but I was most in awe of Omar Sharif, whom I had idolised since watching his most famous film, *Doctor Zhivago*. How astonished was I that he had not only heard of me but was able to recite my exact score from Munich to win the gold medal. I discovered later that he had a head for figures (in more ways than one), being an accomplished bridge player.

The most memorable part of the event, however, was the reaction to my arrival on stage. When my turn came, some voice off stage began intoning the words, 'Twenty years ago this little girl from Ballymena won a sack-race …' I'd had a couple, so I pulled my long gown down over my knees and hopped across the set to my chair alongside the famous interrogator. It was pretty evident that Russell had been concentrating so hard on his questions that he hadn't heard that introductory line. He looked at me as though I had either taken complete leave of my senses or else become stricken by some awful affliction which his researchers had forgotten to tell him about. I shall never forget the horror on his face or my own cringing embarrassment.

Embarrassment of another kind came in October 1972, when I was invited on to Bruce Forsyth's *The Generation Game*. I nearly didn't make it to the studio as the taxi driver they sent refused to believe I was his fare. I'd had to wait for ages while he simply stared at me without opening the door. Finally, it dawned on him. 'I was told to pick up a pair of heaters,' he protested!

Then, once onstage, they for some reason asked me to demonstrate to contestants how to throw a discus, even though it wasn't one of my disciplines, but thankfully, the one they gave me was made of polysterene, which was just as well as I had to throw it into the audience! Then my medal caused something of a small sensation when it was discovered that the reverse side bore a kind of relief map of two fairly well-endowed gentlemen standing about without any clothes on.

Bruce had wanted to know if the medal was solid gold. It isn't, it's gilt silver dipped in gold. By the time I had walked out into the stadium in Munich to receive it, it already had my name and my discipline – in common language, my event – engraved round the rim. I can hardly remember anyone wanting to see my Commonwealth Games golds for which I had worked so hard but everyone wanted to see and touch my Olympic medal; so many that I took to carrying it around with me in my handbag.

One morning, going into the gymnasium, I stopped as usual at the army barrier that stood at the end of Upper Arthur Street. A young soldier with a beret, flak jacket and an automatic gun stepped out from his wooden guard post with its sandbags and whorls of barbed wire, and gave me a thorough twice-over with that piece of electronic machinery that was known locally as the Geiger counter. Each time, while hovering over my handbag, the instrument emitted a high-pitched protest. The soldier gave me a cold, hard, mistrustful look and said, 'There's a large lump of metal in there.' I was mortified. There were a number of people close around me waiting to be electronically frisked. I dreaded being questioned further and then made to open my bag to prove it wasn't a gun. I said, 'It's a medal.'

It rang a bell somewhere in the soldier's mind. He looked at me again and I knew he recognised me. Fatigue and strain were engraved on his face. He didn't enthuse or smile. In a flat, dead voice he said, 'Pass on.'

Then it was from 'Brucey' to Blobby and my encounter on Noel Edmonds' *Saturday Night House Party*, a massive ratings hit at the time. On one show I had been swooning over the handsome face of Omar Sharif, on another I was appearing alongside a rotund pink figure covered in yellow spots, with a permanent toothy grin and green jiggling eyes.

I was on with the England World Cup winning hero, Sir Geoff Hurst, and my fellow athlete Steve Cram. Having been advised beforehand not to wear any expensive clothing, due to the likelihood of being 'gunged' – audiences loved this segment of the programme, where Blobby doused his celebrity guests with what can only be described as slimy, green blancmange – Steve and I were surprised to see Geoff Hurst rock up in a very smart suit. Then, we discovered, his agent had insisted a condition for his appearance was that he wouldn't be subject to any indignity. So, while Steve and I were promptly 'gunged', Sir Geoff remained a picture of sartorial elegance ... until Steve and I plastered him with ours, much to the delight of the studio audience.

*A Question of Sport* was a particular favourite of mine and I appeared on the popular BBC quiz show many times, including the 250th anniversary episode. David Vine and David Coleman were the first presenters in my time but my favourite was Sue Barker. Few people realise that, back then, the BBC filmed four episodes in one day (the first I was involved in was shot in a church hall in Manchester before moving to a proper studio). That meant sixteen guests all milling around at various stages of the day, some of them quite precious, and, despite her busy schedule, Sue made time for everyone.

Down the years I fielded questions alongside my dear friend Cliff Morgan, Bill Beaumont, Henry Cooper, Ian Botham, Bobby Charlton, Ally McCoist, John Parrott, Phil Tuffnell and Matt Dawson. We had so much fun, on and off camera. Cliff and Henry would take the train up from London and spend their £50 fee on dinner, drinks and jollity on the return journey. There were some very funny moments on screen, worthy of *It'll Be Alright on the Night*, that would probably be outtakes today.

During a 1987 picture board round, Emlyn Hughes identified Princess Anne as John Reid, the Northern Ireland jockey, and Princess Anne appeared on the 200th edition of the programme, shortly after. In another episode, Ally McCoist failed to identify himself in a clip and didn't recognise his Rangers boss at the time, Walter Smith. During mystery guest rounds, Sue Barker has been variously guessed as Ray Clemence, Chris Hoy, Alan Minter, and Dennis Taylor. I like to think I acquitted myself well with the questions, though perhaps it was a little too well. On one particular programme, I was getting so many right that my captain, John Parrott, remarked, 'Get her some theatre tickets ... she needs to get out more.'

Mind you, there was never much money in television in those days – £25 if you were lucky, and that was swallowed up in travel and clothing expenses! And while usually, I would be part of a panel or group of guests while on screen, twice I found myself taking centre stage.

The first was a cloak and dagger affair as friends collaborated to get me on to *This Is Your Life* with the larger-than-life Eamonn Andrews in January 1973. I had suspected something was going on when I was spirited to London, supposedly for lunch with Marea Hartman. Prior to that there had been suspicious phone calls to my health club in Lisburn. When I answered, the caller would hang up, and when others picked up, there would be whispered conversations.

It was all very mysterious, but I twigged as we sat down to lunch in London. I secretly slipped a note into Buster's jacket pocket, saying, 'We are going to do *This Is Your Life*, aren't we?' And before he could read it, Eamonn Andrews appeared and 'surprised' me with his famous red book. We were quickly taken to the studios where I was handed a glass of bubbly and parked in a back room so as not to see the other guests. They give you an hour or so to compose yourself after the initial shock, and all that while I was wondering only one thing: had they brought my brother, John, over from Australia? Then it was lights, cameras, action as a procession of old school friends, teammates and my rival from Munich,

Heidi Rosendhal, stepped out from backstage to share their memories of me. I really was disappointed when John suddenly came up on film, talking from outside his home in Sydney saying he was sorry he couldn't share in my evening, being on the other side of the world.

Then right at the end of the programme there was a voice that literally made my heart miss two beats. Imagine my surprise, delight and tears at the programme climax when, from around the corner of the set came John. I hadn't seen him for twelve years. That was the best of very many good days – a magical memory.

But if the intrigue leading up to *This Is Your Life* was slightly outside my comfort zone, I was much more at home, quite literally, when Loyd Grossman came calling for an episode of *Through the Keyhole* – a show in which panellists in the studio tried to guess the owner of a house from its contents. Thank heaven I keep my house tidy!

My athletics memorabilia should have been an easy giveaway. I can't remember who got it, but I do recall Loyd's answer to his trademark rhetorical question, 'Who lives in a house like this?': 'Hansel and Gretel,' he suggested, as the perfect description of my little cottage by the river, just outside Belfast. And he must have left a trail of breadcrumbs on the way out as he returned for a follow up episode a few years later.

During the Beijing Olympics in 2008, I was one of a group of former gold medallists invited to London to press the button for the Saturday night lottery draw. I released the balls hoping there would be a Northern Ireland winner, but sadly not. Anyway, it was an enjoyable experience. A friend and I were installed in a top-class hotel for two nights and took in *The Lion King* West End show, all for half an hour's 'work'. On returning home, I telephoned the TV producer who had arranged it all to say thanks, only to be meet with silence. Eventually she explained, 'We've been doing this for nearly fifteen years and no-one has ever said thank you before.'

From that experience I always tell young people to remember the importance of those two words … thank you. After all, manners cost nothing but are worth so much.

In the 1980s I took part in a BBC TV sports series *Maestro* and arrived for a meeting with one of the producers from London at the old Conway Hotel at Dunmurry. Hotels then were much different to now, with set meal times and kitchen hours. Lunch had already been served but the pushy producer, believing he was still in London, demanded sandwiches. 'I'm sorry, sir, but the kitchen is closed,' said the friendly barman. 'Just get me some,' our visitor rapped back. I could have died a thousand deaths at the way he spoke, but a while later, the barman returned bearing a tray of sandwiches he had clearly made himself. 'Thank you, now bring the same again,' ordered the hungry Beeb man.

I couldn't get away quickly enough, so imagine my shock a few weeks later, on returning to the hotel for a function, to be taken to one side by the general manager, a former rugby player, who kissed me from wrist to elbow and apologised profusely for 'having let you down' on my previous visit. It turned out the man from the Beeb was friendly with a boss from the hotel parent company back in London and had complained. I was mortified and could only think to joke, 'Don't worry, just send up the champagne later!'

I thought nothing of it until a while later the doors of the reception room flung open and my manager friend wheeled in the champers. I didn't know where to look. His hotel had been the innocent party all along.

And just to complete the mortification, as I exited down the grand staircase, treading carefully in my high heels and linking arms with my good friend, the great raconteur and wit, Victor Haslett, for balance, the manager hove into view at the bottom of the stairs, winked conspiratorially, and whispered, 'If you ever need a room, I'm here.' For once, Victor was left speechless.

The camera can be deceptive, though. One of my most iconic pictures, one that people most remark upon, is of me sipping a glass of champagne, surrounded by the Rolling Stones. It looks as though I am living the high life, partying with the most famous rock band in the world at the time.

In reality, it was a PR stunt.

The truth is we met for no more than five minutes (they had no clue who I was and couldn't wait to get back to their screaming fans outside). They were appearing in a Belfast theatre and I was collecting an award at the hotel next door ... a quick-thinking PR saw a golden photo opportunity to promote the event and whisked me in and out in a 'Jumpin' Jack Flash'.

# 19

# For Queen and Country

It has always been very important for me that I give back to my adopted home. In the years immediately following my win I was even approached to go into politics, by members of both the Conservative and the Alliance parties. But politics, professional party politics, has never been my way. I am not a political animal. My philosophy is simply that life is very precious and that every hour of every day must be lived positively, and this was the example I tried to set on the running track. I ran in the name of Belfast and Northern Ireland to attempt to show the world that our spirit was not dead.

Along the way, through failure and success, I know that my efforts were not wasted on the ordinary people at home, and I am incredibly grateful for the honours and titles I have received over the years. In 1973, I was honoured to be made a Member of the Order of the British Empire (MBE) for services to athletics, and in 1990 was promoted to Commander (CBE). I was made a Dame Commander (DBE) in 2000, and a Member of the Order of the Companions of Honour (CH) in 2015.

I am particularly proud of my five-year tenure as Lord-Lieutenant of Belfast (2009–2014); it was an honour and a privilege to be asked to become the Queen's official representative in Belfast. Prior to my appointment, I had been one of twenty deputies, serving under my predecessor, Lady Romayne Carswell, until she retired, as is required, at the age of seventy-five. I had no expectation of succeeding her. In my deputy role, I had been to Hillsborough Castle once or twice a year and had attended a few funerals. That was all I knew. But during a Christmas function at Hillsborough as Lady Romayne's retirement approached, a government official took me to one side for a 'discussion'. I was asked if I would be prepared to allow my name to go forward to the Queen as Lady Romayne's successor.

'Are you sure I am up to the job?' was my immediate response.

'We wouldn't ask if we weren't,' came the reply!

I couldn't wait to get home and google the position. That's where I found out the role included 'working closely with voluntary services, charities and local businesses but primarily arranging visits by members of the Royal family and escorting Royal visitors to Northern Ireland.' All purely voluntary, of course.

Within days, a letter arrived from the then prime minister, Gordon Brown, asking officially if my name could go forward to the Queen. I replied in the affirmative and then sought a meeting with Sir Jonathan Phillips, the permanent secretary of the Northern Ireland Office, as I had some questions of my own.

Firstly, did I have to wear a hat? Only in the presence of the Queen.

I'm a non-church goer, but was willing to attend services – would that be a problem? Not at all.

Are there clothing expenses? The response to this one was less clear …

According to the rules, Lord-Lieutenants are not paid and only receive expenses such as travel costs incurred on official duties. Male Lord-Lieutenants wear a grand uniform on official duties, and can therefore wear the same thing time and again, but we ladies were expected to look our best in our own attire, and when you are being photographed at engagements, sometimes three in a week, we couldn't be seen to be wearing the same dress. The only trapping provided with the office was a beautiful, official brooch, which I was to always wear. It cost £5,000 and we were told we must insure it ourselves and to always keep it in a safe place between engagements. And I did … at the bottom of my knicker drawer!

So, while I would say I ended up out of pocket on that front, it was worth every penny for the sense of duty I derived, my pride at serving my monarch and, of course, the people I met. That brooch made over 250 appearances in those whirlwind five years representing Her Majesty, and during that time, I accompanied the Queen on all her visits to Northern Ireland, and to this great city of ours. Belfast, it turned out, was a place close to her own heart. I remember accompanying her on a tour of the city in 2002 as part of her Golden Jubilee celebrations around the UK and the comment she made on the welcome she received: 'Belfast won hands down.'

But then, my abiding memory of Her Majesty, over 54 years of up close and personal encounters will always be of her human touch and how down to earth she really was in those private moments. The tone had been set at our first meeting, back in 1968. After the Mexico Olympics I had been invited, as captain of the British Women's athletics team, to a reception at Buckingham Palace. There we shared our experiences with the Queen, who had also been to South America. She nodded, knowingly, as we related how eight of us athletes had shared an apartment in the Olympic Village. Conditions were spartan, we washed our clothes in the bath and often, when taking a shower, the lights would go out. 'Oh yes, that happened to me, too,' replied the Queen.

On another occasion at the palace, as I attended a birthday party for Princess Anne, I was alone in a state room admiring the gifts laid out when I heard this familiar voice behind me, 'Have you seen Philip anywhere?' Never in my life had I expected to be asked by the Queen where her husband had got to!

Even more bizarrely, I once found myself escorting Prince Philip on a tour of the bleak, Victorian-era Crumlin Road Gaol in Belfast, which at its overflowing peak capacity, had held some of the most notorious terrorists of the Troubles. Our visit occurred long after it had been closed down and turned into a tourist attraction. It was still a grim, forbidding place whose walls echoed with memories of darker days. We were following the Queen, who was being guided by the then First and deputy First Ministers, Peter Robinson and Martin McGuinness, when Prince Philip broke the ice with a risqué joke about prison life, which I shall not repeat for fear of ending up in the Tower. Suffice to say, those walls echoed with laughter for once!

As did the walls of the Ulster Television studios in Belfast in 2010 when, during the Queen's tour around the building, she was brought to

Studio One to see the technology used for weather forecasts by popular presenter and weatherman Frank Mitchell, with whom she struck up an instant rapport. The Queen didn't need the technology to observe that it was 'rather wet'.

Over the course of the five years, I was at the steps of the aircraft to greet the Queen and Prince Philip, Princess Anne, Charles and Camilla, William and Kate, Andrew, Edward and Sophie, Duchess of Gloucester. Another distinguished visitor I had the privilege to accompany was the then President of Ireland, Mary McAleese, a native of Belfast. Such a gracious lady, always beautifully dressed and so hard working, President McAleese could carry out as many as eight engagements in a day and make even the last one seem like her first.

And yet, for all the famous and titled people I would meet in my Lord-Lieutenant's role, my favourite moments were the citizenship ceremonies I was called upon to perform at Hillsborough Castle. I treasure pictures I have with children from all over the world being officially welcomed as UK citizens, integrating into our society. A particular pleasure was bestowing citizenship on a man I know, originally from China, who was a coach at the Salto Gymnastics club in Lisburn, of which I am president. And then there was the woman from Kenya who came forward to accept her British passport. An official of the UK Passport Office was on hand to receive her Kenyan passport as part of the ceremony. 'I don't have one,' she said. 'Well how did you get here?' the incredulous official asked. 'On my sister's,' the lady smiled innocently. Sometimes the less you know, the better.

The Lord-Lieutenancy was demanding, but I loved every single day and still managed to carry out my other commitments at the track, to my trust, to many other charities, and honour the invitations I had accepted before accepting the role. One of the earliest was a school prizegiving at Dungannon Girls High. I had been invited to lunch at the palace with Her Majesty on the same day to discuss the Lord-Lieutenant role, but explained to the Royal Household that I had a prior engagement. When the school heard, they were most apologetic and offered to change the date of their prize-giving, but I insisted we go ahead, believing it was the honourable thing to do. A commitment is just that, in my book.

When I retired, I was asked what gift I would like as a thank you. I replied that my greatest gift had been doing the job. And there were more gifts like that to come ...

In 2017, I was made a Dame of the Order of Saint John (DStJ) and in 2019 I was astonished and deeply honoured to be invited by the Queen to become a Lady of the Garter, a member of the oldest and most senior Order of Chivalry in Britain. Again, as with my Lord-Lieutenant appointment, I turned to Google and found I was one of only a small group of people outside the aristocracy to have ever been invited on to the distinguished list of names, which dates back 675 years. Her Majesty makes these personal honours and that she had chosen me, a commoner of no aristocratic background, to be a Lady of the Garter was just out of this world.

I remember thinking, 'If I am going to become a lady, I had better start acting like one!' Though I must admit that, throughout all the honours bestowed upon me, I have tried to remain grounded. Like the time I got the bus into Belfast one day. A lady kept looking at me and finally asked: 'Are you Mary Peters?' 'Yes,' I replied. 'Well, what are you doing on a bus?' she exclaimed. 'Because it's free,' I said, waving my bus pass. At the end of the day, the title I really prize is that of 'Our Mary', which is how I am often greeted by people of all sections of the community. So, just as I did when I became a dame and people began asking what they should call me, I would reply, 'Just call me Mary P.'

There were so many things to think about in preparation for the honour, including deciding upon my own coat of arms. I was invited to attend the College of Arms and they were quite surprised to see that I had already compiled a list of the elements I wanted included: 'Usually we have to interview people to see what their interests are,' they said. We talked about all the elements that I'd like included, then they asked me what my motto would be.

I went to school at Portadown College, whose motto is *Fortiter et Humaniter*, meaning 'with courage and courtesy'. I rang the school and asked permission to use that and they were very happy.

On my garter shield, the background of the coat of arms is divided into blue and red, echoing the Union Flag. Five interlaced gold rings are in the centre, a reference to my Olympic experiences. These sit within a circlet of ten white oak trees with gold acorns which are a tribute to my father – outside the nursing home in Australia where my stepmother had lived was a big oak tree and my father always said that it was his little bit of England – but also to Derriaghy, where I live, a name that means oakwood. They also refer to the ten oak trees planted at the Mary Peters Track to mark my retirement from the Lord-Lieutenancy. On the left is a springer spaniel with a collar of red and white roses: we always had springer spaniels at home, and my brother and his wife bred springers in Australia, winning best of show on many occasions; while the roses are a reference to my grandparents coming from Lancashire and Yorkshire. On the right is a liver bird holding a flaming torch and wearing a collar of flax flowers: the bird is a reference to Liverpool, where I was born; the flax is for Northern Ireland; and the torch is to represent my charity, the Mary Peters Trust and the Olympic flame, but the flame is also a symbol of Lisburn, for which I hold the freedom of the city.

The badge comprises the dome of the city hall in Belfast, for which I also hold the freedom of the city, and it has a Ulysses butterfly sitting on top of it, in honour of my brother, a world authority on butterflies.

My installation on 'Garter Day' took place alongside that of the 7th Marquess of Salisbury, Robert Gascoyne-Cecil, who became a knight companion, while the rehearsal ahead of the ceremony had the king of Spain, king of the Netherlands and Lord Salisbury in attendance. The main event was held at Windsor Castle in June 2019, with the investiture ceremony in the morning, prior to the Garter Day procession, where the Queen and her knights paraded in velvet robes and plumed hats; a tradition of nearly 700 years, now being carried on by King Charles III. My personal seat at St George's chapel is where former prime minister William Gladstone once sat; next to me is Sir John Major. I was delighted that my brother, John, his wife, May, their daughter, Vanessa, and her husband, Grant, travelled from Australia to be with me on the day.

Windsor Castle and St George's Chapel will therefore always be special places to me and there was a certain poignancy in finding myself there again on the occasion of Her Majesty's funeral in September 2022.

I was present in the chapel at the service when the royals said their final farewells to this most revered of monarchs. To be there as an ordinary citizen at an epic moment in British history was overwhelming. I was left feeling humble but also recognised the absolute privilege of the role that had cast me into such a position. The magnitude of it all was brought home to me as I watched the sceptre and orb removed from the coffin as it was made ready for burial. Then, next morning, I was taken back to the chapel to see the marble stone over the vault where the late Queen now rests with her late mother, father and husband. The whole experience was so moving, and while I wish King Charles and Queen Camilla the utmost goodwill in the enormity of the roles they are taking on, no one will ever replace Her Majesty.

Eight months later, on 6 May 2023, I bore witness, up close and personal, as the pages of history turned once more at the joyous and uplifting coronation of King Charles III and Queen Consort Camilla.

I attended in my official capacity as the representative of the Order of the Garter, and was part of the actual procession, leading the King and Queen to their crowning in front of 2,300 specially invited Westminster Abbey guests and hundreds of millions viewing on television globally. I walked behind my good friend Lord Seb Coe who, I later discovered, had in a national TV interview outside the cathedral, demoted me from Lady Mary back to Dame, but I forgave him as we go way back to a time when I was plain Mary P., managing him in the British Olympic team.

My mind was racing as I tried to take in the magnitude of the occasion, the pomp and ceremony, the rich and famous, world leaders and ennobled on either side of the aisle as we walked down. My overriding thought was of what my late parents would have made of seeing me not only present at the coronation but actually walking in front of the King and Queen at this most historic moment in time.

My, it was a long day: a 6.30 a.m. start from the hotel nearby, where I had been staying since Thursday's full dress rehearsal, until bedding down at 10 p.m. on the Saturday night. With road closures and security, a fifteen-minute walk to the Abbey in the morning turned into a journey of two and half hours in the evening in lashing rain as I returned to my hotel. But I savoured every minute.

People have since asked how I managed to go for so long without sustenance. Well, we were given a Jammie Dodger and glass of water as we donned our robes in a marquee outside the Abbey at 9.00 a.m. before being taken to the Cloisters at 10.20 a.m. to await the arrival of the new king and queen. It was all very precise.

From being centre stage in the procession, we had a much less favourable view from our seats in the West Chancery and ended up watching the ceremony on television! We could hear everything loudly and clearly, from the wonderful music to the ceremonial exchanges, but could only see the actual proceedings, including the moment the crown was placed upon the Royal head, on our TV monitors. I had taken some peppermints and sugary sweets into the Abbey to keep me going, so it was as well we were out of sight.

Watching on, I found myself trying to take in every detail. Camilla, I felt, looked radiant and carried herself with great dignity. I was especially delighted to see that she had chosen to have images of her two little rescue dogs embroidered on to her dress, a lovely thought. I also found myself wondering what was going through the King's mind. Initially, I thought Charles looked slightly anxious and vulnerable, being an older gentleman – we tend to forget that, at that moment he was seventy-four years old. Then there was that awkward moment when the Archbishop of Canterbury adjusted the heavy crown to fit and I saw then that Charles was overcome with emotion and by the enormity of it all.

Charles, I feel, is misunderstood by many people looking at him from afar. In reality, I have always found him genuine and sincere. Once, during my Lord-Lieutenancy, I was struck down by an attack of shingles and imagine my surprise when a bouquet of flowers was delivered to my door with a get well soon card, personally signed by Charles. When we next met, he asked if I was fully recovered, which I found remarkable, considering the number of people he meets. We also had a deputy Lord-Lieutenant go into hospital for heart surgery. He awoke to find a bottle of Isle of Islay special blended whisky by his bed, with a handwritten note from Charles assuring him the 'wee dram' was for medicinal purposes.

Of the younger Royals, William and Kate are shining lights who will illuminate the family firm for another generation. I attended their wedding as Lord-Lieutenant and my elevation to the Order of the Garter was announced by William as he casually pulled pints in the aptly named Empire pub in Belfast as I accompanied the couple on a visit. That simple act, which the cameras loved, showed how down to earth and in touch with people they really are.

Yet, for all the dignitaries, presidents and royalty surrounding us, my eyes were drawn most to the seven girls from Methodist College, Belfast who sang as part of the coronation choir. I spoke with two of their teachers and told them how proud I was of their students. They will remember that day for the rest of their lives. Who wouldn't?

I know I shall be pinching myself to make sure I didn't dream it for the rest of mine.

# 20

# The Heart of the Matter

I faced the greatest physical challenge of my life, not on the athletics track, but on a hospital operating table in November 2018. It all began with an unplanned check-up and ended in major heart surgery.

Unaware of any problems, in 2013 I opened a facility at Kingsbridge clinic on the Lisburn Road and was offered a full health check which showed that a heart valve was not working as efficiently as it should. I was unperturbed. There were no noticeable symptoms and because I was fit and leading a healthy lifestyle, walking four miles daily, it didn't register with me that this could be something serious lying in wait up ahead. I carried on doing what I was doing, working for the Trust, fundraising, taking part in activities and then becoming immersed in my Race to a Million project.

Then in January 2018 I came down with a bad cold. I was out walking and experienced a bit of a problem walking uphill. Soon after, I was at an event at the Track, where there is a steep incline on the way out, and as I was walking away, I found myself becoming short of breath. I actually bent down and pretended to tie my shoelaces so no-one would notice, I hoped. This time I paid heed and made an appointment with my GP, who sent me to a consultant for cardiogram and echo tests. I spoke to a good friend, Malcolm Crone, who is a consultant at the Ulster Independent Clinic, and sought his advice. He recommended that I go for surgery.

My Trust, at that time, had an arrangement with the clinic whereby injured young athletes were fast-tracked for treatment to get them back into action as quickly as possible, an initiative funded by the then Rory McIlroy Foundation. I had the option to undergo the operation privately at the clinic, but instead I chose to join the NHS waiting list as I neither wanted nor expected preferential treatment.

When the time came, the surgeon at the Royal Victoria Hospital who was to carry out my operation, Alastair Graham, explained that an aortic valve had calcified, preventing blood from circulating as it should. It didn't matter that I had led an active and healthy life. There had been a gradual deterioration through age, and because of the nature of the problem, there was no option but to open me up. I was told that, without the operation, I would have a life expectancy of no more than two years (I learned after the surgery that, in reality, it was more likely to have been only one year). A new valve could give me another ten good years.

I was a little apprehensive about being admitted, simply because of the unknown, but I wasn't afraid. I have always had this mechanism whereby I compartmentalise by shutting out thoughts of anything I don't want to do and replacing them with more positive ones. Like when I go on a long-haul flight, I never ask how many hours, I just shift my focus on to something else until we get there.

So, despite the risks inherent in all surgery, it never occurred to me that I might not come through the operation, and I agreed to the procedure.

For all that, I was unprepared for being in hospital. I expected to walk in and straight back out again in a matter of days and initially everything was going to plan. The operation itself took six hours – or so I was told as I wasn't awake for it – and was deemed a success. Alastair and his NHS staff were such experts. They knew what they were doing and I would have no hesitation putting my trust in their hands again.

Afterwards, I was sitting up, welcoming visitors and telling them I would be out by the weekend. Then I had a setback when irregular heart rhythms were detected, and I was back in bed hooked up to tubes and monitors again. I was in a low place those few days. Having blood taken and all manner of tests carried out was alien to me. I was in a state of shock. One of the nurses treating me said the effect on the body of such prolonged surgery was akin to being hit by a bus. That is when I realised what exactly I had come through. I wasn't in pain, which was a surprise in itself to my nurse friend, but there was a great deal of trauma to deal with. I hadn't asked for too many details about my operation beforehand, so it wasn't until I watched a television programme months later about open heart surgery which showed the same operation I had gone through. I was initially quite interested, until the programme showed the surgeon cutting into the breast bone. Then I had to turn away.

The aftermath too, was a total shock to the system. All the medical and nursing staff who attended to me at the Royal, and later while recuperating in the Somme Nursing Home, were marvellous. I can't speak highly enough of them. But I went from leading an extremely active life, on my feet sometimes 24/7, to being confined to quarters. This, even if it was just for a few weeks, was very difficult to come to terms with. I had never been ill in all my 79 years until then, and had only been hospitalised once, when I required surgery on an injured shoulder.

My physio urged me not to rush things but I can't change the way I am. I was on a Zimmer frame at first and it bugged me. I had received fantastic care from everyone at the Royal but it was an important step in my recovery to be able to leave, and within a few days of arriving at the Somme Nursing Home, I blossomed again. Finally, I had time to quite literally smell the roses. I had television, my phone and iPad, and I began to draw up a to-do list for when I got home. Towards the end of my stay there, I was able to go outside and tentatively take my first few steps unaided down the road outside, using lamp posts as a yardstick and going one further each day.

I was also cheered by the number of cards and bouquets that began to arrive from well-wishers as word of my operation spread. I had visits from Jim Kirkwood and from Mike Bull, who brought along an old black-and-white pic of us competing at Crystal Palace in 1972. But most all, my good friends Gillian Hetherington, Terry Crothers and Georgina McCloskey were towers of strength for me all the way through. Gillian is executive manager of the Trust while Terry is a director and former BBC NI sport administrator and member of the NI Commonwealth Games council, recently retired. Georgina has been a long-time friend. They helped restore some normality to my life as I recovered in the Somme.

When it was finally time to leave, I was reminded that I had to take things gently, which is not in my DNA: there would be no driving for six months, and no lifting – not even a kettle. As they told me all that, I couldn't help imagining what my doctors would have made of me abseiling down the side of Belfast Castle months earlier in a Trust fundraiser, back when the extent of my heart condition wasn't yet known. I had been scared clambering over the parapet and had thought to myself, 'Do you realise what age you are?' but it was an achievement, and I was going to do it.

But that's me. I am not one for resting on my laurels when there is work to do. I have never failed to meet a challenge in my life, and I wasn't going to allow the small matter of heart surgery to change that. I'd already had to miss taking part in a zip-wire crossing of the Lagan at the Queen's Bridge in August that year because I had to have treatment for cataracts in my eyes. The nurse then had said I wasn't to do any window cleaning or vacuuming for a while and I'd replied, 'What about a zip-line?' You can imagine the response.

It took a while for me to get my confidence back for meeting people. It sounds irrational, but I felt people would be looking at me, as if they knew I'd just had surgery. It was all in my head, I know, but I needed to prepare myself mentally. Going out to a local cafe for a coffee with Terry helped. I knew then I was ready to face the world again.

I felt so grateful to have been given a second chance, one that I was determined to make the most of. I may have needed major surgery, but six weeks is a comparatively short time to change your life for the better.

Life is precious and I can honestly say I have lived mine to the full and will continue to do so for as long as I am able. Thankfully, I am fortunate to have been blessed, for the most part with good health.

I have made many great friends down the years and met so many people I wouldn't otherwise have had an opportunity to meet, had it not been for my athletic career and everything that came from that. It has enabled me to help so many young people develop their skills through my Trust, which I continue to serve. I love what I do and that work has never been for any reward other than the joy of seeing those young people flourish. I was lucky to have been able to fulfil all my dreams and nothing pleases me more than to put others on the pathway to theirs.

For all that I have achieved and the honours that have come my way, I have one sole regret ... that my late mother did not live to see all of that: my gold medal win at Munich, becoming a Dame and then Lady of the Garter, and on to my role in the Coronation of King Charles. But I know she would have been so proud and that thought consoles me.

For now, I hope my story will empower and inspire all who read it to never give up on their dreams.

# Acknowledgements

First and foremost, I want to personally thank everyone who has played a part in our journey so far; stars from the world of sport and entertainment but mainly our own Northern Ireland public who have been most generous.

To anyone who has given their time or money to help the Mary Peters Trust, thank you. You are helping our brightest prospects achieve their sporting ambitions locally and globally. This would have been enormously difficult without your financial help and encouragement.

Finally, I would like to thank Ian and Sarah Wooldridge, Derek Gallop, Gillian Hetherington, Roy Bailie, Terry Crothers and Malcolm Brodie, and give a special mention to my good friend and author of this book, Jim Gracey, who generously gave his talent and time to update and complete this life story.

# Index

Agostini, Mike, 24
Aitken, Sir Max, 113
Andrew, Duke of York, 178
Andrews, Eamonn, 172
Andrews, Mark, 95
Angelova, Nedyalka, 90
Anne, HRH Princess, 111–2, 136, 157–8, 172, 177, 178
Archer, Sir Jeffrey, 158
Armagh, County Armagh, 17
Athens, European Games, 87, 144
Athletics NI, 152
*Athletics Weekly*, 87
Australia, xiv, 18, 26, 37, 92, 96, 106, 172, 180

Ballymena Academy, 8
Ballymena Athletic Club, 15
Ballymena Model School, 8
Ballymena, County Antrim, 7, 8, 15, 20, 169
Banks, Gordon, 112, 114

Barker, Sue, 157, 171, 172
Bayi, Filbert, 128
BBC, xi, 17, 33, 65, 95–6, 100, 111, 112, 114, 117, 131, 133, 138, 147, 150, 157, 158, 161, 164, 171, 173, 186
Beaumont, Bill, 171
Becker, Ingrid, 66, 187
Bedford, David, 84, 94
Beijing, Olympic Games, *see* Olympic Games
Belfast City Council, 152, 153, 156
*Belfast Telegraph*, xiv, 98, 103, 104, 105, 125, 133, 148, 149, 166
Belfast, County Antrim, 2, 5, 7, 13–18, 20, 22, 24, 27, 28, 29, 32, 33–4, 37, 38, 41, 43, 53, 54, 69, 71, 72, 73, 79, 89, 91, 94, 100, 106, 110, 111–2, 113, 114, 115, 116, 119, 122, 126, 127, 130, 137, 140, 146–52, 155, 156, 157, 161, 163, 165, 166, 167, 173, 174, 175, 177–8,

179, 180, 182, 183, 187
Belgrade, 65
Bignal, Mary, *see* Rand, Mary
Birmingham, 19, 22, 113
Board, Lillian, 67, 144
Bodner, Christine, 75–6, 84, 90
Botham, Ian, 171
Brandt, Willy, 94
Brasher, Chris, 96
British Amateur Athletic Board, 41
British Boxing Board of Control, 164
British Pentathlon Championships, 19
Brodie, Malcolm, 148, 189
Brundage, Avery, 22, 35, 130
Bryant, John, 142
Budapest, 56
Budd, Zola, 134, 139, 141, 152
Budgett, Richard, 143
Bull, Mike, 69, 70, 121, 129, 186
Byers, Lord, 70
Bystrova, Galina, 48–9

Calcutta, India, 37
California, 11, 71, 119–21, 153
Camilla, HM Queen, xiv, 178, 181, 182
Canada, 16, 29, 92, 129, 133, 161
Cardiff, Commonwealth Games, *see* Commonwealth Games
Carpenter, Henry, 164
Carrickfergus, County Antrim, 115
Carswell, Lady Romayne, 175
Catherine, Princess of Wales, 178, 182
Chappell, Ted, 79
Charles III, HRH King, xiv, 69, 178, 180–2, 188

Charlton, Bobby, 171
Cherryvale, *see* Queen's University running track
Chizhova, Nadezhda, 59
Christchurch, New Zealand, 118, 121–5, 127, 128, 145, 155, 160
Christchurch, Commonwealth Games, *see* Commonwealth Games
Christie, Sir William, 110
Chudina, Aleksandra, 141
Churchill Memorial Scholarships, 70, 73, 154
Churchill, Lady, 73
Clarke, Darren, 156
Clarke, Derek, 50
Clarke, Tom, 114
Coleman, David, 171
Comăneci, Nadia, 132
Commonwealth Games i, ii, 21–7, 28, 34, 38, 42, 43, 51–9, 60, 63, 68–9, 75, 80, 88, 117, 120, 121–130, 138, 145, 155, 156–7, 160, 161, 164, 170, 186
  Cardiff (1958), 21–5, 27, 28, 42, 43
  Perth (1962), 34, 38
  Kingston (1966), 51–9, 60, 68
  Edinburgh (1970), 68–9, 75
  Christchurch (1974), 117–8, 121–130, 145, 155, 160, 161
Commonwealth Paraplegic Games, 127
Conlan, Michael, 156
Cook, Bill, 88, 123, 126
Cooper, Henry, 112, 157, 171
Cooper, Malcolm, 143
Corry, Ian, 155

Cosford, 68
Cowdrey, Colin, 70
Craig, Flora, 116
Craig, Tom, 116
Cram, Steve, 152, 171
Crone, Malcolm, 184
Cropper, Pat, 88, 101
Cross, Martin, 143
Crothers, Terry, 186, 189
Crump, Jack, 41
Crystal Palace, London, 62, 73, 106–8, 147, 186
Cunningham, Dorothy, 129

*Daily Express* Sportswoman of the Year award, 112–4
*Daily Mail*, xiii, 139–40, 142, 150–1
*Daily Mirror*, 30
Davies, Dickie, 95, 97
Davies, Lynn, 134, 138
Davies, Sharron, 133, 135
Dawson, Matt, 171
Dean, Christopher, 157
Decker, Mary, 140–2
Derry, County Londonderry, 13, 164, 165
Dors, Diana, 169
Duffin, Harriet, 109
Duncan, Sandy, 99

Edinburgh, Commonwealth Games, *see* Commonwealth Games
Edmonds, Noel, 169, 171
Edward, Duke of Edinburgh, 178
Elizabeth II, HM Queen x, xiv, 24, 175–83

Ellison, Adrian, 143

Empire Games, *see* Commonwealth Games
Europa Hotel, Belfast, 106, 136, 157–58
European Championships, 45, 56, 58, 85
European Games, 63, 87, 160
Ewing, Pat, 131
Exeter, Lord, 94

Firth, Bethany, 157
Forde, John, 71, 121
Forsyth, Bruce, 170–1

Gallagher, Kelly, 156
*Generation Game*, 170
George, Mluleki, 165
Germany, 2, 43, 78, 95
Gibson, Cathryn, 156
Given, Jenny, 136
Gold, Arthur, xiv, 75, 93
Goodbody, John, 92
Goodhew, Duncan, 138
Gordon, Mr, 10–11, 14
Gorman, Ruth, 133
Graham, Alastair, 185
Grainger, Katherine, i, 158
Gray, Janet, 156
Graymount Girls' Secondary School, 27
Grey, Lord, *see* Lord Grey of Naunton
Grossman, Loyd, 173

Halewood, Liverpool, 5

Hamilton, Holly, 158
Hartman, Marea, 42, 55, 57, 64–6, 77, 81, 83, 99, 101, 130, 133–4, 172
Harty, Russell, 169
Haslett, Victor, 174
Heath, Edward, 94, 99–100, 106
Hetherington, Gillian, 156, 186, 189
Hillsborough, County Down, 155, 176
Hillsborough Castle, 140, 158, 176, 178
Holmes, Andy, 143
Holmes, Kelly, i, 153
Hopkins, Thelma, 14–15, 21, 22, 23, 45
Howell, Denis, 151
Hoyte-Smith, Joslyn, i, 158
Humphreys, David, 156
Hurlingham, 42
Hurst, Sir Geoff, 171

Ibbotson, Derek, 97
International Amateur Athletics Federation, 139, 143
International Athletes' Club, 106–7
International Olympic Committee, 22, 34
Ipswich, 111
Isle of Man, 7, 123

Johnson, Dr Wilson, 54
Jones, Diane, 124, 125
Jones, Emlyn, 108
Jones, Les, 114, 152

Kemp, Peter, 78

Kingston, Commonwealth Games, *see* Commonwealth Games
Kirk, Katie, 144
Kirkwood, Jim, 156, 186
Knowles, Linda, 65
Kyle, Maeve, 15, 22, 25, 127–8

Lancashire, 5, 41, 80
Larmour, Davy, 129
Lascelles, Dorothy, 123
Lascelles, Ross, 123
Le Masurier, John, 77, 87, 124
Lisburn, County Antrim/Down, 13, 153, 162, 172, 178, 180
Liverpool, xiv, 5–8, 12, 16, 19, 43, 44, 82, 106–8, 116, 165, 180
London, ii, ix, 14, 21, 22, 37, 41–3, 54, 65, 65, 66, 84, 86, 92, 96, 100, 103, 106, 107, 108, 109, 111, 112, 115, 128, 131, 138, 142, 144, 147, 151, 161, 163, 164, 165, 172, 173–4
London, Olympic Games, *see* Olympic Games
Londonderry, *see* Derry
Lonsbrough, Anita, 133
Lord Grey of Naunton, 157
Los Angeles, Olympic Games, *see* Olympic Games
Lynam, Des, 133
Lynch, Jack, 114

Mack, Karen, 77, 90
*Maestro*, 173
Major, John, 164, 180
Manchester, 171

# Index

Mandela, Nelson, 164–5
Martin, Stephen, 156
Mary Peters Health Club, 162–3, 166, 172
Mary Peters Track, xiv, 137, 140, 148–53, 154, 155, 156, 162, 166, 178, 180, 184
Mary Peters Trust, ii, xi, xiv, 136, 144, 154–9, 162, 178, 180, 184, 186, 187, 189
McAleese, Mary, 178
McBride, Violet, 136
McCawley, Debbie, 128, 129
McClelland, Kenny, 9, 10, 89
McCloskey, Georgina, 186
McCoist, Ally, 171, 172
McCoubrey, Larry, 117
McDowell, Graeme, 156
McGuinness, Martin, 177
McIlroy, Rory, 185
McKillop, Michael, 157
McShane Health Club, 34, 38, 161
McShane, Margaret, 52–3, 104, 112–3, 115–7, 161
McShane, Robert Terence 'Buster', x, 2, 27, 28–40, 41, 43–4, 50, 51–3, 58, 60, 62, 68, 69–73, 75, 77, 80–81, 83, 84, 85, 86, 87–90, 92, 93, 94, 96–97, 98, 99–106, 111, 115-8, 119, 121, 122, 126, 129, 145, 147, 149, 151, 153, 161, 172
Meade, Richard, 11
Melchett, Lord, 166
Mexico, Olympic Games, *see* Olympic Games
Miskimmon, Irene, 36

Mitchell, Jean, 36
Mitchell, Robin, 155
Monteith, Deryck, 115–6, 117, 122–3, 126
Montreal, Olympic Games, *see* Olympic Games
Moore, Dr John, 154
Moores, John, 152
Morgan, Cliff, 131, 171–2
Moses, Ed, 152
Mr Blobby, 169, 171
Munich, Olympic Games, *see* Olympic Games
Murray, Derek, 127
Murray, Granny, 27
Murray, Helen, 27

Nash, Charlie, 164
Nevill, Lord Rupert, 100
New South Wales, 26
New Zealand, 24, 25, 118, 119, 121, 127, 128, 144, 155, 161, 163
New Zealand, Commonwealth Games, *see* Commonwealth Games
Newcastle, County Down, 13, 15
Newham, London, 117, 164
*News of the World*, 45
NI Amateur Athletics Association, 132
Nikolić, Vera, 67
*Noel's House Party*, 171
Nordwig, Wolfgang, 81
Northern Ireland Women's AAA, 21, 64, 148

Oakley, Margaret, 134
Ohuruogu, Christine, 158

Oliver, Jay, 104–5
Olympic Games
   Tokyo (1964) 38, 46, 48–50, 60, 65
   Mexico City (1968) 57, 60–7, 68, 87, 120, 144, 177
   Munich (1972) x, xi, xiii, xiv, 1, 9, 38, 57, 68–73, 74–82, 83–91, 92–103, 105, 106, 110, 111, 122, 123, 153, 154, 157, 163, 169, 170, 172, 188
   Montreal (1976) 117, 131–3
   Moscow (1980) x, 133–4, 143, 144
   Los Angeles (1984) x, 134, 139–144
   Seoul (1988) 144, 148
   Barcelona (1992) 144
   Atlanta (1996) 144
   Sydney (2000) 144
   Athens (2004) 144
   Beijing (2008) 173
   London (2012) ii, ix, 138, 144
   Tokyo (2020) 135
Olympic Villages, 1, 64, 66, 67, 74, 75, 83, 88, 98, 98, 101–3, 121–2, 127, 129–30, 132, 134, 137, 138, 141–3, 177
Oshikoya, Modupe, 125–6
Ovett, Steve, 134, 137, 138, 152

Packer, Ann, 46
Paisley, Eileen, 110
Paisley, Revd Ian, 110
Palmer, Dick, 135
Parrott, John, 171, 172
Pasadena, California, 71, 72
Pascoe, Della, 101
Pearl, Bill, 73
Pearl, Judy, 71
Perth, Commonwealth Games, *see* Commonwealth Games
Peters, Arthur, 5–9, 11, 12, 13, 15, 16, 17, 18, 20, 26, 35, 39, 41, 44, 92, 95, 96, 97, 100, 106, 107, 108, 114, 123, 180
Peters, Doris (née Waterhouse), 16, 17
Peters, Hilda, xiii, 5, 6, 7, 13, 15, 16, 17, 19, 33, 53, 188
Peters, John, 5, 6, 7, 8, 10, 11, 17, 18, 19, 26, 172, 180
Philip, Duke of Edinburgh, 142, 177, 178
Pirnie, Bruce, 129
Pollak, Burglinde, 2, 7, 76, 78, 79, 83, 84, 86, 87, 89, 90, 92, 93, 94, 117
Portadown Golf Club, 11
Portadown, County Armagh, 8, 9, 10, 11, 17, 18, 179
Poulsen, Barbara, 125, 126
Press, Irina, 48
Princess Anne, *see* Anne, HRH Princess
Pryce, Pat, 46
Puică, Maricica, 141

Queen's University Belfast, 39, 54, 148
Queen's University running track, 14, 39, 73, 148, 149
*Question of Sport*, 171

Rand, Mary (née Bignal, then Toomey), 44, 50, 62, 63, 68, 119, 123, 126, 127, 128

# Index

Rand, Sidney, 120
Redgrave, Steve, 143, 157
Rice, Tim, 157
Robinson, Bridget, 22, 23
Robinson, Peter, 177
Rolling Stones, 174
Romano, Joseph, 102
Romayne Carswell, Lady, *see* Carswell, Lady Romayne
Rook, Jean, 113
Roseman, Ray, 107, 108
Rosendahl, Heide, 2, 75–8, 83–90, 91, 92, 93
Ross, Sir Alexander, 127
Rowley, Margaret, 20
Royal Air Force, 111 Squadron, 111
Royal Ulster Constabulary Sports, 13
Royal Victoria Hospital, 185
Rush, Hilary, 36
*Russell Harty Show*, 169, 170
Russell, Hugh, 138

Sanderson, Tessa, 134, 138, 140, 142, 142, 152, 157, 158
Scott, Sue, 62
Sharif, Omar, 169, 171
Shaw, David, 133
Sherlock, John, 153
Sherwood, Sheila, 82, 101
Simpson, Janet, 88, 101, 102
Somme Nursing Home, 186
Sophie, Duchess of Gloucester, 178
South Africa, 45, 47, 139, 140, 141, 165
Spartan Ladies' Athletic Club, 42, 64

Sports Council NI, 150, 155, 162, 165, 166, 167
Sports Writers' Association, 115
Stevens, Jocelyn, 113
Stewart, Charlie, 125, 126
Stewart, Jackie, 112
Stirling, Rosemary, 1
Stormont Castle, 151
Stranmillis Training College, 17
Strong, Shirley, 152
Sydney, Australia, 18, 26, 144, 173

Thatcher, Margaret, 135
*This Is Your Life*, 172, 173
Thompson, Daley, 133, 134, 136, 138, 143, 157
Thompson, Elliot, 137
*Through the Keyhole*, 173
Tikhomirova, Valentina, 83, 84, 85, 90
Tokyo, Japan, 38, 46, 48–50, 60, 65, 135, 138
Tokyo, Olympics Games, *see* Olympics Games
Tomelty, Joseph, 115
Toomey, Bill, 120
Toomey, Mary, *see* Rand, Mary
Torvill, Jane, 157
Tossa de Mar, Spain, 42, 43, 44
Tuffnell, Phil, 171

Ulster Arts Club, 106
Ulster Independent Clinic, 184
Ulster Sports and Recreation Trust. *See* Mary Peters Trust
Ulster Television, 106, 133, 177

Victoria Friendly Society, 5
Vine, David, 115, 171
*Voices of Sport*, 150

Walker, John, 152
Wallace, Joan, 41
Watman, Mel, 87, 89
Watt, Jim, 164
Watts, Denis, 43
Weinberg, Moshe, 102
Wells, Allan, 138
Whitbread, Fatima, 134, 143, 152
White City Stadium, London, 21, 41
Whitehead, Nick, 134, 142
Whitelaw, William, 97, 151
William, Prince of Wales, 178, 182
Wilson, Ann, 62, 74, 76, 85, 92, 125, 126
Wilson, Denis, 149
Wogan, Terry, 131
Wolfe, Geoffrey, 151
Women's AAA, 21, 64, 148
Woodman, Donald, 9, 17, 89
World Dwarf Games, 152
World Police and Fire Games, 152
World Transplant Games, 152

Young, Val, 57